F. C. Woodhouse

Monasticism, Ancient and Modern

F. C. Woodhouse

Monasticism, Ancient and Modern

ISBN/EAN: 9783337379124

Printed in Europe, USA, Canada, Australia, Japan

Cover: Foto ©Lupo / pixelio.de

More available books at **www.hansebooks.com**

MONASTICISM

ANCIENT AND MODERN

ITS PRINCIPLES, ORIGIN, DEVELOPMENT, TRIUMPHS, DECADENCE AND SUPPRESSION;

WITH

AN ENQUIRY AS TO THE POSSIBILITY OF ITS REVIVAL

BY THE

Rev. F. C. WOODHOUSE, M.A.

AUTHOR OF
"THE MILITARY RELIGIOUS ORDERS," "THE LIFE OF THE SOUL IN THE WORLD,"
"A MANUAL FOR LENT," ETC., ETC.

All men cannot receive this saying, save they to whom it is given . . . he that is able to receive it, let him receive it.

London
GARDNER, DARTON AND CO.
3 PATERNOSTER BUILDINGS

PREFACE

THE following pages represent an effort, not only to give a succinct historical account of the rise, progress, and decay of Monasticism, but also to investigate its fundamental principles, and to discover, if possible, the causes that have led to its abandonment, to a large extent, by the civilized nations of the world. From our vantage-ground at the end of the nineteenth century, we can look back upon this very remarkable system, and appraise its character with special facility; and it is interesting and instructive to set out the opinions respecting it of writers of every school of thought. The dry pages of ancient authors, and the romantic and legendary stories of mediæval chroniclers, have, to a great extent, lost their value in the eyes of modern readers, who desire rather to hear the judgment of the men of their own day, and to form their own opinions by an unbiased consideration of the verdict of those to whom they look up, and whom they regard as their proper and most qualified teachers, because they have lived in the full light of modern research, and with documents in their hands that were unknown to past generations.

Moreover, the thoughtful English Churchman can hardly rise from the study of the annals of so powerful and long-honoured an agency both of conservative and aggressive Christianity, without asking whether it is indeed dead and gone; or whether it may not be advantageously revived and adapted to the wants of the Church of to-day. He cannot help considering whether this old weapon of the Church militant is to lie henceforth numbered and labelled, as it were, in the glass case of a museum, to be talked about and criticized by learned and dispassioned antiquarians, or to be stared at and ridiculed by the gaping crowd of ignorant sight-seers; or whether, like the stout blade that lay forgotten and rusting behind the altar of the Church at Fierbois, it will not some day be sought by a divinely-inspired enthusiast like Jeanne D'Arc, and in a pure and powerful right-hand be brandished once more in the front of the Church's battle, and wave on eager hosts to victory and honour. The enemies of God and man have set their battle in array; the Church's warriors are discouraged and perplexed; is there no man, like David, chosen and anointed of God, who will meet giant foes fearlessly, strong in faith, armed, not with the borrowed armour that has so often failed to deliver and defend its wearer, but in the every-day garb of simplicity and integrity, and with no other weapon than that of the poor but brave and true shepherd of the sheep of Christ's flock?

CONTENTS

CHAP.		PAGE
I.	THE THEORY AND PRINCIPLE OF MONASTICISM	1
II.	THE ORIGIN AND EARLY HISTORY OF MONASTICISM	37
III.	THE GROWTH AND WORK OF MONASTICISM ...	67
IV.	MONASTICISM IN BRITAIN	131
V.	THE CORRUPTIONS OF MONASTICISM; ITS ABUSES, DECAY, AND SUPPRESSION ...	218
VI.	THE REVIVAL OF MONASTICISM IN THE CHURCH OF ENGLAND	270
	NOTES	384
	INDEX ...	401

MONASTICISM
ANCIENT AND MODERN

CHAPTER I

THE THEORY AND PRINCIPLE OF MONASTICISM

> If thou wilt be perfect, go and sell all that thou hast, and give to the poor, and thou shalt have treasure in heaven; and come and follow me.—*St. Matt.* xix. 21.

THE student of post-pagan literature is constantly confronted with the fact of Monasticism. It is found to be an inseparable element in all departments of knowledge and experience. Monks stand out as the conspicuous men in Church and State; they sway the counsels of kings; they are the authors of great changes and progressive reforms; they come frequently from the noblest and purest blood of the land, and are forced by their innate genius, and by the will of the people, to become rulers of men, and the guiding spirits of the world's destinies in their times. Europe is covered to-day with towns that bear the names of monks, and which originated in the cell of an anchorite, which grew into an abbey. Literature is indebted to Monasticism for the preservation of books, and for the desire and the ability to read them. Architecture had a new birth, and attained a marvellous maturity, as the abbey with its church and dwellings grew up, majestic, beautiful, useful. Painting was encouraged and patronized by the cloister. Agriculture, as we understand it, was created by monks; cattle-breeding and fruit and vegetable growing come from the same source. The dignity of labour, the free tenure of land, the relief of the poor and unfortunate, the education of the gifted, the cultivation of music, the employment of women, and their elevation to positions of responsibility and power—these and a multitude of other valued features of our present civilization owe their origin, more or less directly, to the monastic system, or to men whom it created and developed.

But if we, on these accounts, should imagine that Monasticism consists in these things, or in any of them, we should be greatly mistaken. There was, indeed, during the ages a steady advance from the lonely cave of the ascetic in Egypt, to the mitred abbey with its stately church, its wealth, its princely governor, its throng of inmates and dependents, its cultivation of the arts, its influence upon the nation and the world; but the theory of Monasticism, the spirit that gave it birth, that made it grow and become powerful, that animated alike the breast of the dweller in the desert, while Rome was still standing and ruling, and that dwells to-day in the faithful Carthusian, or the brown-frocked Friar, whose house has escaped the general ruin, and in the Sister who is trained at Clewer, or who goes forth into the slums from East Grinstead—this spirit is simply the passionate love of the devout soul for God, and the irresistible desire to separate itself from all and everything, within and without, that would hinder its communion with Him whom it loves above all things.

The teaching of St. Thomas Aquinas, on this subject, is thus summed up by Prof. Allies—" Christian perfection consists in charity. Now there are four degrees of charity; the first is to love God as much as He is lovable, that is, with a love as infinite as Himself. This degree of charity belongs only to the Three Persons of the Blessed Trinity. The second is to love Him, not as much as He is lovable, but as much as the creature can love Him; and in this consists the happiness of the blessed, whether angels or men. The third degree is to love Him neither so much as He is lovable, nor so much as the creature absolutely is capable of loving Him, but so much as a mortal creature can love Him, who removes every impediment in the way of that love, and surrenders himself wholly to it. This is the perfection aimed at by the religious life. The fourth degree is to love Him, less indeed than this, but yet so much as to love nothing more than Him, and nothing equally with Him. And this degree is enjoined upon all men."

And again—" Look at Europe at the end of fifteen centuries. In all the countries from the Mediterranean to the furthest inhabited northern land, great houses are found in which men or women live, who each by a distinct solemn act accepted and bound themselves to the Virginal Life. At that time there were houses which numbered thirty continuous generations of men among their inhabitants, who from age to age chose poverty instead of riches, humility and subordination to others, and resignation of their own will, instead of pride; purity and self-denial instead of bodily pleasures and the heart's affections. St. Augustine has given us both the order of their birth and the power of their life. 'No corporeal fecundity produces this race of virgins; they are no offspring of flesh and blood. Ask you the mother of these? It is the Church. None other bears these sacred virgins but that one espoused to a single husband, Christ. Each of these so loved that beautiful One among the sons of men, that, unable to conceive Him in the flesh as Mary did, they conceived Him in their heart, and kept for Him even the body in integrity.'"[1]

Following the same idea, St. Chrysostom said—"χριστὸς ἐκ παρθένου. γυναῖκες παρθενεύτε, ἵνα χριστοῦ γένησθε μητέρες."

This fundamental principle of Monasticism has been discerned by all who can divest their minds of distracting considerations, and who can strip off all the accidents, all the accretions, all the abuses that have attached themselves to the monastic system, and look upon it in its essence, which time does not affect, and which varying circumstances and environment leave untouched. Thus Montalembert says—"Among so many founders and legislators of the

[1] *Formation of Christendom* Part I., Lecture vi. (Burns and Oates).

religious life, not one has dreamt of assigning the cultivation of the soil, the copying of manuscripts, the progress of arts and letters, the preservation of historical monuments, as a special aim to his disciples. These offices have been only accessory—the consequence, often indirect and involuntary, of an institution which had in view nothing but the education of the human soul, its conformity to the law of Christ, and the expiation of its native guilt by a life of sacrifice and mortification. . . . Every man who believes in the Incarnation of the Son of God and the divinity of the Gospel, ought to recognize in monastic life the most noble effort which has ever been made to overcome corrupted nature, and to approach to Christian perfection."[1]

"I desire nothing more," said Marie Alacoque, "than to be blind and ignorant as regards human affairs, in order perfectly to learn the lesson I so much need, that a good nun must leave all to find God, be ignorant of all else to know Him, forget all else to possess Him, do and suffer all in order to learn to love Him."[2]

In the same persuasion Dr. Newman writes, "Monachism ultimately took up many works, but originally it was simply flight from the world, and nothing else. In its innocency of life, it realized the poet's dream of Arcadia, or the reign of Saturn."[3] And Mr. Lecky, with all his hostility and bitter

[1] *Monks of the West*, vol. i. (J. C. Nimmo).
[2] Quoted by A. J. C. Hare in *Biographical Sketches*.
[3] *Historical Sketches*, vol. iii. (Burns and Oates).

invective against Monasticism, nevertheless cannot help confessing that, "The monastic system, in its central conception, that the purely animal side of our being is a low and a degraded side, reflects with perfect fidelity the feelings of our nature."[1] Bossuet says of the Rule of St. Benedict, "It is an epitome of Christianity, a learned and mysterious abridgment of all the doctrines of the Gospel, all the institutions of the holy Fathers, and all the counsels of perfection. Here prudence and simplicity, humility and courage, severity and gentleness, freedom and dependence, eminently appear. Here, correction has all its firmness; condescension all its charm; command all its vigour, and subjection all its repose; silence its gravity, and words their grace; strength its exercise, and weakness its support." And another writer says, "The Rule of St. Benedict may be summed up in two words—labour and obedience. He said that our life in this world is like the ladder which Jacob saw in his dream: in order to reach heaven, it must be planted by the Lord in a humble heart; we can only mount it by distinct steps of humility and discipline. He demanded long trial and probation to discover whether the candidates for admission really had a vocation for the life of a monk."

But we may go further even than all this. Let any dispassionate person read for the first time our Lord's Sermon on the Mount, and he will probably come to no other conclusion, than that the life of the ascetic is distinctly ordained by Christ. "The Counsels of

[1] *History of European Morals*, vol. i. (Longmans).

Perfection" form the rule of conduct there provided. Other declarations of our Lord Himself are of the same kind; for example, "There went great multitudes with Him; and He turned, and said unto them, If any one come to Me, and hate not his father, and mother, and wife, and children, and brethren, and sisters, yea, and his own life also, he cannot be My disciple; and whosoever doth not bear his cross, and come after Me, cannot be My disciple."[1] St. Augustine tells us in his *Confessions* how these words came like an arrow to his heart, and forced him then and there to give up the world, and follow the rule of Christ. St. Bruno and St. Francis, in the same way, became convinced that for them there was no possible way of life but that of the Sermon on the Mount, in its literal acceptation; and from St. Anthony to the present moment similar conversions take place.

Peter the Venerable, Abbot of Cluny, exclaims, "What else is it to say, 'Omnia quæ habes, da pauperibus, et veni sequere me,' but, 'Become a monk.'"

"A convent of Religious," says Hugo of St. Victor, "is a paradise, having the tree of life in the midst of it, yielding shade and fruit; that is, Christ giving life."

St. Anselm says, "The object of the monastic discipline is purity of heart, and the end everlasting life," and Antonio de Guevara declares, "A perfect man makes the world a monastery, and the profane man makes a monastery the world."

[1] St. Luke xiv. 25—27.

"The first especial cause of all monastic life is the desire to avoid the occasions of sin, to declare war with the perverse world, and to be delivered from the danger of its snares."

Cowley says, "To be a philosopher is but to retire from the world, or rather to retire from the world as it is man's, into the world as it is God's."

"The monastic life was a reducing to practice the mystery of Holy Saturday; it was the life hidden in Jesus Christ; a perpetuation of the Epistle for the day, 'Ye are dead, and your life is hid with Christ in God.'"

The Christian then, with the New Testament in his hand, does not feel called upon to apologize for Monasticism; while, at the same time, he recognizes the high possibilities of sanctity in the ordinary secular life, believing that the Apostles knew the mind of Christ, and had received from Him instruction for all time respecting that utterance of His—"Every man cannot receive this saying; he that is able to receive it, let him receive it"; but he still acknowledges the existence of a higher vocation for all those to whom our Lord says, "If thou wilt be perfect . . . follow Me."

"Le catholicisme cherché l'idéal de la vie Chrétienne, et considéré le Monachisme comme la perfection de la vie Chrétienne, perfection relative assurément. Mais il est faux de dire . . . qu'il est pour nous Catholiques *la* vie Chrétienne; c'est *un* idéal, et *un* idéal auquel tout le monde n'est pas appelé. . . .

"Entre le Monachisme et l'Eglise il n'y a pas

d'opposition de principe; le Monachisme est une portion de l'Eglise, une portion de choix, un état privilégié, mais un état exceptionnel, exceptionnel en ce sens, qu'il sera toujours et forcément l'état de la minorité. C'est un état qui requiest une grace, un appel tout particulier."[1]

"Christians have but one faith," says M. Bulteau, "which prescribes to them the giving up of earthly things; one baptism, by which they are consecrated to the service of the Blessed Trinity; one rule, the Gospel; one model, Jesus Christ; one hope, the blessedness of heaven . . . . since the precept to love God above all things, and without reserve or limits, is given to every one, one might say that every one is called to perfection. But it is certain that all men are not compelled, as they are not capable of embracing this rule. Penitence, prayer, fulfilment of the duties of life, are commanded to all as precepts; but the Gospel enjoins only by way of counsel to sell one's goods and give them to the poor, and to abstain from marriage. Those who do not practise these things may not be blamed. So St. Bernard said that 'he who cannot fly as an eagle, may at least fly as a little bird.'"[2]

Thus "we find the Church gradually dividing itself with more definiteness into two classes—those whose calling was in the world, and those who were called to the regular practice of asceticism in one or more of its features. Such a division within

[1] *Revue Benedictine*, July 18, 1895.
[2] *Essai de l'Histoire Monastique*, Book I. ch. iii. iv.

the Christian body had always been contemplated by our Lord Himself, for He speaks at times not to all, but to those who are able to receive His words. As time went on, and the first fervour of love declined, asceticism could scarcely be practised at all without separation from the bulk of Christians, who ignored even that part of its practice which was incumbent upon all." [1]

Closely connected with the love of God, as the root-motive of Monasticism, is the overwhelming sense of the unsatisfying nature of all things temporal. When the "Pearl of great price" has been found, the finder lightly esteems everything else, and will gladly part with all that he has that he may possess the treasure in peace. Thus an early ascetic says, "What is our prosperity here below?—a dream, a vapour, the foam of the sea. God grant that the possession of present good may not hold to us the place of future recompense, that the abundance of that which perishes may not be followed by the dearth of that which endures." In the latter period of the Roman Empire the state of morality was so hopelessly bad and depraved, that many godly men felt that flight was their only security. Esteeming the world as it then was to be the doomed Babylon, they literally obeyed the call, "Come out of her, my people, that ye be not partakers of her sins, and that ye receive not of her plagues; for her sins have reached unto heaven, and God hath remembered her iniquities." But there is, moreover, a conviction of the unfitness of the world,

[1] J. H. Blunt.

even at its best, to fulfil the aspirations of the soul. It is not only sour and selfish pessimists like Schopenhauer who become possessed with a deep sense of the transitory and disappointing nature of human life; nor is it worn-out debauchees only, like the Preacher, who have tasted all the fruits of the earth, permitted and forbidden alike, who cry out that "All is vanity and vexation of spirit;" but in all ages, and wherever men have thought and reasoned, and weighed and appraised calmly the pains and pleasures that flesh is heir to, there has been a conviction in a certain number of minds that it is wise to retire as much as may be from the world, and to seek for happiness in simple pursuits, and in meditation upon higher things. "In the depths of human nature there exists without doubt a tendency, instinctive, though confused and evanescent, towards retirement and solitude. Its manifestations are found in all the epochs of history, in all religions, in all societies except perhaps among savage tribes, or in the bosom of that corrupt civilization, which by its excess and over-refinement too often leads humanity back to a savage condition."[1] "Every man who has penetrated the mysteries of life and death, has got the truth in solitude, and in a mighty travail of body and spirit, generally upon a mountain."[2] Eckart says—"Man must be silent before he can hear the divine Voice. . . . They shut their eyes to earth so that they might the better open them to heaven. They struggled

---

[1] Montalembert, *Monks of the West*, vol. i.
[2] H. S. Olcott, *Religion and Occult Science*.

up to those regions of serenity, where the sounds of life grow hushed and dim, and all space is filled with the pervading presence of the Divinity." "A few individuals imagine that this is a satisfactory and happy world, but in every age the voice of humanity has risen in wondering sorrow to the silent heaven. The Hindú sages perceived that our life was utterly undesirable. This drove Gautama Búdha from his throne to the jungle, and it underlies all his religion, expressed in the Buddhist prayer, 'All is transitory; all is misery; all is void; all is without substance.'"[1]

Side by side with this idea of the imperfection of this world's best, has come the belief that the soul may be more or less freed from the trammels and debasing influence of the body by mortification of the fleshly instincts and desires. "All great religious movements have been due to ascetics. Buddha, Moses, Mahomet, Calvin, Fox, Wesley were all men of austere principles. Luther was perhaps the one exception to this rule. He was a man of coarse and vigorous animalism, but he was naturally endowed with immense power, and his seclusion at Wartburg served to concentrate his forces. . . . The ascetic instinct is intimately united to the religious instinct. There is scarcely a religion of ancient or modern times, Protestantism excepted, that does not recognize asceticism as an element of its system. The principle of asceticism is abstinence from lawful pleasures, the subordination of certain faculties to others, and the restraint of certain propensities. Buddha taught his

[1] A. Wilson, *The Abode of Snow* (Blackwood).

disciples a religion of abstinence. Brahminism has also its order of ascetics. From the earliest Vaidic age Hindû thought turned to self-immolation. Mohammedanism has its fakirs, subduing the flesh by their austerities, and developing the spirit by their contemplations and prayers. Fasting and self-denial were required of the Greeks who desired initiation into the Mysteries. The Egyptian priests passed their novitiate in the deserts. They renounced all commerce with the world, and lived in contemplation, temperance, and in absolute poverty. The natives of North America fast for days before they are initiated into the rights of manhood. The Peruvians and the Mexicans had severe rules of fasting and mortification both for individuals and for the nation, and there were ascetic orders for men and women. In the divine regulations of the Jewish nation fasting and self-abnegation found an important place. . . . . Suffering is found, by all experience, to be necessary in order to bring out whatever is best and highest in man. Men with no specially religious feeling admit this principle in their practice, and the vagaries of the Alpine Club are but a grotesque caricature of the spiritual joy of triumph won by endurance. Consequently a religion which puts suffering aside, not only fails to have any further relation with the great majority of mankind, whose daily lot it is to endure, but it fails to awaken any ideal in its own followers which may nerve them to exceptional exertion. The ascetic cuts himself off as much as possible from all means of wasting force. His voluntary celibacy and abstinence from active work place at his disposal all that force which would be discharged by a man in the world in muscular action and in domestic affection."[1]

"This is the meaning of the life of sacrifice; it has ever before it a positive rather than a negative end, and it aims at life, not death—death only as a gateway to a better life. It looks with no puritan eye of contempt at the fair things that the world has, or at those whose lives are less stern; it only gives up what it does surrender to gain something better. For the power to give up many things—every earthly thing—is at bottom a power of not being able to do without other things. He to whom honour is necessary can do without money. He who must have goodness can get along without praise. He who must have God's communion can do without the sweet companionship of fellow-men ... and on the other hand, as you grow worse ... the highest necessities let you go, and the lowest necessities take tighter hold of you. ... You come down at last where you cannot do without a comfortable dinner and an easy bed, but you can do without an act of charity or a thought of God. ... The abiding in Christ, then, demands a surrender of all that hinders the union of the soul with Him. There is no broad rule that can be laid down beforehand; it is an individual matter between each soul and Christ."[2]

---

[1] S. Baring-Gould, *Origin and Development of Religious Belief*, vol. i. (Longmans).

[2] *Some Principles and Practices of the Spiritual Life*, by the Rev. B. W. Maturin, p. 177.

"In the Asiatic mind there prevails an idea that knowledge can be assimilated once and for all; that if you can obtain it, you immediately possess the knowledge of everything. This is the reason of the prolonged fasting and solitary meditation of the ascetics. They believe that by attenuating the bond between soul and body, the soul can be liberated, and can temporarily identify itself with other objects, animate and inanimate, besides the especial body to which it belongs, acquiring thus a direct knowledge of those objects, and they believe that this direct knowledge remains. The ultimate difference between the Asiatic saint and the European man of science is, that while the former believes all knowledge to be directly within the grasp of the soul under certain conditions, the latter denies that any knowledge can be absolute, being all obtained indirectly through the bodily senses, a medium not absolutely reliable." [1]

Other thoughtful writers dwell upon the universality of the spirit of asceticism. Thus Mr. Lecky says, "The Therapeutics mentioned by Philo were probably pagans; and indeed in Asia and Africa the monastic type has always existed, and has assumed forms very similar to those among Christians." [2] And again "Among the Jews—whose law, from the great stress it laid upon marriage, the excellence of the rapid multiplication of population, and the hope of being the ancestor of the Messiah, was peculiarly repugnant to monastic conceptions—the Essenes had constituted

---

[1] F. Marion Crawford, *Mr. Isaacs.*
[2] *Rationalism*, vol. ii. (Longmans).

a complete monastic society, abstaining from marriage, and separating themselves wholly from the world. In Rome, where practical genius was, if possible, even more opposed than that of the Jews to an inactive Monasticism, and even among those philosophers who most represented its active and practical spirit, the same tendency is shown. The Cynics of the later Empire recommended a complete renunciation of domestic ties, and a life spent mainly in the contemplation of wisdom. The Egyptian philosophy, that soon after acquired an ascendency in Europe, anticipated even more closely the monastic ideal. On the outskirts of the Church many sects surpassed and stimulated the private penances of the orthodox. The soil was thus thoroughly prepared for a great outburst of asceticism, whenever the first seed was sown."[1]

Pliny speaks with astonishment of a solitary people, who dwelt among the palm-trees near the Dead Sea, who subsisted without money, and who derived from the disgust and repentance of mankind, a perpetual supply of voluntary associates.

Indeed it has been truly said, " It has been with Monasticism as with every other intellectual movement. An idea exists long in a state of free solution, till the master-mind is revealed, destined to give it fixity and permanence ; and from that time it becomes a nucleus around which system gathers and crystallizes."[2]

It has been strangely imagined by some that

[1] *European Morals*, vol. ii. p. 103.   [2] J. H. Blunt.

Monasticism was instituted for and maintained by the weak and morbid, and that asceticism implies feeble mental power, and that it produces invalids and low physical energy. Thus Chateaubriand says, "If there are refuges for the health of the body, permit religion to have such also for the health of the soul, which is still more subject to sickness, and the infirmities of which are so much more sad, so much more tedious and difficult to cure." Nothing could be more untrue to facts. Most of the early abbots were of royal or at least of noble birth. They were aristocratic because they were the best men of their day. No one can read the lives of these men without admiring their manly vigour, their indomitable endurance, their reckless courage. The resistless energy that sends men to posts of danger to-day, that inspires the soldier and the sailor, the explorer of wild lands, and the rescue-party at the coal-pit or the fire—this found its congenial occupation in the life of the primitive missionary. The hot blood of the chief still stirred in the veins of the cowled monk, and there were often seen strange contrasts in the conduct of the man, whose inherited passions drove him into violent outbursts of anger or indignation, while his acquired sanctity made him generally the most gentle and patient of Christians. St. Columba was a remarkable instance of all this. He came of a family accustomed to command and to be obeyed; he was immovably convinced of the rectitude of his own aims and motives; and he found it difficult, and sometimes impossible, to subdue his words and his gestures in the face of sturdy wrong-doing and obstinate resistance; so that his biographers are obliged to apologize for the occasional appearance of the likeness rather of the lion than of the lamb in the saint's demeanour. Nor does St. Columba stand alone in monastic hagiology in respect of these characteristics. So that Montalembert justly says, " Monasteries were never intended to collect the invalids of the world. The religious life, far from being the refuge of the feeble, was, on the contrary, the arena of the strong." "Resolute to escape, as much as was in nature, from the empire of falsehood and wickedness, from the instability of human things, these athletes sought to put their life into harmony with their convictions; and by a warm and pure inspiration of their free-will, they consecrated to the service of their neighbour, to the love of God, to the profit of the soul, a virgin energy of which nothing had yet tarnished the purity or enfeebled the force."[1]

A very different mind comes to the same conclusion. "A prudent regard to our future prospects and interests; an abstinence from unlawful pleasures, because they will entail the loss of greater pleasure by and by, or perhaps be paid with pain—this is called virtue now. If Christianity had never borne itself more loftily than this, do you suppose that those fierce Norsemen would have fashioned their sword-hilts into crosses, and themselves into crusading chivalry? The first preachers of Christianity went

[1] *Monks of the West*, vol. i.

forth on their warfare with evil, preaching not enlightened prudence, but purity, justice, and goodness, holding out no promises except of suffering, as their great Master had suffered; and the crown of glory to come was no enjoyment at last of what they had surrendered in this life, but to lose themselves in Christ whom they loved."[1]

So too among ourselves, those who are most widely removed from primitive and Catholic Christianity, are seen to adopt the fundamental principle of asceticism in acts of self-discipline and sacrifice of ease and comfort for others. In her autobiography, Miss F. P. Cobbe confesses that in her early years, when under the influence of extreme puritanical ideas, she made all sorts of severe rules for herself, and if she broke them, manfully mulcted herself of any little pleasures, or endured some small self-imposed penance. And again, speaking of her friend and companion in work among the slums of Bristol, she says, "It was a wonderful spectacle to see Mary Carpenter sitting before the large school gallery, teaching, singing, and praying with the wild street boys, in spite of endless interruptions caused by such proceedings as shooting marbles into hats on the table behind her, whistling, stamping, fighting, shrieking out 'Amen' in the middle of the prayer, and sometimes rising *en masse* and tearing like a troop of bisons in hob-nailed boots down from the gallery, round the great school-room and down the stairs, out into the street. These irrepressible outbreaks she bore with

[1] J. A. Froude, *Short Studies* (Longmans).

infinite good-humour; and what seemed to me more marvellous still, she heeded, apparently, not at all the indescribable abomination of the odours of a tripe-and-trotter shop next door, which, together with the *bouquet du peuple* of the poor little unkempt scholars, rendered the school on a hot summer's evening little better than the ill-smelling *giro* of Dante's *Inferno.*"

And may we not venture to say, that whatever measure of success has attended the work of the Salvation Army, is due, not to its drumming and screaming, not to its revival meetings, and strange doctrines of instantaneous conversion, and such like, but to the self-denials practised by its more devoted members, its care for the poor and suffering and lost, and the demands made upon every new member of money payment, and the giving up, not only of immoral habits, but of the bodily gratifications of beer-drinking and smoking?

But this instinct of asceticism is found also in very unlikely places. For example, there are many singular communistic societies in the United States, all intensely modern and anti-Catholic in their constitution and general aims, but nevertheless almost all of them adopt some of the principles of asceticism, and even, probably quite unconsciously, follow many of the old monastic rules and practices. They eat in common and in silence; clothing is provided; a probation of two years is required before new members are admitted; they demand unreasoning submission to their superiors; they have daily religious meetings; individual confession is demanded of all. They feed and lodge strangers freely. Most of them are celibates, but some allow marriage as an inferior condition. They leave the business of their societies to appointed members, that the rest may give themselves entirely to a spiritual life. The women hide their hair with a close head-dress.[1]

We see then that the fundamental principle of Monasticism lies deep down in the very constitution of human nature; that it received the sanction of our Lord's own teaching, and that He Himself set the example of framing His life according to its threefold rule of Chastity, Poverty, and Obedience. Our Lord "came not to destroy the Law and the Prophets"; He did not set Himself against all that was good and true in man, or in the teaching of seers, and prophets, and wise men in past ages, but He gathered up the vague and disjointed fragments of truth that the Holy Spirit of God, "who lighteth every man that cometh into the world," had given to mankind, "in sundry times and in divers manners;" and "sitting as a refiner and purifier," He separated the dross from the fine gold, and taught the truth, unmixed with human error and perversions. We sometimes read objections against Christianity on the ground that many of its precepts are not original, but may be found in the writings of oriental sages, and the founders of other religions. Such objections do not seem reasonable. There was doubtless an original

[1] Vide *The Communistic Societies of the United States*, C. Nordhoff.

revelation of faith and practice to mankind; and the spirit of man, compassed as it is with infirmity, and biased by many influences, nevertheless, as it came from God, so it strains ever upward towards God; and there is still light within, and a recognition of the great principles of right and wrong, and a yearning after the same great objects of the soul's desire.

St. Paul at Athens recognized this. He was, by his liberal education, acquainted with the wisdom of the ancients, and quoted their words with approbation. Just in the same way the teaching and practice of the primitive Church allowed all that was true and good in paganism, winnowing the chaff from the wheat, turning heathen temples into churches, and substituting Christian festivals for the commemoration of the gods, and the seasons of the year. A timid policy would have feared to encourage asceticism, because those "who followed not" Christ had inculcated it; just as the Iconoclasts argued against the use of images; but the Church was strong in her grasp of the truth, and was able to see good everywhere, and, like David, was ready to use her giant enemy's weapon to destroy the error which it had been formed to defend and enforce. And so, although the Pythagorean ascetics abstained from flesh, from strange ideas respecting the transmigration of souls, and others followed a similar course from equally subtle and fanciful theories, the Church encouraged the temperance and abstinence of her Nazarites, while the apostolic canons condemned all pagan and superstitious motives for such practices, and the enforcing them as binding upon every one, as "abominating the good creatures of God."

The original and fundamental principle of Monasticism, then, was the love of God. From this came the practice of mortification, that the divine spirit within might not be hindered by the lusts of the flesh from communion with the Spirit of God without and above. From this too arose the flight of the ascetic from the evil influences of the world, and the companionship of ungodly men. Next was seen the element of labour. Idleness was ever known to be the mother of many vices; and therefore the primitive hermit employed his time and his thoughts, when not engaged in prayer, worship, and meditation, in some handicraft. He hollowed out a cave for his habitation, or built a rude hut; he cultivated the ground to supply his slender repasts; or he wove mats or baskets that could be exchanged for money or for food. Through all the developments of the monastic system, these two employments, Labour and Prayer, never varied or disappeared. The Rule of St. Benedict, which systematized and formulated the principles and practice of the religious life as they had been carried on for centuries, specially insisted upon the unalterable necessity of these two elements for the welfare and even the existence of Monasticism. The wisdom of this provision was sadly proved in after ages, when the wealthy and lordly monk said his offices by deputy, and kept servants and dependents to do his manual work.

The next out-growth of the principle of Monasticism

was work for others. The world was very evil, and the godly man fled from it in horror, lest he should be corrupted by it, and be partaker in its sins and its doom. There was misery, and ignorance, and suffering, and there was no helper for the weak, no defender of the oppressed, no voice to call the sinner to repentance, or to tell the proud evil-doer of judgment to come. The solitary in his desert recalled the mission of Elijah, and the preaching of the Baptist, and his spirit stirred within him as he thought that God was without witness and prophet, and man without warning and good example. He pondered over the life of his Lord, and remembered that after His sojourn in the wilderness, after His years of toil at Nazareth, He had gone forth teaching, the helper of the suffering, the friend of sinners. Already men had found his retreat, and come to him, some to remain and follow his life of abstraction and prayer and labour, but more to return to their work and duties in the world. Already this and that recluse had been persuaded, or forced, to leave his cell and become a bishop, and a preacher of the Gospel of Christ in some busy town. Far as he was from cities and the thoughts and doings of the time, there came ever and anon to the hermit's ears sad and stirring accounts of crying evils, desperate crimes, urgent crises that demanded a man with strong will and high principle and the sacrifice of self, to turn the tide of men's thoughts, and to inaugurate a much-needed reformation. The devout soul would suddenly discern new light thrown upon familiar words—" He that will save his life shall lose it ; and he that will lose his life for My sake, shall save it." "He that loveth not his brother, whom he hath seen, how can he love God whom he hath not seen?" "Inasmuch as ye have done it unto one of the least of My brethren, ye have done it unto Me." "Go ye into all the world, and preach the gospel to every creature." He would hear a voice crying to him—

> "'Wake,
> Thou deedless dreamer, lazying out a life
> Of self-suppression, not of selfless love.'
> . . . . . .
> And in his heart he cried, 'The call of God!'
> And called arose."

Lacordaire says, "It would be singular if Christianity, founded on the love of God and man, should end in withering up the soul in respect to everything which was not God. Self-denial, far from diminishing love, nourishes and increases it. The ruin of love is self-love, not the love of God; and no one ever met on earth with affections stronger and purer, more ardent, more tender, and more lasting, than those to which saints gave up their hearts, at once emptied of themselves and filled with God."

"Human society has one motive power for its actions, the love of money; and the divine society has another, the love of God. . . . Nor will human society neglect works of mercy, which not only approve themselves to the natural feelings, but enter into the true doctrine of political economy. It will have salubrious buildings, able physicians, well-instructed nurses, duly-provisioned chaplains. Only the basis of all is, in some shape or other, adequate remuneration."[1]

So it was that Telemachus left his hut in the Nitrian desert, and begged his way to Rome, and there bounding into the arena of the Coliseum, placed his body between the gladiators, and called upon them to put up their swords. The thousands of spectators, ranged tier upon tier, yelled and cursed, and the stolid gladiators soon despatched the poor zealot. But that heroic act was the signal for the suppression of all such brutal sports, and an imperial edict soon after forbade their exhibition for ever. So it was that Basil, and Gregory of Nazianzen, and Chrysostom, and others, after a period of solitary training, came forth to positions of influence, and left their mark upon the world. So it was that oftentimes the great cities were astonished by the apparition of a crowd of weird and passionate men, who would not be silenced till they had been heard, and their will obeyed. So it was that Columbanus, and Aidan, and Boniface, and Augustine, and a goodly succession of mission monks, went forth and spread the Church of Christ, and taught the wild heathen to aspire to a gentler and higher life than that of the savage beasts, whose manners they had adopted, and whose very names they assumed with pride for themselves.

The repeated invasions of the barbarians not only swept away the civilization of Rome, and all the culture that had grown up gradually from the old world, but actually destroyed the population of large

[1] *Formation of Christendom*, Prof. Allies.

tracts of Europe, and reduced them to a wilderness, strewed with ruins. First came the Goth; but he was converted by his victims from barbarism. Next came the Hun; he was irreclaimable, but he did not stay. But then came the Lombard; and he kept his ground and his savageness, and under him Roman civilization crumbled to ruins. Thus Pope Gregory says, "The cities are destroyed; the land depopulated; no one remains in the country, scarce any one in the towns; and still the poor remains of humanity are daily smitten, carried captive, mutilated, murdered. Pestilence and earthquakes were added to the miseries. Twenty-nine public libraries were swept away. Every town was sacked and burned. Man and his works ceased from the earth. The waters spread unchecked and drowned vast regions, stopped thoroughfares, and obliterated the very sites of cities in pestilential morasses; torrents carried down rocks into the plains; forests haunted by wild beasts covered fair lands; the dwindled race of men lived in huts of mud, or amid the ruins of marble palaces." [1]

Of this period Bishop Creighton says in his recent Lectures—"Civilization was attacked from all sides, and would have entirely disappeared if it had not happened that at this time the Christian Church made its influence felt. What was the meaning of the growth of the Christian Church at a time when everything else was going to pieces? It was simply this, that the basis of character having disappeared, there was no way of re-establishing man but by the

[1] J. H. Newman, *Historical Sketches*, vol. iii. (Longmans).

influence of Christianity, and Christianity had to undertake the work of re-making character.

"It was very difficult work, for all kinds of reasons. The Christian knew what it was to be a man, and then he wanted to act like a man. But when everything else and every one else was going wrong, how was he to do so? That was the difficulty that faced the early Christians. As they pondered over this problem the answer that forced itself upon them was —We cannot do anything in the world as it is: the only thing we can do is to get out of it, and form the nucleus of another world in which the life we desire to live shall be possible. Some left the crowded cities and went and lived in the deserts, and little by little the practice spread until, at the end of the second or the beginning of the third century, monasticism really was the natural tendency of the men of the times. It was the outcome of the desire to re-make character, and of the consciousness of the impossibility of doing anything in the world as it was. The circumstances of the times seemed to require that a protest should be made."

It was amidst the dense forests and savage wastes of desolated Europe that the missionary monks settled down, building huts for themselves with the trees they felled. There they lived, and worked, and taught, and often were martyred. But others took their place, and the work went on, century after century. "Every monastery became a centre of charity. By the monks the nobles were overawed, the poor protected, the sick tended, travellers sheltered, prisoners ransomed, the remotest spheres of suffering explored. During the darkest period of the Middle Ages, monks founded a refuge for pilgrims amid the horrors of the Alpine snows. A solitary hermit often planted himself with his boat by a bridgeless stream, and the charity of his life was to ferry over the traveller. When the hideous disease of leprosy extended its ravages over Europe, and men's minds were filled with terror, not only by its loathsomeness and its contagion, but also by the notion that it was in a peculiar sense supernatural, hospitals overspread Europe, and monks flocked in multitudes to serve in them."[1]

"The genius of the age expended its highest efforts to provide fitting tabernacles for the divine spirit which they enshrined; and alike in village and city, the majestic houses of the Father of mankind and His especial servants towered up in sovereign beauty, symbols of the civil supremacy of the Church, and of the moral sublimity of life and character which had won the homage and admiration of Christian nations. Ever at the sacred gates sat Mercy, pouring out relief from a never-failing store to the poor and the suffering; ever within the sacred aisles the voices of holy men were pealing heavenwards, in intercession for the sins of mankind; and influences so blessed were thought to exhale around those mysterious precincts, that the outcasts of society—the debtor, the felon, and the outlaw—gathered round the walls, as the sick men sought the

[1] Lecky, *European Morals*, vol. ii. (Longmans).

shadow of the apostle, and lay there sheltered from the avenging hand till their sins were washed from off their souls. Through the storms of war and conquest the abbeys of the Middle Ages floated, like the ark upon the waves of the flood, inviolate in the midst of violence, through the awful reverence which surrounded them."[1]

But in spite of all the records of history, there is a deep and bitter prejudice against Monasticism. Its abuses and faults are remembered, its beneficent work and its high and noble principles are forgotten; and it is imagined that its day has passed for ever, and that it is not possible to revive it, or to adapt it to the needs of the present time.

Forgetting his own favourable testimony, Mr. Lecky, for example, adds his voice to the common slander that Monasticism is synonymous with idleness.[2] Or taking another standpoint, he condemns it with singular misapprehension of its fundamental principles. Thus, he says, "The ascetic, proclaiming the utter depravity of mankind, seeks to extirpate his most natural passions, to crush the expansion of his faculties, to destroy the versatility of his tastes, and to arrest the flow and impulse of his nature, and is thus striking at the very force and energy of civilization. Hence the dreary sterile torpor that has characterized those ages in which the ascetic principle has been supreme, while the civilizations which have attained the highest perfection have been those of ancient

---

[1] J. A. Froude, *Hist. of Eng.*, vol. ii. (Longmans).
[2] Vide *Rationalism*, vol. ii.

Greece and modern Europe, which were most opposed to it."[1]

In the same way, Thos. Carlyle, in his usual style, speaking of monks, says, "These singular two-legged animals, with their rosaries and breviaries, with their shaven crowns, hair-cilices, and vows of poverty, masquerade so strangely through our fancy; and they are in fact so very strange, an extinct species of the human family." And Gibbon, with all his knowledge of the past, is so blinded by prejudice, or envenomed by hatred of Christianity, that he can speak of monks merely as "a race of filthy animals." "They embraced a life of misery, as the price of eternal happiness." "These unhappy exiles from social life were impelled by the dark and implacable genius of superstition. Reason might subdue, or passion might suspend this influence, but it acted most forcibly on the infirm minds of children and females. It was strengthened by secret remorse, or accidental misfortune; and it derived some aid from the temporal considerations of vanity or interest." "Monasteries were filled by a crowd of obscure and abject plebeians, who gained in the cloister much more than they had sacrificed in the world. Peasants, slaves, and mechanics might escape from poverty and contempt to a safe and honourable profession, where apparent hardships were mitigated by custom, by popular applause, and by the secret relaxation of discipline."[2]

One specimen may suffice to illustrate modern

[1] *Rationalism*, vol. ii.   [2] *Decline and Fall*, vol. vi.

feeling with respect to Monasticism; and such quotations might be almost indefinitely multiplied. "Must we not, looking on the ten thousand thousand hearts broken in monasteries and nunneries all over Europe, admit that historical Christianity has not only done good work in the world, but bad work also, and that, diverging widely from the spirit of Christ, it has been far from uniformly beneficent?"[1]

How strangely do such words read by the side of the testimony of so many to the happiness which reigned in the hearts, and displayed itself in the faces and in the lives of ascetics in all ages! For instance, we are told of St. Francis of Assisi, that "he found so much joy in his terrible mission and its sufferings, that he often cried out to God not to give him his blessedness on earth." So Montalembert says, "Of all the erroneous conceptions of religious life, there is none more absurd than that which would persuade us to regard it as a life sad and melancholy. History demonstrates precisely the contrary... When the spirit of the world penetrated the cloister, and ended by stealing it away from the spirit of God, when it had introduced the *commende*, then, doubtless, that which had been a rare and guilty exception became an abuse too habitual and general; then, doubtless, there was a crowd of vocations false or compulsory, and of bitter sorrows, stifled under the frock or the veil. But whilst it was permitted to the monastic orders to flourish in freedom melancholy was unknown." "They had no sadness," is the testimony of

---

[1] *Life of F. P. Cobbe*, vol. i.

St. Chrysostom; "they wage war with the devil as if they were playing." So Orderic Vital, speaking of himself, tells us, "I have borne for forty-two years, with happiness, the sweet yoke of the Lord." And St. Anselm writes, "Behold and see with what lightness the burden of monastic life is borne by Christians of each sex, of every age and condition, who fill the entire world with their songs of joy."[1]

"It would be a mistake to imagine a community of sour faces, their mouths puckered with discontent or grim despair. No words can give an idea of the glad cheerfulness, the holy joy, the serene composure which reigned in the little world, as it still reigns to-day unimpaired in many of Teresa's convents. Melancholy in the convent! God forbid! Teresa dreaded melancholy as the plague; a person infected with it was to be refused admittance, and she sought her nuns with clear and serene understandings and unclouded brows."[2]

There is a whole world of literature in the writings of monks and nuns, quite unknown to the ordinary reader, in which there runs an undercurrent of happiness and innocent enjoyment, that breathes the spirit of childhood, and helps us to understand our Lord's mysterious precept to His disciples, that they should be as "little children." The soul that has freed itself from the tyranny of fashion, and lives under a law of liberty to do and be as God has made it, has reverted to the unconsciousness and simplicity of childhood,

---

[1] *Monks of the West*, vol. i.
[2] *Life of St. Teresa*, G. C. Graham.

and experiences the joyousness that comes naturally to the healthy mind happily ignorant of evil habits and desires. The condition of subjection to superiors, intolerable to the rebellious pride of unsanctified human nature, delivers the pure heart from many difficult dilemmas. Obedience to a higher nature, which is trusted and loved, creates the "service which is perfect freedom." If Schopenhauer's theory has any truth in it, that the will is the source of all human unhappiness, the absolute sacrifice of the individual will to the guidance of another will, removes the cause of discomfort and insatiable craving. The supply of "daily bread," without luxury, and without the anxious toil of procuring it, does away with that "carefulness" which our Lord deprecates, and realizes in man the beautiful dependence of the "fowls of the air, and the lilies of the field." The mutual love and trust between the child and the animal, which are seen before sad experience has taught each to fear the other, are found also in the lives of the recluses; many of whom are said to have had as companions beasts, or birds, whom they regarded, with St. Francis, as "brothers and sisters." The love of their poor homes and their surroundings; the tender affection which members of the same community had for one another, of which there are abundant evidences, are further instances of the similarity between the devout and consistent Religious and the unsophisticated child. It may be objected that such gentle natures are out of place in the rough ways of the world—the battle-field, the senate, the counting-house, the colony; but still such natures exist, and they have therefore a right to live as suits them best. Besides, gentleness is not synonymous with weakness. There are instances enough where recluses, like St. Anselm, have been torn unwillingly from their retirement to take front places in the world's rudest struggles, and who have then shown themselves as manly and strong and inflexible as they were mild and childlike before. The gentle man will be tender and pitiful to the weak, but brave as a lion where courage and endurance are required.

"Few can be persuaded to look upon the ancient monk as anything better than a personification of all that is sensual in our corrupt nature, and whose self-indulgence was the great business of his life, although it was concealed beneath the uninviting cloak of an austere discipline. Hypocrisy is considered to be the principal science which was pursued within the walls of a monastery; and that for many ages the real character of its inmates was kept a profound secret, which enabled them to rest like an incubus upon society, while they preyed upon its vitals." "The fallacy seems to be at length giving way, which identifies the very name of monastery with the worst errors and corruptions of the Church of Rome, and fills the mind with reminiscences of nothing but sin and profligacy. But we should always recollect that these abuses are not the natural fruits of Monasticism; their source is rather to be traced to that deeply-seated propensity to evil which is inherent in our fallen nature."[1]

[1] Fox, *English Monasteries* (Masters).

The grievous fact is, that the evil spirit of the world corrupted the Religious Life, and then, like many tempters, turned round and abused its victim for the sins which it had forced it to commit.

Prejudice dies hard; but truth is great, and will at last prevail. Already Sisterhoods have won their way, and have obtained the respect and the gratitude of English men and women. Brotherhoods are surely coming, and when God's good time arrives, the men will be found whom God has appointed and fitted for this work; and then we shall marvel how the Church of England lived so long without it; or we shall understand that her weakness and failures were caused by the want of this powerful and blessed instrument for working the work of God.

CHAPTER II

THE ORIGIN AND EARLY HISTORY OF MONASTICISM

> If any man come to me, and hate not his father, and mother, and wife, and children, and brethren, and sisters, yea, and his own life also, he cannot be my disciple. And whosoever doth not bear his cross, and come after me, cannot be my disciple. For whosoever will save his life shall lose it; but whosoever shall lose his life for my sake, and the Gospel's, the same shall save it. For what shall it profit a man, if he shall gain the whole world, and shall lose his own soul? or what shall a man give in exchange for his soul?

THE interior motives of Monasticism, as we have seen, lie deep down in the nature of man, and have always found expression in the irresistible impulses of certain individuals. A love of solitude, a distaste for the lower gratifications of the senses, a deliberate judgment that human life—in its ordinary experiences of pain and pleasure, of marriage and paternity, of riches and poverty, of health and sickness, of youth and age—cannot satisfy the higher instincts of the soul, and that the mental and spiritual faculties should be cultivated at the expense of the animal propensities and instincts, these convictions have, in all ages and in every country that has attained any degree of intellectual progress, ever been evidenced in the lives of ascetics, recluses, and philosophers.

Christ, in His teaching, and by His personal selection of a life of self-sacrifice, gave His sanction to the practice of asceticism. But although some of His precepts seemed to demand the pursuit of "perfection" by all His followers without exception, it is certain that He did not in reality lay any such command upon His Church. His Apostles, who were specially instructed by Him "in the things concerning the Kingdom of God," evidently did not so understand His will, for they inaugurated no such universal and absolute renunciation of the world. They themselves followed their Lord's example literally, and the frequent surrender of personal property, the community life, and the practice of virginity, so early found in the primitive Church during the lifetime of the Apostles, prove that the "Counsels of Perfection" were preached and practised as part of the Christian system of Ethics from the very first. At the same time the case of Ananias, and the general adoption of marriage, prove that one and all of these counsels were left to the discretion or the vocation of individual Christians, and that those who did not feel bound to give up their possessions, and those who believed they were called to adopt marriage, and to follow secular occupations, were perfectly free to use the liberty they claimed, without incurring reproach, or even rendering themselves liable to be classed as unworthy and lukewarm disciples of Christ.

Monasticism, then, has been said to be "de jure divino, non precipiente sed consulente." The Church, in her corporate capacity, never established Monasticism, nor did she ever institute a single Religious Order. The undivided Church put forth Creeds. Everywhere she insisted upon the necessity of the Sacraments, and the three orders of the ministry. She preached the words of Christ, and held up His example for all to follow; but she did not make hard and fast rules, or attempt to cast her children's character in one iron mould of absolute uniformity. Our Lord Himself declared that the Holy Spirit of God, dwelling in His Church, would lead her into all truth. This is the true "Theory of Development" of Christian doctrine and practice. The growth of the Church's system is like that of a tree, from the original deposit of life and truth within; and that growth may be modified and fostered in one direction or another, according to the environment of the moment; just as European fruits and flowers and vegetables assume new characteristics when they are planted in the tropics or the antipodes, and some spring forth into hitherto unknown luxuriance.

If we take a comprehensive glance at the progress of discovery, we notice that man does not in his collective capacity make advances, or gain steps upward in knowledge, but that he depends upon gifted individuals, who possess, by the providence of God, powers of mind that do not belong to the rank and ole of humanity, to raise him to some higher level of skill, or material comfort and prosperity. Just in the same way the spiritual advance of mankind has always been obtained by the leading and teaching of individuals, fitted and called by God to be prophets, reformers, and founders. Abraham, Moses, David are examples of this. Nor must we altogether exclude from such a list, Confucius, Mahomet, Buddha, and others. And it seems possible, on this assumption, that Adam may have been an exceptional man among the primitive race of lower humanity, selected by God as the fittest to inaugurate a higher order of beings, more intelligent, and above all, more spiritual than those inferior men who had hitherto peopled the earth.

Christ, the Son of God, is the last of a long series of prophets of God. Moses foretold His coming as his successor, but also as his superior. So the Baptist spoke of himself and of Him who should "come after him." Our Lord in His parables represents Himself as the King's Son, sent as a final messenger to those who had rejected His predecessors. The Epistle to the Hebrews assumes the same order of God's providences, and declares that the prophets had spoken "in divers manners, and at sundry times," before Christ came; and He Himself says that He came not to contradict that which God had already revealed, but to explain it, to enlarge its boundaries, and to add new revelations that had hitherto been kept secret.

The history of science, of the nations, of progress and discovery is but the history of a few men. The unnumbered, unrecorded multitudes of beings are of no account in the broad features of human advancement. They have no power to originate, or to lead;

their part is only to follow, and to profit by the divine gifts and powers that are bestowed, once in a century or yet more rarely, upon the appointed benefactors and teachers of their race. Democracy, Socialism, Communism, and other modern theoretical systems find no countenance in the history of the world, nor in the economy of God's dealings with mankind. Men are not equal; and if it were possible to destroy individuality, and to level all down to one uniform standard, genius would be smothered in its birth, and mankind would degenerate rapidly towards beast-life. Everywhere, throughout the universe, we discern law and obedience; some ruling, many ruled; liberty within bounds; but subjection always, and by all to some higher power; up to the Highest, who alone is "unlimited."

Monasticism, then, like other great institutions, can best be described by relating the history of some few men who have been its authors, its promoters, its reformers. ANTHONY, PACHOMIUS, HILARION, MARTIN, BASIL, BENEDICT, these are the names that meet us as we turn to the records of the past to learn how Monasticism began, and what were its original characteristics. There are many other men whose influence helped the creation of this mighty power in the history of the Church and of the world, whose zeal extended its influence, either in their own countries or throughout Christendom, whose reforming genius restored discipline and brought back lost integrity to failing or corrupted communities; and it will generally be found that while the spirit of the age, or the dead weight of human frailty dragged men downwards to crime and moral degradation, it was ever the stirring words, the indignant remonstrance, the indomitable courage and zeal, the exalted spiritual attainments of some saintly man that arrested the fatal course of nations or of men, and setting up once more the standard of Christ and His Cross, taught the better souls to follow it, and silenced and shamed the average professors of Christianity into a more consistent life. It has been said that the world does not know its greatest men. Certain it is that many who are "called benefactors" will with shame have to take "the lowest room," when "the last shall be first, and the first shall be last," and He "by whom actions are weighed" shall give to every man according to his works.

Monasticism had obscure beginnings. At first, there were no monasteries. Like the kingdom of heaven, Monasticism was as "the mustard seed that is the least of all seeds." Like the seed itself that is buried in the ground unseen, so that no one can record its first budding into life and vigour; like the wondrous organism of body, soul, and spirit that is presently known as the great man of his day, but which was "day by day fashioned" in secrecy and darkness, none knows how; so that which in the progress of the ages covered the earth had such a humble and obscure commencement that we search in vain for certain and accepted annals of its birth and infancy. Some authorities unhesitatingly declare that Anthony was the founder of Monasticism, while others, with equal certainty, assign it to a totally different origin; and there are not wanting those who pronounce that Anthony never existed, and that he was but the mythical invention of a superstitious age!

There seems, then, an unavoidable groping in the dark, and a necessary contentment with mere probabilities, when we ransack the pages of antiquity, and ask the opinion of those who seem best qualified to satisfy our inquiries, as to the earliest phases of that which ultimately developed into Monasticism. If there is one point upon which there is, on the whole, unanimity of opinion, it is that we must look to the East for the embryonic sources of Monasticism; and with almost equal agreement the best authorities declare that Egypt was the country of its birth. It is probable, however, that there were hermits and ascetics in other countries, like John the Baptist, living solitary and mortified lives in the wilderness; while the Carmelite Order boldly claims Elijah as its founder, or at least its primogenitor and example. On the other hand, it is maintained by learned authorities that it was the Decian persecution in the third century that caused many to flee to the deserts, that they might practise their religion without interference or danger. It is quite likely that this attack upon Christianity may have added to the number of those who retired to Nitria and other inaccessible regions, but it is difficult to believe, in the face of the accounts we have of recluses, even before the Christian era, that there were not some, if not many, who retired from the world from other and higher motives than that of fear of torture and death. Indeed, Bossuet says—"Persecution made fewer solitaries than the peace and triumph of the Church. The Christians, who were such enemies to luxury, feared a peace which flattered the senses more than they feared the cruelty of tyrants. The deserts became peopled by innumerable angels who lived in mortal bodies, without holding to the earth."

Of this multitude of persons of both sexes, scarcely any names have come down to us. It is hardly possible that it could be otherwise. Not only is the time remote, not only were historians and chroniclers few, but these men and women deliberately hid themselves in obscurity, and desired nothing so much as to live and die unknown. PAUL, the hermit, is known to us because he was visited by Anthony, but little more is told us of his history. St. Jerome says of Monasticism, "Hujus vitæ auctor Paulus, illustrator etiam Antonius." The records or legends of desert life begin with ANTHONY. Born about the middle of the third century, of wealthy and noble parentage, at the age of twenty he heard the Gospel story of Christ's reply to the rich young man who came to ask Him what he must do to inherit eternal life, and, unlike that rejecter of the call to "perfection," he literally obeyed our Lord's instructions. He went at once and sold all his possessions, and leaving friends and home and the world itself, he retired into the desert, and passed years in solitude, prayer, and the severest mortifications. There is a difference of

opinion among his biographers as to his education
and mental acquirements. St. Athanasius maintains
that Anthony always possessed a love of reading, and
that he employed himself during his retirement in
the study of the Scriptures; but St. Augustine says
that Anthony could not even read, and that his
parents had not allowed him to be taught lest he
should read immoral and injurious books. He continued this hermit life till his fifty-fifth year, when,
in obedience to the repeated entreaties of other recluses, he became their head, and practically established the first monastery. This is said to have been
at Phaium, in Upper Egypt. He is reported to have
visited Alexandria during the persecution commenced
by Maximius, and again, about 355, in order to
oppose the spread of the Arian heresy, but he was
always anxious to return to his monastery, saying,
"As fish die if they leave the water, so does a monk
if he forsakes his solitude." His fame spread far
and wide, and many persons, out of devotion or from
curiosity, visited him; and the Emperor Constantine
and his sons wrote a letter to him, commending themselves to his prayers. The fame and example of
Anthony gave a fresh impetus to the ascetic life; many
persons joined his monastery, and other communities
were formed upon the model which he had established.
It is said that in the days of St. Jerome nearly fifty
thousand monks were sometimes assembled at the
Easter festivals; that in the desert of Nitria alone
there were, in the fourth century, five thousand monks
under a single abbot; that an Egyptian city, named

Oxysynchus, devoted itself almost exclusively to the ascetic life, and included twenty thousand virgins and ten thousand monks; that Serapion presided over ten thousand monks; and that at the close of the fourth century, the monastic population in a great part of Egypt was nearly equal to the population of the cities.

We have thus arrived at an important epoch when monastic life really began, as distinguished from the solitary retirement of individuals from the world. There was the greatest difference between a multitude of ascetics, however numerous, living in the same neighbourhood, but altogether independent of each other, and having no common rule of life, praying, fasting, and working each as he pleased, and a community of monks under the headship of an abbot, to whom they owed obedience, and by whose orders they regulated their devotions and their labour.

At this time, and for a long period afterwards, each monastery was absolutely independent of all others. There was no order of monks, and no rule for the guidance of monastic life generally. Each abbot ruled his society according to his own ideas, following, as he thought best, the traditions that had been handed down orally by a long succession of hermits and recluses. Nor must we, while we use the word monastery, suppose that there was anything in common in outward appearance, between the primitive community of monks in the Eastern deserts and the stately European abbey of the fourteenth century. We must picture to ourselves a number of caves, or wattled huts, each inhabited by a half-naked man, with unkempt hair and unwashed body, praying, making baskets or mats, or digging the ground and cultivating a few herbs or roots, at certain not very regular hours, determined for the most part by the rising and setting sun; a wooden mallet struck upon a suspended board was the signal for these wild-looking devotees to assemble for united worship, or to hear some address or instruction from their abbot. Sometimes a brother would be sent on an errand to a distant town; sometimes a visitor of importance would arrive; sometimes a novice would be received into the body; sometimes death would put an end to the unchronicled existence of a brother, whose emaciated body would be laid in a nameless grave, and whose hut would presently be tenanted by another brother, who would lead the same changeless life, and die in the same way, and be forgotten. Sometimes, however—especially in the latter period of this phase of Monasticism—the monks would leave their home in a body, or in considerable numbers, and betake themselves to the towns to join in the violent controversies of the day. We read of such demonstrations in connection with Arianism and the Iconoclastic movement; and the tragic fate of Hypatia, at Alexandria, was brought about by one of these monkish raids. At other times " wandering in bands through the country, the monks were accustomed to burn the temples, to break the idols, to overthrow the altars, to engage in fierce conflicts with the peasants, who often defended with desperate courage the shrines of their gods, and were quite unmoved by the grandeur of the Serapeum, or of the noble statues of Phidias and Praxiteles."[1]

But notwithstanding such fanatical outbursts, the monastic system afforded an asylum for noble and pure souls, who revolted from the degraded state of society during the later years of the Roman Empire. "The monastic system called into existence a body of men who, in self-denial, in singleness of purpose, in heroic courage ... have seldom been surpassed. Abandoning every tie of home and friendship, discarding all the luxuries and most of what are deemed the necessaries of life, scourging and lacerating their bodies ... wandering half-starved and half-naked through the deserts with the wild beasts for their only companions, the early monks almost extinguished every natural sentiment, and emancipated themselves as far as it is possible from the conditions of humanity. Ambition, wrath, ease, and all the motives that tell most powerfully upon mankind, were to them unmeaning words. No reward could bribe them, no danger could appal them, no affection could move them."[2]

The creation of monasteries, which was inaugurated by Anthony, in the deserts, soon spread to the towns, and this itself caused considerable modifications in the rules and discipline of the communities, and prepared the way for the further development of Monasticism in hitherto unknown directions. The abbot

---

[1] Lecky, *European Morals*, vol. ii.
[2] Lecky, *Rationalism*, vol. ii.

became a personage of importance. The monk was no longer ignorant of the events in the world around him. In troublous times, when a strong hand was wanted to quell disorder, or an opinion and advice were needed unbiased by party prejudice and greedy self-seeking, or a bishop could not be found among the secular clergy qualified to rule a great diocese, it was in the cloister that search was made for the man filled with the Spirit of God, uncorrupted by contact with the world, without family ties, without ambition. Or, greatness and goodness, hide themselves as they might, would nevertheless become known, and the saintly abbot, or the humble but much-loved preaching monk, would be dragged by force from his happy obscurity into the full glare of the world's notoriety, and into the uncongenial turmoil of controversy, war, or political strife. And later still, when the repeated invasions of the barbarians not merely devastated the fairest countries and reduced the small remainder of the population to despair, it was in the monastery that brave and patient men refused to give up hope, and not only preserved much of the old civilization, but performed the harder task of converting savages into reasonable men, and then into practising Christians.

The next name that emerges dimly from the mists of monastic antiquity is that of PACOMIUS. He was contemporary with Anthony, and was a native of the Thebaïd. His parents were heathen, but he was early converted to Christianity through the charity of some kind-hearted people who relieved him when in distress. He had been carried off as a conscript by the Emperor's recruiting agents, and being treated with great cruelty, was fed and cared for by the Christians of one of the towns where he and his comrades stayed for a time on their way to the army. As soon as he obtained his release from the service he made his way back to his benefactors, and was instructed and baptized. He then betook himself to a hermit, and placed himself under his direction, and ultimately adopted his way of life. After some years he went to Tabenna, a small place near the first cataract of the Nile, and there gave himself up to the practice of austerities and to meditation and prayer. Others soon joined him, and before long there were a hundred devout men living with or near him. For the guidance of these he drew up a Rule of life, which is believed to have been the first monastic Rule committed to writing. Many other monasteries were established in the neighbourhood of his foundation, which were visited by St. Athanasius, who has left an account of what he saw, mentioning among other particulars that there were three thousand monks in that one locality. Before his death the number of monks under the authority of Pacomius had reached the surprising aggregate of seven thousand. The Rule of Pacomius was observed for many centuries, and over a wide area in the East, till it was superseded by the Rule of St. Basil.

During all this time convents for women had also been established; so St. Chrysostom writes—" Go to the Thebaïd, and you will find there a solitude still more beautiful than Paradise, a thousand choirs of angels under the human form, nations of martyrs, armies of virgins, the diabolical tyrant chained, and Christ triumphant and glorified."[1] There had been women-hermits and ascetics before there were communities of nuns. The female relations of Anthony, Pacomius, and others had followed them into the desert, and imitated their mode of life. The names of some of these primitive devotees have been recorded by historians. Alexandra, Euphrosyne, Eugenia, Mary, Thaïs, Pelagia, Euphrasia, are lauded for their extraordinary austerities; some virgins or widows, having given up rank and wealth; others having been converted from a life of pleasure and profligacy; while others, such as Paula and Eustochium, who placed themselves under the direction of St. Jerome at Bethlehem, were distinguished for learning as well as for devotion.

Another early father of Monasticism was AMMONIUS, a contemporary of St. Anthony, and of the same nationality. He was a married man; but he and his wife agreed to separate and devote themselves to the religious life, and each became the head of a large community of monks and nuns respectively. It is said by some writers that there were two brothers of this name, and that they both retired from the world.

MACARIUS was a native of Alexandria. In 335 he gave up his business and took up his abode in Thebaïs as a hermit. He is said to have been remarkable, even among the numerous ascetics of his

[1] In Matt. Hom. 8.

time, for extraordinary fasting, and for supernatural gifts and powers.

HILARION was the first to introduce the eremitical life into Syria, of which country he was a native. He was sent to Alexandria for education, and there became acquainted with the fame of St. Anthony, and visited him. After imitating his manner of life for some years in Egypt, he returned to his own country, and established a monastic community at Gaza. He afterwards visited Cyprus, and induced many to follow his mode of life, and there he ended his days.

NILUS was the first of many ascetics who settled themselves in the neighbourhood of Mount Sinai, where numerous monasteries were established afterwards.

EPIPHANIUS, EPHREM, and others were pioneers in the introduction of Monasticism, in its most primitive form, into various parts of the East; so that in Mesopotamia, Armenia, Persia and India, Africa and Asia Minor, there were thousands of religious of both sexes, who vied with one another in the practice of mortifications. Some were called "Browsers," because they lived entirely upon raw herbs; others, like Simon Stylites, who lived for more than forty years upon the top of a pillar of stone, invented new and unheard-of austerities; while many were put to death by the Emperor Julian, by the Persians, and other pagans, and were reckoned among the martyrs.

We now meet with the name of one who was one of the most influential promoters of Monasticism,

BASIL, who was born about 329 at Cæsarea. His parents were of noble rank. Basil displayed so much youthful talent and ability that he was sent to Constantinople to complete his education, and from thence he went to Athens. Here he became intimate with Gregory Nazianzen, who continued to be his friend throughout his life. Basil returned to Cæsarea and practised at the bar, while he also opened a philosophical school. He soon attained eminence and reputation, but with Gregory he discoursed much upon the variety of human life, and they resolved to give up their secular occupations and to take up the religious life. Basil then left his home and visited many of the most celebrated monasteries. Returning once more to Cappadocia, he was ordained deacon, and then retired to Pontus, where he gathered other like-minded men, and formed them into a monastic community, and with them devoted himself to religion and to sacred literature. After some years he was ordained priest, and ultimately became Bishop of Cæsarea. He came into conflict with the Emperors Julian and Valens, the former endeavouring to stamp out Christianity, and to revive paganism; the latter persecuting the Catholics, and seeking to propagate the Arian heresy in place of the faith of Nicæa.

But the great work of Basil was the lasting service that he rendered to Monasticism in the formation of the Rule, which has ever since been the law and guide of life to all the oriental Religious Orders. Hitherto every founder, and practically every abbot, had been free to govern his monastery or monasteries in his own way. The ancient traditions provided on the whole a uniform system as regards poverty, chastity, and obedience; but there were manifold variations in the discipline and practice of different communities. Basil gathered up all these traditions, and digested them into one system, which rapidly commended itself to general adoption, and still rules supreme in the religious houses of the eastern branches of the Catholic Church. The Rule was twofold, and was called the Longer and the Shorter Rule. Basil in these codes lays it down that the cenobitic life is, on the whole, better than the eremitical, thus introducing a variation from the original practice of ascetics, which has ever since regulated the conduct of those who desire to give themselves to the religious life. Another important point was the insistence upon the monk's external and even internal submission to his superior; curtailing the individual liberty that had been claimed and exercised by each separate hermit. There was also a special provision that the monastery should afford hospitality to strangers, travellers, and the poor; at the same time, there was the practical and common-sense safeguard against imposition and the abuse of charity, in the hint that the clothing and diet of the monk should be inferior to that of ordinary persons living in the world. Indeed he orders but one meal a day, and that without flesh, and curtails the hours of sleep, by requiring that all monks should rise at midnight to commence their devotions for the day. At the same time he displays a broad and enlightened apprehension of the supremacy of the spirit of Monasticism over the mere letter of hard and fast rules and regulations by saying, "If fasting hinders you from labour, it is better to eat like the workmen of Christ that you are."

"The transition from the eremite to the monastic life involved not only a change of circumstances, but also a change of character. The habit of obedience, and the virtue of humility, assumed a position which they had never previously occupied. The conditions of the hermit life contributed to develop to a very high degree a spirit of independence and spiritual pride. . . . But in the highly organized and disciplined monasteries of the West, passive obedience and humility were the very first things that were inculcated . . . and as the monk represented the highest moral ideal of the age, obedience and humility acquired a new value in the minds of men. . . . The entire mode or tenor of the monastic life was designed to tame every sentiment of pride, and to give humility a foremost place in the hierarchy of virtues."[1]

The following is a short abstract of

THE RULE OF ST. BASIL.

Chap. I. commands the monks to live together for the sake of mutual help, instruction, and prayer.

Chap. II. ordains that no one be admitted without trial and probation.

Chap. III. lays it down that every one must dispose of his possessions to the poor.

Chap. IV. allows the admission of children, with the consent of their parents.

---

[1] Lecky, *Morals*, vol. ii.

Chap. V. enjoins abstinence in eating and drinking.

Chap. VI. requires plain apparel, and the wearing of a girdle.

Chap. VII. commands obedience to the Superior, next to God.

Chap. VIII. declares the necessary qualities of Superiors.

Chap. IX. directs Superiors to reprove offenders with gentleness, but to deal severely with the obstinate.

Chap. X. forbids the overlooking of the least offence.

Chap. XI. requires the monks to confess their faults to those appointed to this office.

Chap. XII. requires that all things should be common.

Chap. XIII. enjoins that property should be given up to those of kin, and some portion to the poor.

Chap. XIV. forbids any to leave the monastery without special permission.

Chap. XV. orders that defamation of any Brother be punished by excommunication.

Chap. XVI. enjoins that no one does his own will.

Chap. XVII. requires the free admission and fair trial of postulants.

Chap. XVIII. commands the Superior to regulate the eating and abstaining of the members.

Chap. XIX. orders members to receive a garment when it is offered.

Chap. XX. says that those who do not come to dinner at the appointed time shall eat nothing till the same hour next day.

Chap. XXI. forbids any gift except by the means of the appointed persons.

Chap. XXII. commands care of all the goods of the monastery.

Chap. XXIII. requires each monk to devote himself to some useful work.

Chap. XXIV. orders the wearing of sackcloth in token of humility; and moderation in talking.

Chap. XXV. forbids the monks to speak to women alone.

CHRYSOSTOM, the Archbishop of Constantinople, had much influence in the progress of Monasticism. He wrote a treatise in defence of the Monastic Life, and in his Commentaries on the New Testament he laid down rules as to the right principles which should inspire those who embraced that life. At the same time he severely rebukes those vagabond monks who brought scandal upon their profession, and upon Christianity itself, and he does not for a moment hesitate to speak plainly to the Emperor himself, when he attempts to interfere with the liberties of the Church and of the Monastic Orders.

The General Council of Chalcedon (451) made certain decrees respecting Monasticism, which the abuses of the times demanded. It was laid down that no monastery should be built without the consent of the bishop of the diocese, and that the bishop should be the visitor, and the source of final appeal in all cases of dispute or uncertainty among the monks; and that monks should not be allowed to quit their convent, or to employ themselves in secular business.

The great ATHANASIUS was the first and principal instrument for introducing the monastic system, which had originated in the East, into the various countries of the West, where Christianity had taken root. He had visited Anthony, and had made personal acquaintance with the system which was already flourishing and spreading in Egypt and elsewhere. Driven from Alexandria by the Arian faction, he sought refuge in Rome, having with him some of the monks from the Thebaïd. The words and outward demeanour of these devout men made a strong and lasting impression upon the Roman Church. There had been some instances of the religious life in Rome and other places in the West, but the visit of Athanasius and his companions stirred up a new enthusiasm, and created a passion for Monasticism which had not existed before, and for ever removed the occidental prejudice against that which had been regarded with something like suspicion as an oriental institution. Athanasius spread this feeling yet more widely by writing the life of St. Anthony, which was soon copied and circulated far and wide. Monasteries rapidly multiplied in and about Rome, and then were founded in various places in Italy, and in the islands of the Mediterranean. The nobility and other men of wealth and position were among the first and most eager to join this new movement, to the astonishment of the heathen, and even of Christians. St. Jerome writes—" Formerly, according to the testimony of the Apostle, there were few rich, few noble, few powerful among Christians. Now it is no longer so. Not only among the Christians, but among the monks are to be found a multitude of the wise, the noble, and the rich."[1]

Many of these wealthy men gave up their own houses to be the homes of the monks; and it is probable that the usual plan of the European monastery was originally derived from that of the larger Roman villas. The remains that still exist at Pompeii and elsewhere show that these houses consisted of courts surrounded by cloisters, into which the principal apartments opened. The northern climate demanded more shelter, and other modifications; but looking at the ground-plans of many of the ancient abbeys in England, France, and Italy, we cannot help being

[1] Epist. 24.

struck with the resemblance between them and the patrician residences of the later Roman period.

"Persecution aroused a passionate, religious enthusiasm that showed itself in an ardent desire for those sufferings which were believed to lead directly to heaven; and this enthusiasm, after the peace of Constantine, found its natural vent and sphere in the macerations of the desert life ... and the extreme luxury of the great cities produced a violent, but not unnatural, reaction of asceticism. The dignity of the monastic position, which sometimes brought men who had been simple peasants into connection with the Emperors; the security it furnished to fugitive slaves and criminals; the desire of escaping from the fiscal burdens which, in the corrupt and oppressive administration of the Empire, had acquired an intolerable weight; and especially the barbarian invasions, which produced every variety of pain and wretchedness, conspired with the new religious teaching in peopling the desert."[1]

The next great name in the annals of Monasticism is that of JEROME. This remarkable man was born either in or near the borders of Northern Italy, in or about 330. His father was a man of rank and means, and took care to give his son a liberal education. At Rome, Jerome pursued his studies with diligence and distinction, but seems to have arrived at man's estate without any personal acquaintance with the duties and restraints of religion. He visited the principal seats of learning in Gaul, and so became

[1] Lecky, *Morals*, vol. ii.

acquainted with the best authors of antiquity, and enlarged his mind and sympathies by converse with the learned and gifted men of his day. But a more important change was made in his thoughts and life by the influence of other men of singular piety and devotion. He became himself a devout and earnest Christian, and in order to deepen and confirm his aspiration, he entered a monastery at Aquileia. After some time spent there he again visited Rome, and then travelled in different directions to make the acquaintance of hermits, ascetics, and monks, of whose fame he had heard, and from whom he desired instruction and edification. In some of his numerous letters he gives details of his mortifications and of his mental trials, and of his final determination to give up secular studies, and to devote himself entirely to the reading of the Scriptures and the cultivation of spiritual advancement. He again spent some time in Rome, and was entrusted by Pope Damasus with important offices. He finally retired to Bethlehem, where he superintended a convent of nuns, founded by Paula, a rich and devout Roman lady. He became an authority, not only in all matters of Scriptural criticism, but especially with reference to the monastic life, and he maintained a large correspondence on this subject with many who sought his advice in almost every part of Christendom.

Monasticism had now (fourth century) become firmly established in the West, and continued to spread and increase. But its success raised envy and opposition. Paganism was dying, but its adherents were especially irritated against the monks and nuns, whose austerities condemned their own vicious lives, and to whose enthusiasm they attributed much of the decadence of the old religion. Ancient and noble families resented the loss of sons and daughters who buried themselves in the cloister, and of the money that was taken away to endow monasteries. Scandalous reports were circulated to rouse the populace, and mobs attacked the religious of both sexes, and clamoured to have them put down by State authority. It was complained that so many men were withdrawn from active life that the army would not be recruited, and that literature would languish. Among those who came forward to defend Monasticism was AMBROSE, the saintly Bishop of Milan. He encouraged the creation of monasteries in his own diocese, and wrote a treatise, *De Virginitate*, in apology for the vocation of women to the Religious Life. It was through the influence of Ambrose that Augustine became ashamed of his self-indulgent life; and it was by seeing the virgin purity and heroic self-conquest of the inmates of the convents that he was stimulated to follow their example. It is a matter of dispute whether AUGUSTINE himself really became a monk, but there is abundant evidence that he adopted the regulated and ascetic life of the cloister, and that in his own diocese he promoted the establishment of religious houses, and wrote in defence of them. It was greatly owing to him that Monasticism spread throughout the African provinces, and it was by his watchful care and wholesome safeguards that abuses, which speedily showed themselves, were checked, and their recurrence rendered almost impossible. This was especially due to the publication (423) of the Rule, which has ever since borne his name, and which has been adopted by many congregations of religious, down to the present time; and to the publication of a book, *De Opere Monachorum*, which was directed against the vice of idleness among monks, and which emphatically insisted upon the duty and dignity of labour, and its necessity for the well-being of Monasteries, and the healthy, spiritual life of its inmates. It is noteworthy that, so early in the history of Monasticism, it should have been found necessary to guard against that fault which, down to our own day, has constantly been attributed to the "lazy monk."

A very remarkable early father of Monasticism was CASSIODORUS, who late in life became a monk, and the founder of an important monastery. He had been the chief minister and adviser of Theodoric and his successors; for although he was himself of one of the oldest and noblest Roman families, he did not refuse to serve under the barbarian conquerors. For fifty years he devoted himself to State duties, and his influence obtained justice and protection for the Catholics from their Arian rulers. When seventy years old he retired (539) from his secular labours and duties, and, instead of enjoying rest and rewards, he became a simple monk in a monastery which he had erected on his estate in Calabria at Viviers. This convent grew to vast proportions, and sheltered a large number of monks, students, and scholars. An extensive library was collected, books were written, and a regular course of study was laid down and pursued. There was also the usual requirement of manual labour; the poor were fed, and the neighbouring peasantry were instructed in husbandry and other arts.

Monasteries were probably not known in Spain till the middle of the sixth century, but hermits and independent ascetics existed at an earlier date. The first record of monasteries that is known occurs in the acts of the Council of Tarragona (516), and the first monastery is said to have been established at Servitarium in Valencia, by DONATUS, a monk from Africa, about the middle of the sixth century. The Rule of St. Benedict was not adopted at first, but afterwards was generally followed. One of the earliest monastic founders, whose name has come down to us, was EMILIANUS, who, like so many others, began his career as an anchorite, and was joined by others, and so became the head of a monastery. Another famous monk was FRUCTUOSUS, a Goth of noble or royal family, who, in the early part of the seventh century, founded the monastery of Compludo, in the valley of Vierzo. Other communities followed, and the district became a kind of Thebaïd.

In Gaul the religious life found a strong advocate and promoter in MARTIN, Bishop of Tours. He himself lived in a monastery that he had founded near his episcopal city; or rather, he and his brethren lived in huts or caves in the rocks on the banks of the Loire, on the spot where in after years the great and wealthy Abbey of Marmoutier stood in its stately magnificence. In other parts similar communities were formed by CASSIANUS,[1] GERMANUS of Auxerre, and other remarkable men, and their monasteries became the centres of civilization and of religion, and endured and flourished for more than a thousand years.

One of the most important foundations was that of LERINS. Like several other influential monastic metropolises, this was established upon an island. Two or three rocky islands lie in the Mediterranean, not far from Cannes, and from these, as afterwards from Iona and Lindisfarne, there came men who did much to shape the religious life of Europe. HONORATUS, a young man of rank and education, gave up all his prospects in life, and, retiring (410) to one of these islands, gathered round him a band of kindred spirits, who formed themselves into a strict religious community, which speedily grew in numbers and importance, and ultimately became a source of devotion and learning famous throughout the Christian world. Bishops for many of the principal sees in Gaul were taken from the monks of Lerins; and writers, such as Vincent of Lerins, were not only justly honoured in their own day, but still hold a high place among the defenders or expounders of the Catholic faith.

"The sea took the place of the desert, but the type

[1] Note A, p. 384.

of monastic life which the solitaries had found in Egypt was faithfully preserved. The Abbot of Lerins was simply the chief of some thousands of religious devotees, scattered over the island in solitary cells, and linked together by the common ties of obedience and prayer. By a curious concurrence of events, the cœnobitic life of Lerins, so utterly unlike the later Monasticism of the Benedictines, was long preserved in a remote corner of Christendom. PATRICK, the most famous of its scholars, transmitted its type of Monasticism to the Celtic Church which he founded in Ireland; and the vast numbers, the asceticism, the loose organization of such abbeys as those of Bangor or Armagh, preserved to the twelfth century the essential characteristics of Lerins. Nor is this all its historical importance. What Iona is to the ecclesiastical history of Northern England, what Fulda and Monte Cassino are to the ecclesiastical history of Germany and Southern Italy, that this Abbey of St. Honorat became to the Church of Southern Gaul. For nearly two centuries—and those centuries of momentous change, when the wreck of the Roman Empire threatened civilization and Christianity with ruin like its own—the civilization and Christianity of the great district between the Loire, the Alps, and the Pyrenees rested mainly on the Abbey of Lerins. Sheltered by its insular position from the ravages of the barbaric invaders who poured down on the Rhone and the Garonne, it exercised over Provence and Aquitaine a supremacy such as Iona, till the Synod of Whitby, exercised over Northumbria. All the more illustrious sees of Southern Gaul were filled by prelates who had been reared at Lerins; to Arles, for instance, it gave in succession Hilary, Cæsarius, and Virgilius. The voice of the Church was found in that of its doctors; the famous rule of Faith—'*quod ubique, quod semper, quod ab omnibus*'—is the rule of Vincent of Lerins; its monk Salvian painted the agony of the dying Empire in his book on the Government of God; the long fight of semi-Pelagianism against the sterner doctrines of Augustine was chiefly waged within its bounds . . . The appearance of the Moslem pirates at once robbed St. Honorat of its old security, and the cessation of their attacks was followed by a new danger from the Genoese and Calabrians who infested the coast in the fourteenth century. The isle was alternately occupied by French and Spaniards in the war between Francis and Charles V.; it passed under the rule of commendatory abbots, and in 1789, when it was finally secularized, the 4000 monks of its earlier history had shrunk to four!"[1]

[1] *Stray Studies*, J. R. Green (Macmillan).

CHAPTER III

THE GROWTH AND WORK OF MONASTICISM

> Verily I say unto you, There is no man that hath left house, or brethren, or sisters, or father, or mother, or wife, or children, or lands, for my sake, and the Gospel's, but he shall receive an hundredfold now in this time, houses, and brethren, and sisters, and mothers, and children, and lands, with persecutions; and in the world to come eternal life.—*St. Mark* x. 29, 30.

BY the end of the fifth century Monasticism had spread all over the Christian world. It still retained its original Oriental characteristics. There were unattached hermits, and there were monasteries independent of each other, each governed by its own abbot without reference to other monasteries. The Rule of St. Basil was taken as the broad principle for the guidance of monastic life, but it was not felt to have any binding authority, and its regulations were modified or rescinded, as circumstances seemed to require, or as the judgment of the abbot determined.

There were seen also, even in this early period, signs of weakness in the system, and a loss of its public estimation. There was a tendency to inaction and coldness, and Monasticism seemed to be settling down into that placid, spiritless condition which still distinguishes and enfeebles the monasteries of the

Eastern Church at the present day. The complaints against the monks and their mode of life, which were heard so frequently in later times, are to be found even in the records of the fourth century. Thus the Emperor Valens issued an edict (373) ordering monks to serve in the army, like other citizens; and there were not wanting those who questioned the sincerity of many religious professions, on the ground that the position of the slave, the peasant, and the fugitive from barbarian invasion, made no sacrifice by entering a monastery, but rather secured a safe and more desirable life than that which he gave up. It was declared to be an unpatriotic act to leave the service of the State at a time when it was weakened by attacks from without; and the still surviving advocates of the old pagan system sneered at the rude habits of the monks, and their ignorance of secular learning.

Thus some writings of the poet Rutilius are extant, composed in the early part of the fifth century. Speaking of a voyage in the Mediterranean, he describes an island, near Corsica, as "full of wretches, enemies of light; they draw from the Greek their name of monks, because they would live without witnesses. Fear of the evils of fortune has made them dread its gifts. They make themselves poor in anticipation, lest one day they should become so: was there ever folly so perverse? There one of my fellow-citizens has lost himself, descending alive into the tomb. He was recently one of us; he was young, of great birth, rich, well-married. But, impelled by the Furies, he has fled from men and gods, and now, credulous exile, lies decaying in a foul retreat. Is not this sect more fatal than the poisons of Circe?"[1]

Gibbon readily adopts this pagan view of the motives of the early recluses.

"The subjects of Rome, whose persons and fortunes were made responsible for unequal and exorbitant tributes, retired from the oppression of the imperial government; and the pusillanimous youth preferred the penance of a monastic to the dangers of a military life. The affrighted provincials, of every rank, who fled before the barbarians, found shelter and subsistence; whole legions were buried in these religious sanctuaries; and the same cause, which relieved the distress of individuals, impaired the strength and fortitude of the empire."[2]

In the first century of their institution, the infidel Zosimus maliciously observed, that, "for the benefit of the poor, the Christian monks had reduced a great part of mankind to a state of beggary."

The first phase of Monasticism had been attained; stagnation was setting in; new life was needed, adaptation to the wants of the times, and some evident merit in the system which should command the respect and admiration of the world. In short, a master-mind was required, a leader, with singular gifts and powers, to stir up the dull average commonplace intellect and will, and to do for Monasticism

---

[1] The poem is quoted at some length by Dugdale, in the Introduction to his *Monasticon Ang.*
[2] *Decline and Fall*, vol. vi.

that good service which great and vigorous men have rendered in every epoch of progress, and in the history of all that relates to man's advancement in knowledge, in politics, in mechanics, in art, and in religion.

Such a man was found in BENEDICT, who was to Monasticism very much the same power that St. Paul was to Apostolic Christianity.

Benedict, like so many men whose names stand out prominently in the annals of the world and of the Church, was of noble birth. His family was ancient and honourable in the town of Nursia, in Umbrian Italy. He was born about 480, and received by his parents' wishes, the best education that was obtainable in his native place. In order that he might carry on his studies to the highest attainments, he was sent to Rome. Here his pure instincts were intensely shocked by the licentiousness which prevailed, and by the precocious depravity of his schoolfellows. Although still a child, under sixteen years of age, he adopted the singular course of fleeing from the corrupting influences that surrounded him, and of taking up the life of a recluse. He stole away to the mountains and settled himself in a cavern at Subiaco, about forty miles from Rome. Here he lived for some years in lonely obscurity, till his fame gradually spread; and when the abbot of a small monastery near Tivoli died, the monks almost forced Benedict to take his place. He did not remain long in this position, but returned to his solitary cave, where many devout persons came to visit him. Among these some left their sons with him to be trained in religious knowledge and practices. Finding himself thus sought for, he fled with a few companions to Monte Cassino, where on the top of a lofty hill there stood a temple of Apollo, in which pagan worship was still maintained. Benedict so wrought upon the people that they embraced Christianity, and pulled down the temple; and on its site was commenced (529) the monastery which gradually attained world-wide reputation, and which was the nursery of the great Benedictine Order, and the source from which religion and the civilization of Europe largely proceeded.

The most important and lasting service that Benedict rendered to Monasticism was the compilation of the RULE which introduced new life into the system, gathering up all its forces into one channel, and ultimately binding into a compact body a multitude of devoted men who formed the army of the Church, both for defence and for conquest. Unity is strength. The world was in a chaotic condition. The ancient civilization had been ruined by the barbarian conquests. The old religions were no longer respected. The invading savages could not impress their wild mythologies and degrading rites upon the more intelligent peoples whom they vanquished. All was unrest, uncertainty, despair. Destruction reigned supreme, and even hope had fled.

In the midst of such moral and social ruin a solid power, animated by ardent faith, unity of purpose, and dauntless courage, was certain to prevail. Order and law could not fail to get the better of disorganized forces, mutually destructive. Men desired leaders whom they could respect and trust, and they found them in the abbots of Benedictine monasteries.

"The rapid decomposition of the entire Roman Empire by continuous invasions of barbarians rendered the existence of an inviolable asylum and centre of peaceful labour a matter of transcendent importance; the monastery, as organized by St. Benedict, soon combined the most heterogeneous elements of attraction. It was at once eminently aristocratic, and intensely democratic. The power and princely position of the abbot was coveted, and usually obtained by members of the most illustrious families; while emancipated serfs, or peasants who had lost their all in the invasions, or were harassed by savage nobles, or had fled from military service, or desired to lead a more secure and easy life, found in the monastery an unfailing refuge. The institution exercised all the influence of great wealth, expended for the most part with great charity; while the monk himself was invested with the aureole of a sacred poverty. In ardent and philanthropic natures, the profession opened boundless vistas of missionary, charitable, and civilizing activity. To the superstitious it was the plain road to heaven. To the ambitious it was the portal to bishoprics, and after the monk Gregory, not unfrequently to the Popedom. To the studious it offered the only opportunity then existing in the world of seeing many books and passing a life of study. To the timid and retiring it afforded the most secure, and probably the least laborious life a poor peasant could hope to find."[1]

The Rule of St. Benedict commences with a paternal address to the novice, couched in the terms of the Book of Proverbs, but inspired with the sweet compelling power of evangelical faith. "Hearken, my son, to the precepts of the Master, and incline to Him the ear of thy heart." In an age of savagery, lawlessness, and cruelty, it pleads with gentlest words, and holds out the promise of peace and blessedness. Labour had been reckoned degrading in the Roman rule of life, and had been relegated entirely to slaves. The savage tribes that poured down upon Italy were mere warriors, ignorant of agriculture and of every art, and despising every occupation but that of war; Benedict's Rule proclaimed the dignity and the necessity of labour, and sent every monk to the field or the workshop, whether he had been a Roman patrician or a Gaulish brave. Pride of independence distinguished the Roman citizen and the untamed barbarous chieftain alike, but in the monastery the first duty taught to each was that of obedience; and the better principles of the human heart at once found a new and unknown joy in the subjection of the will to authority, and in the freedom from responsibility that resulted from it.

Idleness had ever been stigmatized by all moralists as the mother of mischief and of sadness; the Rule of Benedict did away with this source of evil by providing his monks with never-ceasing occupation

[1] Lecky, *Morals*, vol. ii.

throughout the twenty-four hours of the day. Seven times the bell called to prayer and worship in the church; seven hours were spent in manual labour; rest and eating and recreation were all regulated; and in chapter each member of the society confessed his failure to observe the numerous requirements of the Rule, and received correction, or instruction. The abbot was supreme, but he was bound to consult his brethren in all matters of importance, as he was himself elected by the universal suffrage of the community. A certain number of monks were ordained priests, but the Order itself was distinctly intended for laymen. Certain officers were appointed for fulfilling the various duties of the monastery—cooking, buying and selling, building, the care of the sick, and the ministering to guests and the poor. Almost all trades and occupations found employment in a large convent; the clothes were made, repaired and washed, the corn was ground, cattle were bred and tended, books were written, bound and copied, and as far as possible everything was done within the walls, and external interference was rendered unnecessary.

A time of probation was required before any man could be admitted as a monk, and there was always a provision for the retirement from the monastery of any member who desired to leave. The food was of the plainest, and there was usually but one meal in the day, although sometimes two were allowed. The diet was strictly vegetarian, but a small quantity of the wine of the country was generally taken. The dress was that of the peasants of the period, made of the coarsest material. "St. Benedict allowed the habit to vary according to the climate, but for countries of mean temperature he gave it as his opinion that a garment called cuculla, a tunic, and a scapular were sufficient. The tunic was a shirt-like garment, the scapular was without sleeves, reaching to the knees, with a pointed cowl to cover the head. The cuculla was a large mantle, worn in choir, and enveloping the whole person."

"The favour of admission," says Dr. Lingard, "was purchased with a severe probation. On his knees, at the gate, the postulant requested to be received among the servants of God; but his desires were treated with contempt, and his pride was humbled by reproaches. After four days his perseverance subdued the apparent reluctance of the monks; he was successively transferred to the apartments of the strangers and of the novices, and an aged brother was commissioned to observe his conduct, and to instruct him in the duties of his profession. Before the expiration of the year, the Rule was read thrice in his presence, and each reading was accompanied with the admonition that he was still at liberty to depart. At last, on the anniversary of his admission, he entered the Church, and avowed before God and the community, his determination to spend his days in the monastic profession, to reform his conduct, and to obey his superiors. The solemn engagement he subscribed with his name, and deposited upon the altar."

"The Rule of St. Benedict allows parents to offer

up their children under fourteen years of age at God's altar, to serve Him to the end of their days in the cloister. In those lawless times, when acts of violence, rapine, and reckless profligacy were so common, holy parents thought that they could not better protect the purity of their children than by placing them at once under the shadow of a monastery. Monastic vows are in one sense only the completion of the vows of baptism; and it was not thought unnatural that those who, while the child was perfectly unconscious, placed him in the awful contact with the world unseen, implied in baptism, should also put him in the way of best fulfilling the vows to which they themselves had bound him in his infancy.... Every monk was bound to learn the Psalter by heart."[1]

"At first those who, when children, were devoted to the monasteries by their parents, without their own consent, were permitted, when of mature age, to return to the world; but this liberty was taken from them by the fourth Council of Toledo in 633. The Council of Gangra condemned those who taught that children might, through religious motives, forsake their parents, and St. Basil wrote in the same strain."[2]

The following is a short epitome of the several chapters of the Rule of Benedict—

Chap. I. confines the Rule to Cœnobites living under an abbot in a monastery, as distinguished from hermits and wandering ascetics.

---

[1] *Life of Stephen Harding.*—J. H. N.
[2] Lecky, *European Morals*, Pt. 2.

Chap. II. describes the necessary qualifications of an abbot as the representative of Jesus Christ.

Chap. III. requires the abbot to seek the opinion of all his monks before taking any important step.

Chap. IV. summarizes the duties of the Christian life under seventy-two precepts, and declares the monastery to be the fittest place for carrying them out in practice.

Chap. V. enjoins immediate obedience to superiors.

Chap. VI. commands silence.

Chap. VII. describes Humility under twelve conditions in monastic life.

Chap. VIII. orders the first service in church to commence at two a.m.

Chap. IX. arranges the offices and Psalms for the winter.

Chap. X. makes similar rules for the summer.

Chaps. XI. and XII. fix the services for Sunday night.

Chap. XIII. does the same for week-day nights.

Chap. XIV. appoints the offices for Holyday nights.

Chap. XV. defines the period for singing Alleluia.

Chaps. XVI., XVII. XVIII. arrange the day-offices by which the Psalter is sung through each week.

Chap. XIX. reminds the monks of the presence of God and of the angels, and on that account enforces reverence.

Chap. XX. regulates the length of prayers, and the order of leaving the church.

Chap. XXI. requires the appointment of a Decanus, over every ten brethren, in large monasteries.

Chap. XXII. refers to the dormitory, appointing a dean over every room; that a lamp should burn all night in each; that every one must sleep in his clothes, and girded; and that the young be separated from the old.

Chap. XXIII. condemns the disobedient, first to excommunication, and then to chastisement.

Chap. XXIV. punishes light faults with separation from the common table at meals.

Chap. XXV. punishes greater faults with exclusion from the table, prayers, and chapter-meetings.

Chap. XXVI. threatens excommunication to those who company with excommunicated persons.

Chap. XXVII. instructs the abbot as to his dealing with the excommunicated.

Chap. XXVIII. expels from the monastery the obstinate offender.

Chap. XXIX. permits the reception for three times only of those who have been expelled.

Chap. XXX. orders that children and ignorant persons be punished with fasting or chastisement.

Chap. XXXI. lays down the duties and qualifications of the steward of the monastery.

Chap. XXXII. requires the abbot to appoint fit men to take care of the goods of the monastery.

Chap. XXXIII. forbids any monk to possess anything personally.

Chap. XXXIV. orders the just distribution of everything belonging to the monastery.

Chap. XXXV. arranges that the monks must serve by turns in the kitchen and elsewhere, and that they wash each other's feet.

Chap. XXXVI. requires special care of the sick, and gives them certain relaxations.

Chap. XXXVII. grants relaxation of the Rule to the old and the young, as to food.

Chap. XXXVIII. appoints the use of reading during meals, and requires silence, and the use of signs.

Chap. XXXIX. allows each monk two dishes, fruit, and one pound of bread at dinner; but gives the abbot the power of regulating the meals according to the season, and the circumstances of each monk; forbidding the use of flesh-meat except by the sick.

Chap. XL. permits a certain amount of wine.

Chap. XLI. fixes the hours of dinner and supper, both for summer and winter.

Chap. XLII. appoints the public reading of some edifying book daily before evensong, and orders that absolute silence be kept after.

Chap. XLIII. punishes those who come late to church or to meals with loss of wine.

Chap. XLIV. orders excommunicated members to lie prostrate before the church-door, when their brethren are going to say the offices.

Chap. XLV. Mistakes in saying the offices must be acknowledged.

Chap. XLVI. All transgressions must be publicly confessed.

Chap. XLVII. The abbot must give the signal for going to church, and must lead the services.

Chap. XLVIII. Three hours in the morning and three in the afternoon must be devoted to manual labour, and two hours to reading.

Chap. XLIX. lays down rules for the observance of Lent, and forbids any austerities except those ordered by the superior.

Chap. L. Monks travelling or at labour must say the offices wherever they may be.

Chap. LI. Monks are forbidden to eat outside the monastery if they can return the same day.

Chap. LII. The church is to be used for nothing except the offices of devotion.

Chap. LIII. Strangers — especially the poor — are to be honoured as representatives of Christ; their feet are to be washed, and their hunger satisfied.

Chap. LIV. No monk must receive letters or presents, without permission.

Chap. LV. regulates the clothing of the monks.

Chap. LVI. The abbot may call particular monks to his table.

Chap. LVII. Workpeople living in the monastery must have their wages in common.

Chap. LVIII. Novices must be treated with severity before admission; they must have a year's probation, and hear the reading of the Rule frequently.

Chap. LIX. Children may be presented to the monastery, but parents must enter into a bond never to give them any property.

Chap. LX. Priests must observe the same regulations as laymen, before they are admitted as monks, and must not officiate in any way without the abbot's permission.

Chap. LXI. Monks from other monasteries may be admitted to stay.

Chap. LXII. Monks who are ordained to the priesthood must continue to be subject to the Rule, and to their deans.

Chap. LXIII. The order of precedence among the monks shall depend upon the date of their profession.

Chap. LXIV. The abbot must be elected by a majority of all the monks.

Chap. LXV. The abbot appoints and deposes his assistant officers.

Chap. LXVI. regulates the qualifications and duties of the porter.

Chap. LXVII. lays down rules for monks who are obliged to travel.

Chap. LXVIII. A monk must attempt to do what he is ordered, though he may consider it difficult, or even impossible.

Chap. LXIX. Faults are not to be defended or excused.

Chap. LXX. No striking or punishment is permitted except by the authority of the abbot.

Chap. LXXI. Mutual obedience is enjoined. If a superior finds fault, the offender is to prostrate himself before him.

Chap. LXXII. All must be done for love of Christ.

Chap. LXXIII. declares that the Rule is merely one means towards attaining godliness, and is but a beginning of perfection, and that Holy Scripture is the true rule of life.

Such were the principal provisions of the Rule of Benedict. It supplied a want that was generally felt; it summed up the results of the experience of preceding centuries. As has often happened, the man had come who could focus the rays of light that were feeble in themselves, and make them powerful by unity; the master-mind had grasped the vague ideas that were floating far and wide, and had reduced them to practical shape; he had taken the tide at its flood, and he rode triumphantly upon it. At the same time it does not appear that Benedict had any grand and world-wide scheme in his mind. His Rule was designed for himself and his companions at Monte Cassino, but its excellence commended it to general adoption, and the great Benedictine Order and its numerous offshoots carried it into every part of Christendom, and down the ages to our own day. Monte Cassino soon sent out colonies into other parts of Italy, and as time went on Gaul and Spain, Britain, Germany, Scandinavia, and the New World were taken possession of by the

Benedictines, till thirty-seven thousand houses were held by them; and emperors, popes, kings, queens, historians, and learned men were reckoned as members of the Order and disciples of the Rule.[1]

The Abbot of Monte Cassino possessed the following titles—

Patriarch of the Sacred Religion; Abbot of the Sacred Monastery of Cassin; Duke and Prince of all Abbots and Religious; Vice-Chancellor of the Kingdoms of both the Sicilies, of Jerusalem, and Hungary; Count and Governor of Campania, and Ferra de Lavoro, and of the Maritime Province; Vice-Emperor and Prince of Peace.

These magnificent results were hidden and unexpected in the time of Benedict and his successors. The world presented a lamentable aspect. Horde after horde of wild and destructive savages swept over every part of Europe and the colonies of Northern Africa, fulfilling the prophetic descriptions, and like locust-swarms turning fertile and beautiful lands into desolate wastes. The population was massacred, the buildings were reduced to shapeless ruins. Some of the invaders passed on; others settled down, and formed new kingdoms, whose fierce and ruthless rulers were perpetually engaged in warfare. What hope was there that modest and feeble monks could make any impression upon such a world, and upon those wild and beast-like men? Did they not rather flee from them to solitude, and merely ask to be allowed to live in their own way

[1] Note B, p. 385.

unmolested? There was no original idea in Monasticism of the conversion of the world; it came gradually, and was an indirect result of the operation of noble principles which were more powerful than their promoters imagined, and which could not be limited to the fields of exercise for which they were first formulated. The dominion of Monasticism was not sought by its early founders; it was rather forced upon them. The world came to the monks in their retirement, and made them powerful. Monks left the world to work out their own salvation; and they found that they were required to attain their object only by saving others. A few ascetics stole away to the depths of the forest, or to the further side of an unwholesome morass; they prayed, and laboured, and died; they were succeeded by generation after generation of this supernatural family, till there was seen a town where there had been pathless solitude, and rich and fertile land where only wild beasts had roamed. "We sometimes hear," says Archbishop Trench, "the ignoble observation that the monks knew how to pick out the best and most fertile spots for themselves; when it would be truer to say that they knew how to make that which had fallen to them, often the waste or the morass which none other cared to cultivate, the best; but this by the sweat of their brow and the intelligent labour of their hands."[1]

"It was," says Montalembert, "the sober judgment of the wisest and most charitable of the early ages

---

[1] *Lectures on Mediæval Church History* (Paul, Trench & Co.). See Note C, p. 385.

that the world was too bad to mend, and that its destruction was at hand. This feeling died out with the old empire, and the world began a new youth with the new kingdoms of the converted barbarians."

"In an age of turbulence and war, and while force continued to be everywhere triumphant, the uncompromising doctrine of the innate equality of men was slowly producing the most pregnant and remarkable change that has ever passed over the minds of a large section of the race. Even the all-powerful ruling classes could not remain permanently unaffected by a voice which, taking them generation after generation in their triumphs and pleasures, as well as in their most impressionable moments, whispered with all the weight of the most absolute and unquestionable authority that they were in reality of the same class as other men, and that in the eyes of a higher Power they stood on a footing of native equality with even the lowest of the earth."[1]

"The monastic bodies formed secure asylums for the multitudes who had been persecuted by their enemies; constituted an invaluable counterpoise to the rude military forces of the time; familiarized the imagination of men with religious types that could hardly fail in some degree to soften the character; and led the way in most forms of peaceful labour."[2]

Montalembert says—"It is in the preaching of the nothingness of human things; it is by sacrifice of

---

[1] *Social Evolution*, B. Kidd (Macmillan).
[2] Lecky, *European Morals*, vol. ii.

rank, of family, of fortune, and of country, that the monks created monuments and societies most lasting. How many monasteries have flourished, seven, eight, ten, sometimes even fourteen centuries, that is, as long as the French monarchy, and twice as long as the Roman republic."

It was with the utmost difficulty that ancient Rome could support the institution of six Vestals; but the primitive Church was filled with a great number of persons of either sex who had devoted themselves to the profession of perpetual chastity. The Vestals had wealth and the highest honours bestowed upon them, yet their number could scarcely be kept up.

St. Ambrose, in his controversy with Symmachus, dwells upon the contrast between the Vestals and the nuns of his day. He recalls the splendour of the palace of the Vestals, their sumptuous dress, their stately litters, their crowd of servants, their privileges and their pride; and compares all this with the poverty, the fasting, the coarse dress, and the self-sacrificing lives of those women who, from all ranks of society, had devoted themselves to the service of Christ and His Church.

"Monasticism was the natural and spontaneous outburst of society; nay, the highest and most beneficent model of it. It kept alive the brotherhood of men; it interposed a constant barrier between the oppression of the monarch and the nobles on the one side, and the people on the other. If they owned an altogether disproportionate share of power and wealth, they wielded the power wisely and well; the wealth was generously distributed."[1]

The monks may have been rich, but they spent vast sums of money in constructing or embellishing with every known fine art, magnificent churches, which are still the wonder and admiration of all persons of cultivated taste.

From very early times women had followed the example of men in retiring from the world, and living in solitude and in the practice of asceticism. ST. MARY MAGDALEN is claimed by monastic writers as an example of this in apostolic times. ST. PUDENTIANA, ST. THAIS, ST. MARY of Egypt, ST. PAULA, with her daughter, ST. EUSTOCHIUM, and others, adopted the same way of life. In the earliest times women assumed the vows of the Religious life without leaving their homes. So St. Ambrose writes much in favour of virginity, but says nothing of convents for women. But when St. Benedict infused new enthusiasm into Monasticism for men, women also adopted his Rule, and many convents were established. St. Benedict's sister, ST. SCHOLASTICA, became a nun, and the superior of a convent. As Christianity made its way among the barbarous invaders of Europe, women of the highest rank took the veil. ST. RADEGUND, wife of Clotaire, with the permission of her husband, founded a convent of nuns at Poitiers, and became abbess (547). ST. BRIDGET is looked upon as the originator of the houses for women in Ireland. ST. CLOTILDA, after

[1] *Life of St. Theresa*, G. Cunningham Graham.

the death of her husband, Clovis, King of the Franks (511), retired to Tours, and lived as a recluse. The practice of polygamy among the Frankish chiefs led many high-minded women to seek honourable independence in the cloister. ST. WERBURG, ST. ETHELDREDA, ST. HILDA, and ST. BEGA were abbesses in Britain, in the seventh century. ST. GERTRUDE, daughter of Pepin, in France, and ST. WINIFRED, a lady of noble rank in Wales, ST. FRIDESWIDE, an English princess, ST. EBBA, abbess of Coldingham, the empress THEODORA, the empress CUNEGUNDA, ST. MARGARET of Hungary, ST. ELIZABETH of Hungary, ST. CATHERINE of Sienna, ST. THERESA of Spain, ST. JANE FRANCES DE CHANTAL, were all remarkable as members of Religious Orders, in different periods of Church history.

While Monasticism was thus spreading and developing in the Western Church, it was also becoming powerful in the East. Every one of the great oriental patriarchates encouraged and fostered the creation of monasteries. Indeed the number of monks seems to have been excessive, and in many cases evil consequences arose. At Constantinople, Alexandria, and other great cities, tumults and conflicts occurred in which large bodies of monks took an active part. Chrysostom and other bishops indignantly remonstrated and protested, and endeavoured to reform the monastic bodies, and to do away with the abuses that were a scandal to religion.

There were several points of difference between the

monasticism of the East and that of the West. In the East there was no variety of Orders. There were no new creations or reforms; nor do there seem to have been the same faults and corruptions that are found among the Western monks. There was but little learning in oriental cloisters. There were indeed libraries, in which most valuable ancient manuscripts were stored, but little care was bestowed upon them; they were not highly esteemed; and many have perished, the loss of which can only be partially understood by the precious parchments that Mr. Curzon and others have rescued from destruction. Most of the monks at the present time are ignorant, and of the lower orders of society, and are quite satisfied to pass their lives in a system of invariable routine. The oriental idea of Monasticism seems to be that it is the vocation of devout and mortified spirits who practise the counsels of perfection, for their own good and for the benefit of the Church at large; and that it is an instrument for keeping alive ancient customs and principles. The Eastern love of tranquillity and meditation leads many to embrace the life of a hermit, or that of a monk; and the eager restlessness of the European is thought to be a mistake and a fault. The Eastern monks all follow, more or less, the Rule of St. Basil. The bishops, who must be celibate, are always taken from among the monks.

There have been, from time to time, learned and influential men among the monks of the East, such as St. John Damascene; and there has been a vast amount of missionary work done by them, in past centuries. Thus Dr. Neale says, in his *Holy Eastern Church*—

" From the Black Sea to the Caspian the monks of Etchmiadzine braved alike the Pagan and the Fire-worshipper, the burning suns of Tiflis, and the feverish swamps of Imeretia; they subjugated the borderlands of Europe and Asia, and planted a colony half-way up the Great Ararat. Southward, Alexandria sent forth another army of missionaries. Steering through the trackless desert by sun and stars, they preached the gospel as far as the fountains of the Nile, and planted flourishing churches in Nubia and Abyssinia. Solitary monks ventured further into the kingdom of Satan; through the savage Gallas they passed to Melinda or Zanguebar; others committing themselves to the merchant vessels, preached the way of salvation to Cape Guardafui, Zocotra, and distant Ceylon. . . . Northward, latest but most victoriously, Constantinople sent out her envoys. Moscow, Kieff, and Vladimir owned their metropolitans. Tribes unknown to the ancients received spiritual illumination. Undeterred by Sarmatian forest, or Ostiæan swamp, the soldiers of the Cross went on conquering and to conquer, till they stood on the barbarous shores of the 'Sluggish Sea.' Thence their holy chivalry bore them eastward; overleaping the Ural mountains, they forced their way into Siberia; at Irkeutsk, and Sitka, and Tomsk, after centuries of warfare, they have placed a vicar of Christ for the feeding of His flock."

There have been so few changes in Monasticism in

the East that a visit to a monastery to-day will give a good idea of what it was centuries ago. The peninsula of Mount Athos has still twenty monasteries upon it, besides small cells, and hermitages; and there are said to be about three thousand monks, besides a large number of persons employed by them. The services in the church occupy six hours or more of the day and night, the first commencing at about two a.m. The diet is very meagre; no meat is eaten, and on the numerous fast-days there is only one meal in the twenty-four hours. Only a small number of the monks are clergy. Many of the Eastern monasteries are formed partly of natural caves; and others, such as those of Meteora in Thessaly, are built upon the tops of rocks, and the only access to them is by means of ladders, or even by a basket attached to a rope. There are believed to be sixty-six millions of souls in the Eastern Church. There are in Russia 435 monasteries, and 113 convents. In Egypt there are twenty-six Coptic monasteries.

The Nestorian or Chaldæan Church was originally a schismatical body that separated itself from the rest of the Eastern Church after the Council of Ephesus (431).

Gibbon says—"The Nestorians successfully preached to the Bactrians, the Huns, the Persians, the Indians, the Persarmenians, the Medes, the Elamites, and their recent faith was conspicuous in the number and sanctity of their monks and martyrs. The missionaries of Balkh and Samarcand pursued without fear the footsteps of the roving Tartar, and insinuated themselves into the camp of the valleys of the Imans, and the banks of the Selingua."

In the ninth century there were twenty-five metropolitans subject to the Patriarch, and the number of Nestorian Christians was actually greater than that of the whole of the rest of Christendom in the East and West together. The invasions of Tamerlane in the eleventh century almost exterminated the Nestorian Church, and only a small community now exists, continually subject to persecution from the Turks. There are now no monasteries.[1] There still remains on the Malabar coast of India a small community of native Christians who are in communion with the Nestorians, their church having been originally founded by missionary monks of that communion. The Armenians, Jacobites, Copts, and Abyssinians were also bodies that separated from the Eastern Church on doctrinal grounds, but who maintained all external points of similarity, and among them the oriental monastic system. The Maronites originated in the time of St. Chrysostom through the mission of Maro, who founded a monastery near Lebanon, where the patriarch still resides.

The date of the introduction of Christianity into Russia is uncertain, but there is no doubt that missionaries laboured there at an early period, and the Greek patriarch Photius mentions incidentally (866) that there was a bishop among the Russians. Olga, a Russian princess, was baptized at Constantinople (955), and Vladimir himself shortly after

[1] See p. 127.

embraced Christianity, and from that time monasteries were founded.

There was however a difficulty in the way of the success of the Monastic Missions, when they were seriously taken up. Many of the conquering invaders of Europe had been already converted to Arianism. Those who still remained heathen were not slow to use the argument which is so common to-day, "Agree among yourselves before you attempt to persuade us to adopt one or other of your opposing systems." At the same time the Arian priests and bishops made use of force and persecution in order to compel Catholics to conform to their tenets. As Montalembert and others have shown, it was one of the distinguishing features of Arianism that it hated and opposed Monasticism. The Lombards, nominally Arian Christians, certainly brutal savages, burst upon Italy, and forty years after the death of Benedict, burned the monastery of Monte Cassino, and put most of the monks to cruel deaths. A few escaped to Rome, and others retired to inaccessible regions, and became the precursors of subsequent Benedictine communities.

But the most important result of the presence of the fugitives from Monte Cassino in Rome, was the conversion of ST. GREGORY THE GREAT, by their means. Gregory was a man of noble birth, and even when a young man had held important offices and gained influence and respect by the vigour and uprightness of his character. The highest honours and the most lucrative and commanding appointments were within his reach, when, deeply impressed by the words and the example of the Benedictines, he abandoned every worldly ambition, devoted all his wealth to the foundation of several monasteries, and finally gave up his own house in Rome to the Benedictines, and enrolled himself among them as a simple monk. His energy and genius soon made themselves felt in his new life, and against his will he was called to positions of trust and responsibility in the Church, and was finally elected abbot of his monastery of St. Andrew in Rome, and soon after was unanimously chosen Bishop of Rome.

His position was one of the greatest difficulty, and was beset with varied dangers and trials. The Byzantine Emperors were weak and unscrupulous, and their representatives were tyrannical, and they plundered the unhappy provinces which they governed. The patriarch of Constantinople claimed the title of "Universal Bishop," and ignored the traditional rites and privileges of the ancient See of Rome. The Lombards were carrying fire and sword to the very gates of Rome. Donatism was desolating the African Churches; Arianism had become established in Spain; Britain had relapsed into paganism under the Saxons; while in the East the Persians threatened the very existence of the Empire. In his numerous letters Gregory details his troubles and difficulties; history records how manfully and wisely he met and overcame the gigantic obstacles that stood in the way of his far-seeing and beneficent reforms. But in the midst of all his manifold labours and cares, he was always the monk; and by his steady support, Monasticism, which was destined to be the great healer of the world's ills, spread and became organized and efficient. Gregory revised and sanctioned the Rule of Benedict, and it became the authorized monastic guide throughout the Western Church, and even in some parts of the Eastern Church.

Dr. Lingard regards Gregory the Great as the author of the new character adopted by the Benedictine Order. He says—"The regulations which he imposed on his monks were widely different from the statutes of most religious orders. The time which they dedicated to manual labour, he commanded to be employed in study; and while they claimed the merit of conducting their lay disciples through the narrow path of monastic perfection, he aspired to the higher praise of forming men, who by their abilities might defend the doctrines, and by their zeal extend the conquests of the Church."[1]

About fifty years after its destruction by the Lombards, the Abbey of Monte Cassino was rebuilt, and a colony of Benedictines from Rome established themselves there, and resumed the services of the Church, and the industrial labours prescribed by the Rule. The abbey was again sacked and ruined by the Saracens in 857; restored about a century later, it passed through many vicissitudes, but wealth and dignity gradually accumulated upon it, till at the end of the sixteenth century it possessed an enormous income, and its abbot was first baron of the kingdom

[1] *Anglo-Saxon Church*, vol. i.

of Naples, with ecclesiastical and civil jurisdiction that comprised principalities, bishoprics, towns, castles, and a wide territory. The wars that devastated Italy, the general decay of monastic discipline, and the appropriation of its revenues by powerful princes, operated injuriously upon Monte Cassino; till in 1805, under Joseph Bonaparte, it was stripped of almost all its property and power. Under the Bourbons it regained some of its former importance; but after the occupation of Italy by Victor Emmanuel in 1870, the venerable abbey was suppressed, notwithstanding the petitions which were made by Roman Catholic and Protestant powers, that it might be allowed to exist, in memory of the services it had rendered to Italy and to the world.

Even in the lifetime of Benedict colonies were sent out from Monte Cassino. PLACIDUS was despatched to Sicily to establish a monastery upon an estate which his father had made over to Benedict. MAURUS went into Gaul, invited by one of the bishops, and after some delays and difficulties, founded the monastery of Glanfeuil, from which the Benedictine Order spread, till it had abbeys in every part of France, and its original title was merged into that of St. Maur, by which it was generally known. Many of the old monasteries adopted the Benedictine Rule, and the Merovingian princes patronized the monks, founded monasteries, and even gave members of their family to the cloister.

The Order extended itself also into Spain, but whether it was at this time, or later, is a question upon which the Benedictine historians are not agreed; the incursions of the Moors having destroyed many monasteries, and with them the records of their foundation.

The mission of St. Augustine, sent to England by Gregory the Great from St. Andrew's monastery at Rome in 596, led to the establishment of the Benedictines at Canterbury, and to the foundation of other stately abbeys, and to the connection of many of the Cathedrals with the Order.

In Germany, an English Benedictine monk, named Winfred, but afterwards called Boniface, preached and converted large numbers to Christianity, and built many monasteries. The most important of these was the Abbey of Fulda, which was commenced by Boniface in 774, and became the centre and metropolis of the Benedictine Order in Germany. The abbey soon acquired wealth and privileges, among which was exemption from Episcopal jurisdiction, and subjection to the Pope only. The abbot became afterwards a prince of the Empire, and *ex-officio* Chancellor, and exercised authority over a wide area, and received tribute in kind from many other monasteries and ecclesiastical foundations, some of which were at a considerable distance, and even under different civil rulers. From time to time other monasteries were founded by the abbots and congregation of Fulda. This great abbey had a varied and eventful history. Sometimes it enjoyed the favour of princes, and at other times it had to defend itself against attacks upon its prerogatives from dependents, or secular enemies, and it cannot be said that its abbots were always in the right, or that they were free from ambition or greed, and the other evils that usually accompany the possession of riches and worldly rank and power.

There were also other missionary monks, who at the same time, or in succeeding years, pursued the same course as that adopted by St. Boniface, converting the heathen, and founding monasteries, in every part of Europe.

St. Benedict, abbot of Aniane, in Languedoc, has been called the second father of Western Monasticism. He first set about the reformation of his own monastery and then extended his operations to other communities, and with the assistance of the Emperor, Louis le Débonnaire, visited the religious houses of France and Germany, suppressing abuses, restoring discipline, doing away with varieties of practice, and everywhere securing uniformity by the strict observance of the Rule of Monte Cassino; and finally by the decrees of the Council of Aix-le-Chapelle (817) the reformation was extended and enforced.

"During the ninth and tenth centuries the monasteries were the nurseries of true religion and science. Here the simplicity and unworldliness of primitive Christianity were found; to them fled those whose hearts were of finer mould than the hearts of their contemporaries. At an epoch when violence, licentiousness, and barbarism were rampant, when the Church itself was invaded and dishonoured by self-seeking and pride, the monasteries were refuges to which virtue and love of learning escaped, and where they found shelter. But they were more than asylums; they reacted on the outer world. They were schools in which the young were trained in piety and knowledge, at least in respect for something better than brute force. At a period when society seemed to fall into general wreck, something more was needful than an apostle of righteousness lifting his voice in condemnation of evil, here and there. What was needed was institutions which would stand the storms that swept the country, the violence of man, the anarchy, the wantonness of destruction, the dissolution of the old order of society, and which could effect its reconstruction on other bases. The monks were the veritable founders of the culture of the middle ages, and the preservers too of the treasures of classic antiquity. . . . It is impossible sufficiently to recognize the debt we owe to the monks for their diligence in the transcription of books. Never did caligraphy reach a higher standard than in the ninth and tenth centuries, and the elegance of the decoration shows a keen sense of the beauty of form. The monks may be said to have handed on the lamp of art to later ages. They did the same for science."[1]

Nor were the nuns ignorant of artistic and literary pursuits. Like the monks, they transcribed and illuminated books, they embroidered vestments, and

[1] *History of the Church in Germany*, S. Baring-Gould (Gardner, Darton & Co.).

made ornamental hangings for churches, and tapestry. The English convents produced a special kind of work which was named "opus anglicum," which was highly esteemed far and wide. The nuns also studied medicine, and often gained great reputation in the treatment of disease. The writings of St. Hildegarde and other nuns were found in the libraries of most European countries.[1]

It was within the cloister that the great intellectual movements of the Middle Ages began. The names of Abêlard, Arnold of Brescia, Gotschalk, Scotus Erigena, Roscelin, Anselm, Friar Bacon, and many more, are well known for their speculations and their subtle disputations.[2]

The frequent instances of the chiefs of savage tribes entering the cloister, and of proud mediæval barons taking their places side by side with humble monks, seem to be the realization of Isaiah's prophecy of the dominion of the Spirit of God, when "the wolf shall dwell with the lamb, and the leopard shall lie down with the kid; and the calf and the young lion, and the fatling together. And the cow and the bear shall feed; their young ones shall lie down together; and the lion shall eat straw like the ox"; and when fierce warriors laid aside their arms and harness, and toiled in the fields, we remember that other prophecy that there should come a time when men would "beat their swords into plowshares and their spears into pruning-hooks."[3]

[1] See L. Eckenstein's *Woman under Monasticism*.
[2] Note D, p. 386.   [3] Note E, p. 386.

"It was surely good that, in an age of ignorance and violence, there should be quiet cloisters and gardens, in which the arts of peace could be safely cultivated, in which gentle and contemplative natures could find an asylum, in which one brother could employ himself in transcribing the *Æneid* of Virgil, and another in meditating on the *Analytics* of Aristotle, in which he who had a genius for art might illuminate a martyrology, or carve a crucifix, and in which he who had a turn for natural philosophy might make experiments on the properties of plants and minerals. Had not such retreats been scattered here and there, among the huts of a miserable peasantry, and the castles of a ferocious aristocracy, European society would have consisted merely of beasts of burden and beasts of prey."[1]

Pope GREGORY VII. (1073), Hildebrand, who had been a monk of Cluny, among the many changes which he introduced into the Church, was a great reformer of the discipline of monasteries. In order to increase the papal power, and secure the co-operation of the regular clergy, he exempted a great number of abbots from episcopal jurisdiction, and made them subject to the Pope alone. This step, however, led to abuses, for the monks resisted the attempts of the bishops to introduce necessary reforms, and it brought about conflicts with kings, who claimed the right to govern all their subjects, ecclesiastical as well as secular.[2]

The Order of St. Benedict claims to have originated

[1] Macaulay, *History of England*, vol. i.   [2] Note F, p. 386.

12 Monastic Orders, and most of the Military Orders; to have sent forth 30 Apostolic missions to the heathen; to have had in its ranks 15,700 Abbots and Doctors, 4600 Bishops, 1600 Archbishops, 200 Cardinals, 51 Patriarchs, and 46 Popes; more than 240 noble and royal personages; 146 sons of Kings and Emperors, 46 Kings, 4 Emperors, 12 Empresses, 51 Queens, and 55,700 Canonized Saints, and to have published 5260 books.

It required eight large volumes, more than a century ago, to give some account of the Religious Orders.

Great and wonderful as were the missionary efforts and successes of the disciples of St. Benedict, it was not they only who were the pioneers of civilization and Christianity among the wild tribes who had invaded, and conquered, and re-peopled the western provinces of the old Roman Empire. Ireland, which had received the Gospel from ST. PATRICK, a relative of the great St. Martin of Tours, in the fifth century, itself became a source from whence a stream of missionary zeal and enterprise issued. The debt that Ireland owed to Gaul was repaid with usury. ST. COLUMBANUS had become a monk at Bangor, but he was not content to live the Christian life himself, and was fired with a passionate and irresistible desire to be an apostle of Christ and His Gospel to those who were in heathen darkness and ignorance. With twelve other monks he landed in Gaul (585), and by his words, and still more by his holy life, he taught the "more excellent way," to those whose hearts were ready to receive the faith of Christ. After many wanderings and various temporary settlements, he fixed his abode at Luxeuil, in the Vosges (590).[1] Here his influence brought him many disciples; and some of the Frankish chiefs entrusted their sons to him for education, or to become monks in the monasteries which he founded. Like all godly men and apostles of Christ, Columbanus had to endure opposition and persecution. Those who had adopted the Roman computation of Easter were violent in their condemnation of his observances, and of the other practices and customs in which the Irish Christians differed from them. Queen Brunehild and her nobles became hostile to him, and drove him into exile. He wandered to different parts of France, the borders of the Rhine, and Switzerland; and finally settled down at Bregentz on Lake Constance. Here he established a monastic community, and spread the knowledge of Christ among the savage Alamanni. His old enemies ultimately pursued him in his retreat, and he had again to flee for his life. He crossed the Alps, and put himself under the protection of Agilulf, King of the Lombards, by whose assistance he founded a monastery at Bobbio, between Genoa and Milan, where he set himself to oppose the Arian heresy which had made way in northern Italy. Some of his letters and other writings still exist. His Rule was, in some respects, even more severe than that of St. Benedict, but it gained a wide acceptance, and

[1] Note G, p. 386.

seemed at one time to be likely to become generally adopted instead of that of Monte Cassino. Columbanus died in 615. His disciples, Attalus, Bertulph, Sigisbert, and others carried on his work, and founded missionary monasteries; among which that of Dissentis became famous, and has survived in a changed form to the present day. One of the most active successors of Columbanus was ST. GALL, who became the apostle of a great part of what is now Switzerland, and whose memory is still preserved in a multitude of popular legends. He was a native of Ireland, and of noble family. He went to France with Columbanus, and assisted him in his mission, and accompanied him in his exile. After the death of Columbanus, St. Gall continued his work. He refused to become abbot of Luxeuil, and spent the last years of his life in a cell, which afterwards became the site of the great Abbey of St. Gall. This monastery gained a high reputation on account of the number of learned men who were among its monks. Its library was one of the largest and most valuable in Europe, and its school of music regulated Church song for a long period. Poets and musicians were found among the monks, or were attracted to the monastery by the opportunities afforded for the study and practice of psalmody. Ratpert, Notker, Totilo, and others cultivated and spread the knowledge of music, and introduced it into the services of the Church. There appear to have been several monks of the name of Notker, and hymns bearing this name as their author have come down to our own day. Charles Martel, and others, gave it large possessions, and its abbot became a prince of the Empire. In the eighth century the Rule of St. Columbanus was exchanged for that of St. Benedict.[1]

Luxeuil sent out colonies in various directions, and became the monastic capital of a wide district, extending from the banks of the Lake of Geneva to the coast of the North Sea; many bishops and abbots of important places having been chosen from among its monks. One of the great abbeys so founded was that of Jumiéges on the Seine. Others were established at Rebais, Faremontier, Remiremont, Corbie, with many more of less importance. The Rule of St. Columbanus existed side by side with that of St. Benedict in all these foundations, till 670, when the Synod held at Autun enjoined the exclusive adoption of the Rule of St. Benedict.

The first reformation of the Benedictine Order was commenced by Berno, Abbot of Gigny, in France, and was completed by his successor Abbot Odo, and resulted in the establishment of the new *Order of Cluniacs*, which rapidly grew into importance, till more than 300 monasteries belonged to it in France, Italy, Spain, England, Palestine, and even in Constantinople.

The next reformed branch of the Benedictines was that of Citeaux. It originated with Robert of Molesme, in Burgundy, who founded the Abbey of Citeaux, in 1098. The monks were called *Cistercians*, and afterwards Bernardines, after St. Bernard, Abbot of Clairvaux, about 1116.[2]

[1] Note H, p. 387.   [2] Note I, p. 387.

There were also other offshoots from the Benedictine Order, which however never attained much importance. Such was the *Order of Camaldoli*, founded by St. Romuald, in Italy, early in the eleventh century. It consisted of a strict community of hermits, living in separate cells near together, after the Eastern system of the *Laura*. The *Order of Vallombrosa*, founded by Gualbert in 1039, also in Italy, first introduced the custom of admitting "Lay Brothers." The *Order of Grammont* was founded in 1074. The *Augustine Canons* were first incorporated at Avignon, about 1061; and the *Order of Premontré*, by Norbert, in 1120; and the *Order of Fontevraud* in 1100.

A more important Order was that of the *Carthusians*, founded by Bruno at the Chartreuse, near Grenoble, in 1084.

"The Carthusians combined in themselves the severities of the hermits and of the regular Orders. Each member of the fraternity lived in his solitary cell, meeting his companions only in the chapel, or for instruction, or for the business of the house. They ate no meat. A loaf of bread was given to every brother on Sunday morning at the refectory door, which was to last him through the week. An occasional mess of gruel was all there was allowed in addition. His bedding was a horse-cloth, a pillow, and a skin. His dress was a horsehair shirt, covered outside with linen, which was worn day and night, and the white cloak of the Order, generally a sheepskin, and unlined—all else was bare. He was bound by vows of strictest obedience. The Order had business in all parts of the world. Now some captive must be released from the Moors; now some earl or king had been treading on the Church's privileges, a brother was chosen to interpose in the name of the Chartreuse: he received his credentials, and had to depart on the instant, with no furniture but a stick, to walk, it might be, to the furthest corner of Europe."[1]

Mr. Ruskin writes—" I grew daily more sure that the peace of God rested on all the dutiful and kindly hearts of the laborious poor; and that the only constant form of pure religion was in useful work, faithful love, and stintless charity. In which pure religion neither St. Bruno himself nor any of his true disciples failed; and I perceived it finally notable of them, that, poor by resolute choice of a life of hardship, without any sentimental glorifying of 'Holy Poverty,' as if God had never promised full garners for a blessing, and always choosing men of high intellectual power for the heads of their community, they have had more directly wholesome influence on the outer world than any other order of monks so narrow in number, and restricted in habitation. For while the Franciscan and Cistercian monks became everywhere a constant element in European society, the Carthusians, in their active sincerity, remained in groups, of not more than from twelve to twenty monks in any single monastery, the tenants of a few wild valleys of the north-western Alps; the subsequent overflowing of their brotherhood into the Certosas of the Lombard plains

[1] J. A. Froude, *Short Studies*, vol. ii. (Longmans).

being mere waste and wreck of them ; and the great Certosa of Pavia, one of the worst shames of Italy, associated with the accursed reign of Galeazzo Visconti. But in their strength, from the foundation of the Order, at the close of the eleventh century to the beginning of the fourteenth, they reared in their mountain fastnesses, and sent out to minister to the world, a succession of men of immense mental grasp, and serenely authoritative innocence, among whom our own Hugo of Lincoln, in his relations with Henry I. and Cœur-de-Lion, is to my mind the most beautiful sacerdotal figure known to me in history."[1]

It is the boast of the Carthusian Order that it has never required a reform, having been free from abuses and degeneracy.

In addition to the large number of congregations that followed the Rule of St. Benedict, there were also those who professed the *Rule of St. Augustine*. These claimed a greater antiquity than the Benedictines, as their founder, St. Augustine, Bishop of Hippo, in Africa, lived at the end of the fourth century. At first they seem to have been called *The Hermits of St. Augustine*. The invasions of the Vandals completely destroyed them in Africa. The Order, however, was revived in Europe, in different places, and under varying forms. In 1254, Pope Alexander IV. united these bodies into one community, and shortly after the Rule of St. Augustine was revised. Originally the primitive practice of manual labour was inculcated by

[1] *Præterita*, vol. iii. p. 1 (George Allen).

St. Augustine, but in later times the Augustinians devoted themselves chiefly to study and spiritual duties, being usually priests. They were called *Regular Canons*. The Order of Premontré, the Knights of St. John of Jerusalem, the Teutonic Order, and some other communities, besides congregations of women, such as the Brigettine nuns, followed the Rule of St. Austin, with certain modifications.

The pilgrimages that were commonly made from early times to Jerusalem and other places in Palestine hallowed by the memory of our Lord's life, gradually led to the formation of societies of men for the housing and protection of the pilgrims on their way, and during their sojourn in the Holy Land. Hospitals were founded, and those who devoted themselves to the care of the poor travellers who were sheltered in them, were called *Hospitallers*. When the Mahometans attacked, and finally obtained possession of Palestine, these Hospitallers extended their operations, and formed armed bands to conduct and defend the pilgrims. An Order of Military monks was finally incorporated 1104, and called the Order of Hospitallers, or the *Knights of St. John of Jerusalem*. Men of the highest rank enrolled themselves in the Order, and took the three usual vows of Poverty, Chastity, and Obedience, adding a fourth vow to fight against the enemies of Christ. Grants of land were made in various countries of Europe, and monasteries were built where novices were received and trained for their duties in the field. The head-quarters of the Order were first at Jerusalem, afterwards at Cyprus,

Rhodes, and Malta, and it became possessed of great wealth, and did good service both on land and sea in fighting the Saracens and Turks, and in keeping back their invasions, which at one time threatened the greater part of Europe, and made it seem probable that the Moslem faith would supersede that of Christ.

When the Turks obtained permanent possession of Palestine, and the Crusades ceased, the occupation of the Hospitallers virtually came to an end. They continued however to exist, till they were suppressed with the other Religious Orders at various dates in the different countries where they were established.

The Order of the *Knights Templars* took their title from a house which was granted to them in 1118 upon part of the site of the Temple of Solomon at Jerusalem. Their origin was obscure like that of the Hospitallers, and the objects of their mission were much the same. St. Bernard greatly admired the Templars, and the Knights were closely connected with the Cistercian Order, and adopted its Rule. The Order speedily gained favour, especially in France; its ranks were recruited from the best and noblest families. Preceptories, with large landed property, were founded in almost every European country; and in the Crusades the Knights were ever in the thickest of the fight, and gained a reputation for valour, and the gallant sacrifice of their lives for the protection and extension of Christendom. Their services, however, were forgotten when the Crusades were no longer carried on. Philip, King of France, became afraid of their power, and covetous of their wealth. With the connivance of the Pope, who was himself a Frenchman, and owed his position to Philip, the king suddenly issued orders (1307) for the arrest of all the Templars in France, and in 1312 a Papal Brief abolished the Order. The Knights were subjected to imprisonment, torture, and death, and their property was seized by the king. Philip and the Pope, not without difficulty, persuaded the other monarchs to suppress the Order in their dominions, and it became extinct.

The *Teutonic Order* began in a small effort (1128) of a benevolent German and his wife to give assistance to distressed pilgrims of their own nationality at Jerusalem. About 1190, great development having taken place, and considerable numbers of Germans having become associated in the good work, a Military Order was formally constituted. When the campaigns against the Turks were discontinued, the Teutonic Knights, having incorporated a similar Order that had been created in Northern Europe, turned their attention to the defence of that part of Christendom from the attacks of the still heathen population on its borders. They obtained considerable estates in Hungary and Poland, and established their headquarters at Thorn, and afterwards at Marienberg and Königsberg. At the height of its power the Order became the sovereign ruler of a wide territory extending from the Oder to the Gulf of Finland. In 1410 the Knights were attacked and defeated by a large army of Russians, Tartars, and others; the Grand Master, hundreds of knights, and thousands of soldiers were slain. In 1417, an outbreak of the plague inflicted great losses upon the Order. Marienberg was lost in 1460, and soon after the possessions in Sicily. The spread of Lutheranism discredited and disorganized the Order, and Louis XIV. abolished it in France in 1672. It maintained an enfeebled existence till 1809, when it was finally suppressed by Napoleon.

The Military Orders flourished especially in Spain. Not only had the Templars and the Hospitallers large possessions and numerous monasteries, but the Orders of *Calatrava*, of *Santiago*, and of *Alcantara*, which were of Spanish origin, exercised great power, and were associated with much that is noblest in the history of the Peninsula. The long and severe conflict with the Moors not only gave rise to the foundation of these Orders, but ensured them constant employment, and made them popular and honourable, as patriotic defenders of their country, and champions of Christianity against the ruinous advance of the Moslems. The Order of Calatrava was suppressed in 1587, and its resources appropriated by Philip II. The Order of Santiago, at the end of the fifteenth century, possessed 200 commanderies, as many priories, and a great number of castles and estates. There were also houses of Canonesses which were affiliated. The Order of Alcantara did good service in the wars with the Moors, and became wealthy. It was disestablished and disendowed by Ferdinand the Catholic, who, like his contemporary, Henry VIII., was jealous of any authority that interfered with his own absolutism; for the Grand Masters of the Military Orders were really almost independent sovereigns, and the policy of Ferdinand, which brought him into collision with the Pope, demanded the suppression of every other *imperium in imperio*.

There were also many other so-called Military Orders, during the Middle Ages, in different countries, and nominally connected with monastic communities, but they were, for the most part, rather honorary than fighting or ascetic organizations.[1]

Another conventual Rule was that of Mount Carmel. Those who adopted it were called *Carmelites*. This Order sets up the claim for being the most ancient of all religious societies, which its members assert was originally constituted by the prophet Elijah at Mount Carmel. This idea probably arose from the early settlement of hermits on Mount Carmel, just as they sought out other lonely places. Albert, patriarch of Jerusalem (1205), arranged a Rule for the recluses who were living under the oriental system at that time. The Pope recognized them as a Religious Order in 1226. In 1229 they left Syria, on account of its occupation by the Saracens, and settled in Europe. ST. THERESA reformed the convents for women belonging to the Order in Spain, in the sixteenth century. The Carmelites were reckoned among the Mendicant Orders, and were called *White Friars*. ST. SIMON STOCK, an Englishman, became General of the Order in 1245,

---

[1] For full particulars of these, see Helyot's *Ordres Monastiques*; also *The Military Religious Orders*, F. C. Woodhouse (S.P.C.K.).

and was the means of increasing the number of its houses in different countries of Europe.

One of the most important epochs in the history of Monasticism is marked by the creation of the two great Orders of Mendicant Friars, the *Franciscans* and the *Dominicans*, in the thirteenth century. This period was especially a time of active thought and of an eager desire for change and progress. A very general feeling of dissatisfaction with the old Orders of monks prevailed. They had, for the most part, given up the active missionary work that had distinguished them in earlier times, and they made little impression for good upon the prevailing degeneracy of morals that surrounded them. It had been decreed by the Council of the Lateran (1215), that no new Order should be created. It was felt that the teachers of religion must be more aggressive, and that more preaching was necessary. As is usually the case, the ideas that were floating in the air, and occupying the earnest thoughts of godly men, took no definite shape, and came to no practical result till men appeared who could embody these impulses in their own minds, and give them shape and method, and themselves become the leaders and exponents of the spirit of the age. Such men were ST. FRANCIS of Assisi, and ST. DOMINIC; the former the son of a tradesman in Italy, the other a member of the noble family of Guzman in Spain. Christianity, which had fled into retreat before the barbarians with Benedict, advanced to conquer with Dominic and Francis.

"The Mendicant Orders," says Archbishop Trench,

"introduced a new idea into Monasticism. Hitherto the monk had been one who, in retiring from the world, had sought in prayer, penitence, and self-mortification, to set forward the salvation of his own soul; now he should be one who in labours of self-denying love, in dispensing the word of life, should seek the salvation of others. Hitherto he had fled from the world, as one who in conflict with it must inevitably be worsted; now he should make war upon the world to overcome it; nothing doubting that in seeking the salvation of others, he should best work out his own. . . . The work of the Friars may be compared with the Methodist revival in England." [1]

Francis was born at Assisi in Umbria in 1182. In 1208 he was greatly impressed by hearing in church our Lord's direction to His disciples, when He sent them forth to preach and teach. "Provide neither gold nor silver nor brass in your purses, nor scrip for your journey, neither two coats, neither shoes, nor yet staves." He felt an irresistible impulse to follow literally this evangelical precept and mission. He first set himself to beg alms for the restoration of a ruined church in the neighbourhood, and then retired to a small hut near a church belonging to the Benedictines, where two or three other young men joined him. He went to Rome (1209), and explained to Pope Innocent IV. his ideas and plans as to the mode of life and work which he proposed to adopt, and although he was at first repulsed, he ultimately

[1] *Mediæval Church History.* See Note U, p 400.

received a verbal approval. The Benedictines soon after bestowed upon him and his brethren the church near his cell, which was called Portiuncula, or St. Mary of the Angels; but Francis refused the offer of a landed endowment, having determined to embrace absolute poverty. He next went to Syria, desiring to convert the Mahometans, or to become a martyr for the Christian faith. Being forced to leave the country without attaining either of his purposes, he went to Morocco, with the same idea, and with similar disappointment. Meanwhile the number of his disciples rapidly increased, and they soon possessed sixty houses in different parts of Italy. In 1212 he extended his system to women; and a devout woman, afterwards called ST. CLARE, became the superior of a body of female Franciscans, which spread and grew, till it had convents in every part of Europe, its nuns being called *Minoresses*, or *Poor Clares*. In 1219 Francis held his first Chapter at Portiuncula, which was attended by no less than five thousand brethren; and in the same year, notwithstanding the recent decision of the Lateran Council that no new Order should be founded, the Pope established the Franciscan brotherhood, and approved the Rule drawn up by its founder.

St. Francis is said to have received the *Stigmata* in his hands, feet, and side, *i. e.* impressions corresponding with the Five Wounds of our Lord, during a solitary retreat that he made on Mount Alvernia in the Apennines. He gave his Friars no special dress, but bade them wear the ordinary clothes of the poor shepherds and peasants of Umbria, which was never much altered in succeeding centuries.

The following is a short abstract of the provisions of the Rule of St. Francis.

> Chap. I. The Rule of the Friars is to follow the precepts of the Gospel, in poverty and charity.
>
> Chap. II. Novices must have a year of probation, and may not leave the Order when once professed. The habit to be worn is described.
>
> Chap. III. The Breviary is to be used daily by the Friars, and the Lay Brothers are to recite seventy-six Pater Nosters daily. Besides Lent, which is to begin at Twelfth-day, fasting is to be observed from All Saints to Christmas. No one is to ride on horseback, and during journeys the Friars are to eat whatever is set before them.
>
> Chap. IV. No money must be possessed.
>
> Chap. V. The Friars must live by the work of their hands.
>
> Chap. VI. They must beg if they are in need, and help each other.
>
> Chap. VII. They must confess their sins to their Superiors.
>
> Chap. VIII. The General is to be elected every third year.
>
> Chap. IX. There must be no preaching without the permission of the Bishop and the Superiors.
>
> Chap. X. The rules of discipline are laid down.
>
> Chap. XI. Convents of women must not be entered; nor must any Friar be a god-father.
>
> Chap. XII. No foreign missions must be undertaken without proper authorization.

After the death of St. Francis (1226), the Order not only increased in numbers greatly, but became powerful, and even wealthy; dispensations having been obtained relaxing the Rule with respect to the possession of property. The Franciscan convents became enormous buildings, with good endowments; the churches were magnificent, like those of the monks; and it was esteemed a privilege worth purchasing to be buried in them. To be clothed with the grey gown of the Order was supposed to confer spiritual advantages upon the dying. Members of the Order accepted positions of importance and honour in the Church, the Universities, and the State; forty-five became Cardinals, five were Popes; entirely against the original commands of their founder. In consequence of this, branches were formed to resume the strict observance of the original Rule. In 1368 PAULET de Foligni inaugurated such a reform, and his Order received the name of the *Observants*. In 1419 ST. BERNARDIN of Sienna once more established the strict observance of the Rule in a branch of the Franciscans. In 1500 the *Recollects* were established in Spain, and in 1525 the *Capuchins* in Italy, and there were other local communities in various places. In 1380 there were said to be 1,500 Franciscan convents, with 90,000 inmates. The Franciscans were sometimes called *Friars minor*, or *Minorites*, and in France, *Cordeliers*. A Third Order was founded by St. Francis, with a mitigated Rule, both for men and women, some living in the world, and some in convents. ST. ELIZABETH of Hungary was a member of the Third Order of St. Francis. A great number of eminent men were Franciscans; among these were ST. BONAVENTURA, ST. ANTHONY of Padua, ST. BERNARDIN of Sienna, ST. JOHN CAPISTRAN, DUNS SCOTUS, and Cardinal QUIGNON. In the fourteenth century the Franciscans became divided into two antagonistic bodies, one claiming the title of *Spirituals*, and professing to maintain the strict Rule of the founder in respect of absolute poverty ; the other availing themselves of a papal dispensation to hold property. Party spirit ran high, and a most unedifying spectacle was presented for many years.

In the sixteenth century the Friars had so completely deteriorated that they lost their early reputation, and became unpopular. The bishops and clergy complained of their intrusion into their churches; the monks were stung with their sarcastic exposure of their failings ; their acrimonious disputes with the Dominicans were a great scandal ; Luther, Erasmus, and other writers unsparingly denounced their inconsistencies and sins of commission and omission ; the people became weary of their greedy exactions; and songs and caricature held them up to ridicule and contempt. They had been called into being to correct the abuses and failings of the clergy and the monks, and in a few years they themselves had fallen into the same faults, and worse.

Generally, men of genius appear singly, and at considerable intervals of time, but, like Adams and Leverrier, St. Francis and St. Dominic were contemporary, and discovered and published at the same time the same remedy for the faults and failings of the Church of their day. There were at first, and still more afterwards, differences of detail in the systems of the two founders, but the fundamental principle was all along the same : the imitation of Christ, the bringing back to Christendom the original truth that the only true apostle of Christ was the man who "denied himself, took up the Cross, and followed Him."

St. Dominic was born in 1170 of an illustrious family in Old Castile. Unlike St. Francis, he never gave way to youthful follies, but from his earliest years displayed strong religious instincts, and manifested that Christ-like, self-sacrificing care for others which distinguished his maturer years. After passing ten years in study at the University of Palencia, he was ordained priest, and became a Canon Regular, in his twenty-fifth year, at Osma. Here his life was a model of piety. In 1201 he accompanied the Bishop of Osma on a journey, and passing through the south of France, he became acquainted with the sect of the Albigenses, who were spreading their tenets with great zeal and success; and he determined to set himself to oppose them. Like so many devout persons of the period, he made a pilgrimage to Rome; and on his return visited the famous abbey of Citeaux, and was deeply impressed by the asceticism and spirituality of the disciples of St. Bernard. There had already been missions to the Albigenses, but the neglect of evangelical poverty, and the want of a consistent life of absolute devotion, had, as usual, deprived the missionaries of acceptance and respect among those who, with all their errors, were often devout and austere in their daily life. Dominic now devoted himself to the recovery of the Albigenses to the Church, and by his eloquence, and still more by his personal piety, he succeeded in gaining over a certain number. For the protection of some of his female converts, with the assistance of Fulk, Bishop of Toulouse, he founded a small convent at Prouille, which afterwards became important, and the mother-house of several other foundations for women. The leaders of the Albigenses had gradually become more political than evangelical; and acts of violence of all kinds were committed by them; till force was met by force, and an army of so-called Crusaders, under Simon de Montfort, having been organized in France at the instance of the Pope, laid siege to Toulouse. The war was carried on with ferocity on both sides, but there does not seem to be any conclusive evidence that St. Dominic had any direct share in the severe measures adopted against the vanquished Albigenses, as some writers assert. About this time he instituted the devotion of the *Rosary*, which has ever since been popular among Roman Catholics. After the capture of Toulouse by the Crusaders, St. Dominic took up his abode there, and with a few companions began a life of devotion and evangelical preaching, which gradually developed into the world-wide mission of the order of *Friars Preachers*, or *Dominicans*. During the eleventh and twelfth centuries religious sects of all kinds had arisen. There was enormous mental activity, but the machinery of the Church seemed unequal to create any adequate influence to direct and control the minds of men. Dominic, like Moses in Egypt and St. Paul at Athens, found his spirit stirred within him, and felt himself irresistibly called to preach a reformation. He went to Rome, during the sitting of the Lateran Council (1215), and, not without difficulty, gained permission to found his Order; having, it is said, met and conferred with St. Francis during his stay in the city. On his return, he called together his brethren at Prouille, and it was unanimously agreed to adopt the Rule of St. Augustine—to which St. Dominic, as Canon Regular, was already committed—with certain modifications, as the standard of life for the new community. The first house of the Order was built at Toulouse, in connection with the Church of St. Romain, which the bishop had made over to St. Dominic (1216). In the same year St. Dominic again went to Rome, and obtained from the Pope formal Bulls confirming the foundation of the Order of Preachers (1216). In 1217 St. Dominic returned to Toulouse, and all the brethren at St. Romain, and the sisters at Prouille, made their solemn profession to him; and the newly-invested preachers were dismissed to their destined missions in various places,— the *Domini Canes*, " the Lord's dogs," as they were afterwards called,—to lead or drive back the wandered sheep of Christ to the fold of His Church.

St. Dominic made another journey to Rome, and there a small church (St. Sixtus) was given to him. He begged money to build a monastery adjoining, and there established a community of his Friars. This house was not long afterwards converted into a Dominican nunnery, and his brethren took possession of the larger convent of St. Sabina, on the Aventine, which then became the mother-house of the Order, till 1375, when the great convent of St. Maria Sopra Minerva was built. New centres were formed in France, England, Spain, Scotland, Italy, Bohemia, Austria, and in the Scandinavian countries. A Third Order was also formed, similar to that of St. Francis. The Dominicans were closely connected with the three great universities, of Paris, Bologna, and Oxford, and many of them became famous for their learning. After the discovery of America, the King of Spain sent a number of Friars Preachers to convert the natives, and Las Casas vainly endeavoured to mitigate the cruelties with which the Spaniards treated the unhappy people of the countries which they had conquered. The Dominicans carried their missions into China, Tartary, India, and other remote parts of the world, and many of their number were martyred. The Order had among its members five popes, forty-eight cardinals, twenty-three patriarchs, fifteen hundred bishops, six hundred archbishops, and a vast number of eminent writers. ALBERTUS MAGNUS, ST. THOMAS AQUINAS, ST. VINCENT FERRER, ST. CATHERINE of Sienna, Fra ANGELICO, Fra BARTOLOMEO, SAVONAROLA, and a multitude of others whose names appear on the pages of European history, were disciples of St. Dominic.

Much odium has been incurred by the Dominican Order through its connection with the Inquisition. This extraordinary tribunal appears to have been created originally in Lombardy for the suppression of heresy. In 1233 Pope Gregory IX. nominated two Dominican friars to proceed against the Albigenses in Languedoc; and as other courts were constituted, members of the Order were again made Inquisitors in Spain, with its American colonies, the Netherlands, France, and other countries; till the conduct of the Inquisition was vested almost entirely in the hands of Dominican Friars. Earl Russell says, "Most of the Inquisitors were men of conscientious convictions and blameless lives." But the spirit of the age favoured the use of persecution and torture, and good men "thought they did God service" by the use of force to compel men to accept what was held to be truth. Roman Catholic and Protestant, Monarch, Bishop, and magistrate thought

"To prove their doctrine orthodox
By Apostolic blows and knocks."

The Inquisition soon became an instrument in the hands of rulers to punish and get rid of troublesome and rebellious subjects; and in Spain it altogether separated itself from papal authority, and refused to listen to remonstrance when its cruelties excited the indignation of those who, in spite of public opinion, desired to follow the Apostles' precept and method, and "overcome evil with good."

Besides the Monastic Orders already mentioned, there have arisen in more recent times several bodies which consist neither of monks nor friars, properly so called, but which have close affinity with Monasticism in some of its fundamental principles. Such is the Order of the *Jesuits*, founded in 1534 by ST. IGNATIUS LOYOLA, which has conducted wide and successful missions among the heathen, and produced many learned men who have taken a leading part in the higher branches of education. Its members have also been largely influential in political movements, and have gained great influence in the papal court; their original and present motive being to oppose the principles of the Protestant Reformation. The *Oratorians* were originated by ST. PHILIP NERI, in 1575, and have devoted themselves to preaching, writing, and to the conversion of the higher ranks of society. The *Oblates of St. Charles* were instituted in 1578, and are a kind of secular Canons, engaged in evangelizing work in large towns. The *Lazarists* (1617), *Passionists* (1725), *Redemptorists* (1732), and *Marist Fathers* (1813), are bodies of priests engaged in mission work at home and abroad. Among the more modern Orders for women are the *Ursulines* (1537), the *Sisters of Charity* (1629), and the *Little Sisters of the Poor* (1840).

The usual localities, and the special work of the several Orders of mediæval Monasticism, are thus described by an old writer—

"Bernardus valles; montes Benedictus, amabat;
Oppida Franciscus; magnas Ignatius urbes."

In the eleventh century there arose in the Netherlands the female Society of *Beguines*, and in the thirteenth century that of the *Beghards*. The members of these societies either lived in their own houses earning their own living, and occupied in works of benevolence, or, without taking life-vows, they lived together under rule, and adopted a common dress.

The *Brothers and Sisters of the Common Life*, of whom ST. THOMAS À KEMPIS was a distinguished member, lived devotional and ascetic lives under rule, and kept themselves free from abuses and disorganization.

There were several later reforms of Monastic Orders. Among the most remarkable was that of *Port Royal*, near Paris. This abbey had been founded in the thirteenth century for Cistercian nuns, but in the seventeenth century the discipline had become entirely relaxed. In 1602 ANGELIQUE ARNAUD was elected abbess, and by her influence a very strict observance of the original Rule was introduced. In later years the community was accused of having adopted the principles of Jansenism, and the abbey was suppressed by order of Louis XIV. in 1709.

Another reformation took place at *La Trappe*. A Cistercian abbey had been founded there in 1140, but great irregularities had gradually crept in. A nobleman named DE RANCÉ, among other preferments was titular abbot of La Trappe, in 1662. Having been converted from a licentious life, he gave up all his property, resigned his other appointments, and retired to his abbey; and there gradually, and not without opposition, he restored once more the original Cistercian Rule, and even introduced greater austerities. A few other monasteries in Spain and Italy adopted the Trappist reform.

Of the marvellous almsgiving of this Poor Order, a writer in the seventeenth century gives the following

account of the beneficence of one of their houses—
"In addition to 1500 to 2000 persons, whom, as I have often counted, they supported by public donations in the dear years, they also sustain privately all the families in the neighbourhood who are unable to work. They receive 4000 guests. They nourish and maintain eighty monks. And all for an income of about 8000 livres. You might ask any one to point out ten households, each with the same income, who do anything approaching to what those sluggards, as some people call them, do with gaiety and edification."

The following quaint description of the duties and occupations of a monk in the Middle Ages is quoted by Fosbroke from a MS. in the Bodleian—

Instructio perbrevis pro novitiis
   in sacra Lirinensi Insula
Attende tibi
Monacho, ad quid venisti
Quare mundum reliquisti,
Cur flocum induisti
Et mundi pompam despexisti.
Nonne ut Deo servires
Et cor tuum custodires?
Cum ergo sic vagaris
Et vana meditaris?
Multum peccas evagando
Tempus perdis otiando;
Evagari non est tutum,
Otiari grande vitium;
Fabulando perdis præmium,
Operando vitæ tædium,
Orando quære subsidium,
Mane ergo in cænobio,
Vive caste sine proprio.

Fuge, tace cum Arsenio,
Sede solus cum Machario,
Sæpe ora cum Antonio,
Jejuna cum Evagrio.
Vigila cum Hilario,
Sustine dolores cum Laurentio,
Despice honores cum Vincentio,
Dilige Jesum cum Ignatio,
Fer rerum damna cum Eustachio,
Confitere Christum cum Tibuitio,
Resiste draconi cum Honorato,
Perfere injurias cum Donato,
Lege, scribe cum Hieronymo,
Canta hymnos cum Ambrosio,
Stude, doce cum Augustino,
Disce mori mundo cum Gregorio,
Perseverando in Monasterio,

Imitare sanctum Benedictum,
Serva verbum tibi dictum,
Bonum est laborare manibus,
Melius orare cum fletibus,
Quære Jesum cum Bernardo,
Cum Hugone, cum Richardo,
Præmiaberis cum Confessoribus,
Si abnegaveris te in omnibus
Cave curiosa legere
Quæ possunt mentem distrahere,
Stude vitia cognoscere,
Et viriliter eis resistere;
Ambula cum simplicibus,
Adhære innocentibus,
Benefac tibi contrario,
Supplica pro adversario,
Et eris gratus Dei filio,
Ac dignus sanctorum consortio.
Monachorum est orare,
Gemiscere et plorare,
Pro suis defectibus
Carnem suam castigare,
Vigilare, jejunare
A voluptatibus,
Linguam refrænare,
Aures obturare
A vanitatibus,
Oculos custodire,
Pedes præmunire
Ab excursibus.
Manibus laborare,
Labris exultare,
Corde jubilare
In Dei laudibus.
Caput denudare,
Basse inclinare,
Genua curvare
Crucifixi pedibus.
Prompte obedire.
Nunquam contra ire
Suis majoribus.
Libenter servire,
Cito subvenire
Infirmis fratribus.
Curas mundi abjicere,
Cœlestibus intendere
Totis conatibus.
Ne vincaris a Dæmonio
Omnia fac cum consilio,
Et non facile aberrabis,
Nescis enim quamdiu hic eris,
Certum est quod morieris.
Numquam tamen desperabis,
Esto internus Deo devotus,
Mundo ignotus,
Et eris semper lætus,
Multum tibi vilis et despectus,
Fratri tuo pius et subjectus.
Maturus et facetus.
De bonis Deo tribue gloriam,
De malis pete veniam,
Omne remittens injuriam,
Sicque per Dei gratiam
Pervenies at Patriam,
Post hujus sæcli miseriam,
Ubi Jesu et Maria
In summa gaudent gloria
Cum tota cœli curia;
Ad quam post multa pericula,
Perducat Agnus sine macula,
Cui laus per æterna secula.
Amen.

The following extracts from the *Book of Canon Law* of the East Syrians, which was translated by

Dean Maclean, while he was one of the staff of the Archbishop's mission, and of which he kindly permits the printing (for the first time), give some account of Monasticism in the remote East, at an early period, and among a body of Christians entirely separated from the Churches of Rome and of Constantinople.

The preface asserts that Elijah, Elisha, the Apostles, and Christ Himself were monks; and that Heb. xi. 38 *et seq.* refers to monks. The following Canons are declared to have been enacted at the Œcumenical Council of Nice: Canon I.—The Head of a monastery must have been brought up in a monastery. He must be subject to the Bishop, Archdeacon, and Chorepiscopus. Canon II.—He gives to each of the monks his proper business. Canon III.—The visitor of the monastery must only take a small contribution. He must not eat or drink with women, nor talk much with them; nor give anything from the monastery to his relations. Canon IV.—Stranger monks, but not laymen, may eat with the monks. If a monk does not work, let his portion be lessened. An accuser, a disobedient person, a despiser of services and fasts, to be immediately expelled. Drunkenness to be forgiven three times, with penance; insult, ten times. Canon V.—Monks may not marry like other clerks or laymen. They may not eat meat, or wear soft clothing, or shoes, but sandals. They pray seven times, at the third, sixth, and ninth hours, besides Evensong and Compline, Nocturns, and Matins. A postulant to be thoroughly examined. Slaves only to be admitted with their master's leave. No one dependent upon their parents to be admitted against their wishes. Married men only if their wives consent, and not at all if there are children. Canon VI.—Work in summer from daybreak till the sun gets hot; then prayer and reading till the sixth hour. After six, light refreshment and rest till the ninth hour. After Nones, work till the evening. Canon VII.—No one to be shut up in houses, or stand on pillars, or let their hair grow, or put irons on themselves, or wander about unattached.

The Canons of Abraham of Fars quote scriptural authority for monastic practices. For quiet: 1 Thess. iv. 11; 2 Thess. iii. 12; Isa. xxxii. 17 *et seq.* For fasting: St. Matt. ix. 15; 2 Cor. xi. 27; Acts xiii. 3. The practice of Christ and the Apostles. For prayer: St. Luke xviii. 1; St. Mark xiii. 33; St. Matt. xxvi. 41; 1 Thess. v. 17. For reading: 1 Tim. iv. 13; Josh. i. 8; Ex. xiii. 9. For hours of prayer: Ps. cxix. 164; Daniel. For silence and solitude: Lam. iii. 27, 28; Jer. xv. 17. For not speaking angrily: Eph. iv. 31; Ps. xxxvii. 8.

In the Fast of Lent no one may go outside his cell without leave. No monk may go to other places without leave. Monks may not murmur against or slander one another. On entering church let monks meditate in the Bible. Fasts may only be broken for illness, the coming of guests, a long journey, or hard work. Any one neglecting fasts to be cut off from the assembly. Novices to stay three years in the Cænobium; if satisfactory, let them build cells for themselves; if not satisfactory, let them be dismissed. A brother finding another guilty of an offence must first rebuke him privately before taking the matter before the congregation.

The Canons of Mar Dadhishu Order—That a monk who errs in the faith, or despises the monastic fathers, must be immediately cut off; that any brother neglecting service on Sundays, except for illness, or after a long journey, is not to be forgiven; that a false accuser, or one who divulges Christian mysteries to outsiders, or one who being censured takes refuge with them, to be publicly rebuked, and on a second offence, to be cast out; that no one be received till he can read; no little boys to be received; that no monk in the cells order one in the Cænobium about a matter done in the cells; that a monk ordered to go on a journey, or to do work, who disobeys, be cut off; that brothers in the Cænobium must not neglect the Hours of Prayer; that if one strikes another, he must be expelled; also the other, if he retaliates; that one who goes outside may be received thrice, but no more; that on days before Feasts and Sundays, which have a vigil, no work is to be done, lest prayers be interrupted by sleepiness; that if a brother neglect the vigil, he may not communicate on the feast; that any one who neglects the four principal services is to be cut off.

Canon of Mar Ishuyaw—No one, under pretence of a monk's garb, may wander about, despise fasting, prayer, and the sacraments, take about with them women dressed as nuns, or live in a monastery where there are men and women. Stranger monks must

s

be recommended by their bishop. Offenders to be disfrocked and excommunicated. New churches and monasteries only to be built by permission of the bishop. Restoring old churches is better than building new ones. Builders of churches and monasteries not to appoint their priests or heads except by command of the bishop. If a monastery fall into ruins, the poorest monasteries inherit its possessions. If none are poor, then the nearest. If two or three are near, let them inherit according to the number of the monks. Failing these, the bishop's house inherits.

It is incidentally mentioned that monks made their only full meal at Compline time.

CHAPTER IV

MONASTICISM IN BRITAIN

> Thy waste and thy desolate places, and the land of thy destruction, shall even now be too narrow by reason of the inhabitants, and they that swallowed thee up shall be far away. The children which thou shalt have, after thou hast lost the other, shall say again in thy ears, The place is too strait for me; give place to me that I may dwell. Then shalt thou say in thy heart, Who hath begotten me these, seeing I have lost my children, and am desolate, a captive, and removing to and fro? and who hath brought up these? Behold I am left alone; these, where had they been? Thus saith the Lord God, Behold, I will... set up my standard to the people: and they shall bring thy sons in their arms, and thy daughters shall be carried upon their shoulders. And kings shall be thy nursing fathers, and their queens thy nursing mothers: ... for they shall not be ashamed that wait for me.—*Isaiah* xlix. 19—23.

THAT Christianity was introduced at a very early period into Britain is certain; but there are no authentic records to fix the exact date, or to determine who were the first missionaries. The earliest British writers lament that they have not any ancient histories to refer to. They tell us, however, that a widely-accepted tradition relates that Joseph of Arimathea came to Glastonbury and founded a monastery there; and many writers, down even to the present day, consider it probable that St. Paul himself preached the Gospel in Britain. There are grounds for concluding that British Christianity came from the East, and although there was constant communication with Rome, certain practices and ecclesiastical regulations of the early British Church were evidently oriental in their origin, and differed from those of the Church at Rome.

The Church in Britain must not only have been fully constituted, but it must have been recognized by and have held communication with the Church in other parts of Europe; for at the Council of Arles (314) a British bishop was present. We must conclude therefore that Monasticism, in its first phase, which was known in Gaul, would also be transmitted to Britain in primitive times. The invasions of the heathen Saxons overthrew the British Church, except in the west of England, and in Wales. At Bangor near Chester, there was a very large monastery, containing several hundred monks, and there were other important British monasteries, which were not only centres of religious life and missionary enterprise, but the seats of learning and the principal places of secular education. The names of DUBRITIUS, DAVID or Dewi, KENTIGERN and others have come down to us, men who were prominent in the British Church, and who, according to the custom of the day, were founders of monasteries, and spent their lives within their walls.

Ireland, at a very early date, received Christianity from Gaul. Legendary accounts state that ST. PATRICK, who was a distant relation of the great St. Martin of Tours, was carried away by pirates, and sold as a slave in Ireland. After some years he regained his liberty, and went to the monastery of Marmoutier, and then to Rome. He was for a time associated with the great champion of orthodoxy, St. German of Auxerre, and under his direction opposed the Pelagian heresy which had taken root among the British Christians. Finally he returned to Ireland as a missionary (440), and by his efforts Christianity was not only established there, but it became vigorous and aggressive, and the mother of other Churches among the Scots, both in Ireland and Scotland, and upon the Continent of Europe.

It was a peculiar feature of this mission that it was almost entirely monastic. The bishops were in some cases abbots, but they often lived in subjection to the abbot, who was only a priest, and they exercised episcopal authority only in conferring orders.

"Travel now through Ireland, and you will find in the wildest parts innumerable remains of Religious Houses which had grown up among a people who acknowledged no rule among themselves except the sword. The monks among these were as sheep among wolves; but the wolves spared them for their character."[1]

"Ireland, in which no proconsul ever set foot, was the only place in the world where the Gospel conquered without resistance and effusion of blood. The first enthusiasm of faith, which elsewhere swept the believers to martyrdom, in Ireland drove the neophytes into monasteries, and St. Patrick rejoiced to see the

[1] J. A. Froude, *Short Studies* (Longmans).

sons and daughters of the chiefs adopt the eremitical life in such numbers that he could not count them. The West had never seen anything like those great foundations, true monastic capitals, Bangor, Clonfert, and Clonard, in each of which were assembled over three thousand monks. But the enthusiasm of the Irish Christians could not be quenched in the retreats of these monastic institutions. They were seized with a passion for missionary work. In dreams and ecstasies they saw the heathen Germans calling to them to come over and help them. They left Ireland in shoals; they carried the light of the Gospel to Scotland, to Northumbria, to Neustria, to Flanders. When, later, the Norsemen landed in Iceland, they found Irish hermits who had gone there to find men to convert, before the island had got inhabitants. These missionaries penetrated the forests of Germany, climbed the Alps, entered Italy and Spain. Christianity in Ireland was wholly monastic. In every abbey were many bishops, and the abbot ruled the community as abbot, and the diocese as bishop. Jurisdiction was in abbatial not episcopal hands." [1]

Montalembert says—"A prince in becoming a monk, naturally became also an abbot, and in his monastic life continued, as he had been in his worldly existence, the chief of his race and his clan. The first great monasteries of Ireland were then nothing else than clans reorganized under a religious form. From this cause resulted the extraordinary number of

---

[1] *History of the Church in Germany*, p. 49. S. Baring-Gould (Gardner, Darton & Co.).

their inhabitants, who were counted by hundreds and thousands."[1]

Nothing remains but ruins to indicate the sites of some of these great centres of primitive Christianity and of secular learning. Monasterboyce, Glendalough, Clonmacnoise, Bangor, and Clonard, once the home of hundreds of monks, have either been swept away entirely, or there are only remains of several churches quite near together, and one of those mysterious round towers.

"Wales was covered with a network of monasteries. The chieftain often became abbot, and the clan the members of his abbey. These Celtic monasteries had a different rationale from that of the later English and Continental monasteries. The great purpose was missionary; daily evangelizing journeys were made into neighbouring districts. Stone crosses were set up to mark the preaching stations, and in course of time a rude building was constructed. Ultimately a suitable church was erected, and called after the name of the mission priest. Thirty-one parishes in Carnarvonshire still bear the names and testify to the missionary labours of the Welsh monks."[2]

ST. BRIDGET (or St. Bride), who was baptized by St. Patrick, became the foundress of religious houses for women in Ireland, the first of which was at Kildare. Probably the Rule adopted in Irish convents, both for men and women, at this period, was

[1] *Monks of the West*, vol. iii. p. 86.
[2] *Social Reform*, by O. M. Edwards.

that which St. Martin had framed for his abbey at Marmoutier; but as yet no monastic rule had been generally accepted, and each abbot ruled his house according to his own ideas of what was most suitable for his monks and their surroundings. Considerable progress was made in secular learning in the Irish monasteries, and students were attracted to them from Gaul and other parts of the Continent. The *Pilgrimage of Brandon*, a poem of very early date, became a classic during the mediæval period.

ST. COLUMBANUS and ST. GALL, Irish monks of Bangor (Co. Down), fired with missionary zeal, left their native land and preached the Gospel in Gaul, Helvetia, and in Germany. They carried with them the traditional customs of their Church, and founded monasteries as the centres of their work, and introduced the peculiarities to which they had been accustomed. When the disciples of St. Benedict extended their missions, they found themselves confronted with monks who followed "the Rule of Columbanus," and much controversy and not a little ill-feeling arose in consequence. But ultimately the Rule of St. Benedict prevailed, and was generally adopted. The principal monastery established by Columbanus was at Luxeuil in the Vosges, from which colonies of monks were sent out, and other foundations were created by them, in which a more strict discipline was observed than that which prevailed in most of the monasteries of Southern Europe.

ST. NINIAN, the son of a British chief, having received instruction and ordination in Rome, returned to his native land and devoted himself to the conversion of the barbarous tribes of the North. He founded a monastery which was called *Candida Casa*, on account of its church, which was built of stone.

In Wales, ST. DAVID carried on the work that had been begun by Kentigern and others, and founded several large monasteries, and introduced the right of asylum, which, in those days of violence and brutality, was often a great boon. Another missionary monk and founder of monasteries was CADOC, who, when driven from his country by the invasions of the Saxons, went to Brittany, and there built a large monastery. He subsequently returned to England, and attempted the conversion of the Saxons, and was martyred by them. Indeed, these savage pagans ruthlessly stamped out the British Church wherever they settled; but beyond their sway bishops and monasteries still maintained the faith of Christ, and adhered passionately to the primitive customs and traditions of their Church; their isolated and remote position making them ignorant of the changes that were taking place in other parts of Christendom.

ST. COLUMBA was a descendant of the royal race of the O'Donnells, and in spite of his subsequent sanctity and devotion to missionary work, often displayed the fiery temper and the love of fighting which distinguished the old Irish chieftains. He was educated at one of the great monasteries, and himself became a monk at an early age, and the founder of monasteries at Derry and other places. His departure from his native country has been variously explained by his biographers, some relating that he became involved in one of the many bloody civil wars between clan and clan that scarcely ever ceased, and that he was sent away by indignant ecclesiastics into banishment; while others maintain that it was only his missionary zeal that led him to go forth into the wild regions of Western Scotland, and to take up his abode among the savage and heathen inhabitants. He landed upon the little desolate island of Hy, or Iona, which afterwards, in memory of his great work there, was called I-Colm-Kill. The first monastery consisted of a few rough huts, built of the coarse undergrowth of the island; for the storm-beaten soil produced no trees; and it is difficult to understand how upon this rocky desert, three miles long by two in breadth, even the meagre food of its ascetic inhabitants could be procured. But in the midst of this desolation the learning of the times found a home, and St. Columba, even to his latest years, employed much of his time in writing copies of the Scriptures and other books. Nor did the remote situation of his island, or the difficulty of access to it, prevent the arrival of a constant succession of visitors, who came to consult this recluse on spiritual questions, or to be taught the rudiments of Christianity, and the principles of the religious life. Many of these visitors remained with their teacher, and soon the place became too small for the largely-increased community. This led to the formation of monastic colonies in various parts of Scotland. There were already settlements of "Scots" from Ireland in the country, who were Christians, at least in name and profession, and these, availing themselves of the teaching of the monks of Iona, learned "the way of God more perfectly." But in the northern wilds of Scotland there were still the tribes of the Picts, who were but barbarous and fierce savages, whose rude religion consisted of cruel rites and bloody sacrifices, conducted by fanatical Druidical priests. To these unpromising subjects for a Christian Mission, St. Columba went, and by his wonderful personal influence he persuaded some of the chiefs to accept Christianity and to be baptized; and before his death, he had the satisfaction of knowing that churches and monasteries stood where all had hitherto been mere wild nature, or degraded superstition. The ancient Irish customs were by St. Columba introduced into Scotland, and the monastic system entirely overshadowed the episcopal dignity; and it does not seem impossible that this long-standing depreciation of episcopacy may have had some influence in later times in bringing about its rejection in favour of the Presbyterian system of Church government. When the Scottish kings became Christian, the custom of a religious service at their coronation was introduced; but this was conducted, not by a bishop, but by the Abbot of Scone, where the famous "Stone of Fate" was preserved, and upon which the anointed king was placed. St. Columba also succeeded in preserving the order of Bards, who had been attached to the heathen chiefs, and who sang of their exploits, and those of their deified ancestors. Native poetry and music were thus not only saved from destruction, but the harps and voices of the Bards were newly attuned to Christian themes and patriotic songs. The monks of Iona were also daring sailors, and in their boats, made of osiers and covered with hides, they navigated the rough northern seas, visiting the Shetland Islands, and even Iceland, evangelizing the wild people, and founding churches for them. They were skilled also in medicine and surgery, as far as those arts were understood in their day. St. Columba died in the Church at Iona, in June 597, and for many years after it became an object of desire with kings and princes and other great men to be buried near his tomb in the monastery churchyard. The abbey was sacked and burned by the Danes in 801, and again in 805, and 877; and after many vicissitudes it was rebuilt by Queen Margaret at the end of the eleventh century.

The next great name that meets us in the annals of British Monasticism is that of ST. AUGUSTINE of Canterbury. The repeated invasions of the Saxons during more than a century resulted in the slaughter or the enslavement of the British people, or their flight to the wilds of the West, or across the sea to Brittany; and the conquering race, with their language and customs, took absolute possession of the whole country. The invading tribes were entirely pagan, and they destroyed without mercy every trace of Christianity. There were continual wars between their kings, and the vanquished were either ruthlessly put to death, or sold as slaves. It was thus that St. Gregory the Great saw and pitied the Saxon children exposed for sale at Rome; and the well-known incident occurred that ultimately led to the conversion of the people of the Heptarchy. St. Gregory determined to send missionaries to teach the religion of Christ to those whose children, as he said, had already "the faces of angels." He commenced his work by purchasing Saxon boys, and placing them for instruction in the monasteries; and finally he selected from the monastery of St. Andrew, which he had founded, its prior, Augustine, with forty monks, to be the first preachers of the Gospel in the distant and barbarous island of the Angles.

The pioneers set out, and in the course of their journey, arrived at the island of Lerins, and rested themselves in the venerable abbey that had once been the home of St. Patrick, the apostle of Ireland. Instead of gathering courage from this fact, they were so terrified at the accounts that were given them of the savagery of the Saxons, and their obstinate adherence to their traditional pagan superstitions, that they refused to go any further, and sent Augustine back to Gregory to beg him to release them from their undertaking. The Pope not only refused to accede to their wishes, but vehemently insisted upon their fulfilling his commands. To encourage them, however, he gave Augustine the rank of abbot, and entrusted him with letters to bishops, abbots, and princes, in which he urged them to help the missionaries on their way, and to give them every possible aid and assistance. After a tedious and toilsome journey, Augustine and his companions landed in Kent, at a place called Ebbsfleet, and sent messengers to Ethelbert, the King of Kent, at his city of Canterbury (597). It was possibly known to Gregory that the King's wife, Bertha, the daughter of the King of the Franks, was a Christian, and had a chaplain who ministered the rites of her religion, in accordance with the agreement made before her marriage. After some delay the King admitted Augustine to an interview, and finally allowed him and his companions to teach their religion to any who chose to listen to them. The little oratory, dedicated to St. Martin, in which the Queen had worshipped, became the church of the monks, and they made themselves some sort of a dwelling near it, being assisted by the bounty of the King; and so the first Benedictine monastery was founded in England, to be the source of the revival of Christianity, and the centre from which it spread all over the land, and became that great Church of England upon whose houses of prayer and worship the sun now never sets.

It is interesting and suggestive to notice that just at the time when the Moslem conquerors were sweeping away the Church in North Africa and elsewhere in the East, the new and vigorous branch of the Church in the far West was being established, as it were, in compensation.

The evangelizing work at first proceeded but slowly; as was indeed to be expected, when it is remembered that the new religion had to contend with a system that was bound closely with the people's traditions and prejudices, and that it ran counter to many of their cherished habits, and was regarded with suspicion as a foreign and alien importation.

The holy lives of the missionaries, their superior knowledge and culture, and the fact that they came from the great city of Rome, of which even barbarous peoples had heard wonderful accounts, gradually gained influence, and converts were made, till on Whitsunday, 597, Ethelbert himself was baptized, and a large number of persons of all ranks speedily followed his example. Augustine now went to France, and was consecrated Archbishop of the English. Ethelbert soon after gave up his palace to be converted into a monastery, in which Augustine lived as abbot and archbishop. The present cathedral of Canterbury occupies the site of the original buildings, and St. Martin's church, whose walls are composed largely of Roman bricks, stands upon the foundations of Queen Bertha's oratory, where King Ethelbert was baptized, and is probably itself part of the ancient structure which was the temporary abbey church of Augustine and his Benedictine monks. There was also at Canterbury a heathen temple which had been built upon the site, and with the materials of an old British church, this, Ethelbert, at Augustine's request, made over to him, and there the archbishop founded another Benedictine abbey, which he dedicated to St. Peter and St. Paul. In later times this foundation was called St. Augustine's, and it became one of the largest and most important abbeys in England.

Suppressed by Henry VIII., its ruins were desecrated by various unworthy uses till, in 1844, Mr. Beresford Hope bought them, and with the assistance of other liberal Englishmen, built upon the site of the abbey the Missionary College of St. Augustine; the original gateways and much of the old material being incorporated into the new buildings (1848).

When Gregory gave Augustine his commission to evangelize the English, he, with true wisdom and charity, bade him respect the remnant of the British Church which had survived the Saxon persecutions, and conciliate its bishops, so as to bring them voluntarily to adopt the customs of the Western Church, where their own practice differed from that which careful reforms had introduced. The British Church had been infected with Pelagianism; it still maintained the quartodeciman method of reckoning Easter; the tonsure of its monks was in the antiquated form which it had seemed well to the most learned and pious authorities to give up; Confirmation was not administered in the same way as that which the Roman Church adopted; and there was, moreover, a strong feeling of animosity against the Saxons and all that belonged to them, the traditional result of the cruel oppression of the invaders, and their bloody destruction of the Church of the conquered race. Augustine endeavoured to persuade the British Christians to conform to the usages of his own communion; and finally he induced the British bishops to meet him at a formal conference on the borderland of the two races, near the Severn (601). There seemed at first to be a good prospect of an understanding and a *modus vivendi* being agreed upon. The British ecclesiastics were conscious of their isolated position, of their ignorance, and of the superior attainments and numbers of the Churches of the Continent; but they clung passionately to all that they had received from the apostolic founders of their Church, and to everything that had been believed and practised by the long line of native saints who had never swerved from the original deposit which they valued more than life itself; and finally their pride and independence seem to have been wounded by the claim of Augustine to jurisdiction over them, in virtue of his commission from Rome, and by some hasty words and a haughty and uncourteous manner, which they assumed to be a sign to them that the new-comer was not a humble and Christ-like man of God. The conference was broken up, and both sides separated with angry feelings, and no further attempt seems to have been made to unite the two Churches. A few years after the conference almost all the monks of the great abbey of Bangor, near Chester, were slaughtered by pagan invaders from the North; and while the British Church decayed and passed out of sight, or was gradually absorbed into the rival communion, Augustine and his successors at Canterbury gradually covered the land with monasteries, and finally established the faith in the Saxon kingdoms, without much opposition and without martyrdoms. The first thirty-eight Archbishops of Canterbury were all monks. In London, St. Paul's was a monastic church; and the great Abbey at Westminster became, and continued for centuries to be, the national Sanctuary of England.

After the death of Augustine a temporary check occurred in the progress of Christianity among the Saxons south of the Trent, through the lapse of some of their princes into paganism; but not only was the faith ultimately triumphant in these regions of England, but it was propagated in the northern division, as it had been received in Kent, by monks, and by the instrumentality of a woman. Ethelburga, who had been married to Edwin, the pagan King of Northumbria, was a Christian, and by her influence, PAULINUS, one of the surviving monks who had come over with Augustine, was consecrated bishop (625), and fixed his see at York, and set about the conversion of the northern Saxons. After a time Edwin himself was baptized, and then his people of all ranks followed his example. Monastic communities were founded at Lincoln, and other places, and it seemed as if all the wide dominions of Edwin were to be made Christian without let or hindrance. But it was not so to be. As in the south, so in the north, there was a revival of heathenism, through the victories of the pagan Penda. Christians were slaughtered; Queen Ethelburga fled to Kent, and became a nun at Lyminge; Paulinus retired to Rochester, and became its bishop; Oswald, the nephew of Edwin, found refuge at Iona. After some years Oswald collected a small army, and attacked the heathen enemies of his kingdom, and gained a signal victory near Hexham, and recovered possession of the whole of Northumbria, and finally became *Bretwalda*, the chief of all the Saxon Kings. His life at Iona had not been without its good effects. He earnestly desired the restoration of his people to the Christian faith, and, as was natural, he applied to the monks of Iona for missionaries and teachers, and one of them, named AIDAN, was consecrated bishop, and sent into Northumbria (635). Instead of reviving the see of York, Aidan founded a monastery at Lindisfarne, a small island on the coast of Northumberland, not unlike Iona on the west, and this insignificant and desolate rock became the spiritual capital of the whole of northern Britain, the residence of its first sixteen bishops, and the centre from which all missionary effort proceeded. Monasteries were founded, boys and slaves were educated, music was taught, and all the influences of enlightened Christianity were brought to bear upon the people, who were civilized and taught social advancement here, as had always been the rule of the primitive monks.

Once more the good work of Christian king and monk-bishop was stopped for a time. Penda again put himself at the head of the heathen population, and attacked Oswald, who was slain in a fierce battle, and the whole of Northumbria was ravaged by the victorious army. Penda, in his turn, was conquered and slain by Oswy, the younger brother of Oswald, and Christianity was restored. Monasteries were founded, or rebuilt, and members of the royal and noble families took vows within them. Oswy's daughter became a nun at Hartlepool; where Hilda, the grand-niece of Edwin, was already abbess. In 658, Hilda erected an abbey at Whitby, which, like some other foundations of early date, provided a house for monks and another for nuns, both governed by the abbess. Among the monks of Whitby was Cædmon, the poet. He was a remarkable instance of the truth of the saying—"*Poeta nascitur, non fit.*" He spent his early life as a cowherd, but his genius was discovered by Hilda and her monks, and he was received into the monastery, and was the author of many religious poems. Another great abbey was commenced at this period (664) at Medeshampsted, afterwards called Peterborough; and at Lastingham, in Yorkshire, a flourishing community was established.

In 674 the important monastery of Wearmouth was built, and soon after that of Jarrow, by BENEDICT BISCOP, a British monk from Lerins. At Jarrow, Bede the historian lived, and died 734. Fursy, an Irish monk, built a monastery in East Anglia, in which King Sigebert became a monk. Teudric, a Welsh prince, retired to the banks of the Wye, where Tintern Abbey afterwards arose; and lived as a hermit.

An Episcopal See was created at Dorchester, near Oxford, and monasteries were founded at Winchester and Malmesbury. Cedd, a monk of Lindisfarne, became Bishop of London (653), and Diuma, another, was consecrated Bishop of Mercia.

In 634, ST. WILFRID was born of one of the

noblest families in Northumbria. After a short military career, he became a monk at Lindisfarne. Desiring to be made acquainted with the practice of the Church in the most civilized countries, he made a journey to Rome, and renouncing the Celtic usages in which he had been brought up, he adopted all Roman rites and customs, and returned to England. These foreign fashions did not commend themselves to his former companions, and he left Lindisfarne, and soon after was made abbot of the newly-founded monastery at Ripon, where he substituted the Roman use as regards the time of keeping Easter, the form of the tonsure, and other observances, for the British traditions. Wilfrid, with all the zeal of a convert, used every endeavour to spread the adoption of the Roman use throughout the Church in Britain, while the successors of Columba and Aidan stoutly maintained and defended their practices. The controversy, which dated from the time of Augustine, now assumed an acute stage, and much angry feeling was displayed on both sides. In 664, a conference was held at Whitby, under King Oswy, to consider the debated questions. Colman, Bishop of Lindisfarne, was the representative and leader of the British party, and Wilfrid was the principal advocate on the Roman side; and his eloquence and his statements respecting the pre-eminence of the See of St. Peter, finally prevailed, and a majority of the assembly voted for the adoption of the usages of Rome, wherever they differed from those of the British Church. Colman, with his followers, refused to agree to this; and going to Ireland, formed a community on the island of Innisbowen, on the west coast, where they could still follow the example of their spiritual fathers. Soon after (664) Wilfrid was elected Bishop of Northumbria; but he fixed his see, not at Lindisfarne, but at York. In this position he not only used all his influence to make the Roman usages generally adopted, but he introduced into Northumbria the Benedictine Rule, which had hitherto been unknown in that remote province.

St. Cuthbert began life as a shepherd, but becoming vividly impressed with religious fervour, he entered the monastery of old Melrose, and after some years became Prior. He next went to Lindisfarne, and ultimately (685) was made Bishop of Lindisfarne, but lived on a small island called Farne, as a hermit. His body was buried at Lindisfarne, and when the abbey was sacked and destroyed by the Danes (793) the relics of the saint were carried to the great monastery of Durham, where a magnificent shrine was afterwards erected to contain them. Adamnan, abbot of Iona, laboured to bring the Celtic monks to adopt the Roman use, and wrote the life of St. Columba.

The Venerable Bede, a monk of Jarrow, born 673, was a man of learning and culture far in advance of his times. His numerous works prove his knowledge, not only of theology and history, but of geography, music, medicine, philosophy, and classical literature. His *History* is almost the only trustworthy record that we possess of the period, whose annals would have been unknown to us but for his labours. He was the pioneer in England of those many literary monks to whom we owe so much.

ST. GUTHLAC was of noble birth, and in his youth served in the army of Ethelred, King of Mercia, but he retired into a monastery in his twenty-fourth year. After passing two years there, he left with two companions and settled in the island of Croyland (699). His ascetic life attracted much attention, and when he died King Ethelbald built a monastery on the site of his hermitage. This was destroyed by the Danes (870), but was restored by Turketil, the Chancellor of King Edred (946).

One of the distinguishing features of the Anglo-Saxon Church was the large number of royal and noble persons, of both sexes, who embraced the monastic life. Thus King Ceolwulf became a monk at Lindisfarne, and his successor Eadbert followed his example. Sigebert, Sebbi, Offa, Coenred, Ethelred, Centwin, Ceadwalla, Ina, all exchanged their crowns for the monkish cowl; some of them making the long and toilsome journey to Rome to effect their purpose. The Saxon ladies also in numerous instances retired from their high positions, and took the veil. HILDA, EBBA, and EFLEDA, as abbesses, possessed great influence and authority. ETHELBURGA and EANSWITH founded and presided over important convents. DOMNEVA, and her daughter MILDRED and even the daughters of the fierce pagan Penda, became nuns. ETHELDREDA, the widow of two Saxon princes, erected the Abbey of Ely, in the midst of the fens, where she was joined by many noble ladies of her own family and others, and her house became famous as a place of education, and a centre and source of religious light and life to East Anglia. CUTHBURGA, sister of King Ina, was abbess of Wimborne, which her brother founded in 705. FRIDESWIDE, the daughter of a Saxon prince, founded an important convent at Oxford, which afterwards bore her name. It was ultimately suppressed by Wolsey, and upon its site was built the College of Christ Church.

"In early Saxon times the monasteries were the means of preserving to our use all the most precious treasures of literature, art, and religion. The monks alone possessed, and handed down to us, contemporary history, laws, manners and customs, which have had a great and powerful influence on the social life of to-day. It was the 'religious houses' that spared the inhabitants of these islands the Sisyphæan task of again toiling up the steps of time from a lower stage of moral, intellectual, and social culture than they had probably attained at the time of the Roman invasion. That some corruption crept into the monasteries there is no doubt, but even were we compelled to believe that they were at certain periods the sinks of iniquity that some have ventured to describe them, this could not have always been the case."[1]

One of the early abuses is mentioned by Dr. Lingard:

"Men of rank and influence, under the pretence

[1] T. Yorke Powell, *Social England.*

of founding monasteries, obtained from the king charters of bocland of the same tenor with those which had been granted to different abbots for that purpose. To ensure the permanence of the grant, it was necessary to comply with the conditions; and therefore they were careful to erect certain buildings, which they called the monastery, and to place in them a certain number of inmates who assumed the name of monks. They themselves were the abbots, though they did not quit their secular offices or pursuits, retaining the property in their own hands, and at their death bequeathing both monastery and lands to their heirs and posterity. . . . By the Council of Cloveshoe it was declared a species of profaneness to give to these places the name of monasteries. . . . After the Council we lose sight of the secular monasteries entirely."

The progress of Monasticism in England was seriously interrupted by the barbarous invasions and devastations of the Danes. These ferocious heathens left their homes in Scandinavia, and landing upon the shores of England, plundered the towns, burned the monasteries, slaughtered the men, and carried the women and children away to be sold as slaves. They first appeared about 787, and the success of their raids induced their chiefs to make other and more formidable expeditions. Almost all the great monasteries were entirely destroyed. Lindisfarne, Wearmouth, Jarrow, Croyland, Peterborough, Ely, Coldingham, and many more, were swept away, and Monasticism virtually came to an end, for a time.

Its revival commenced with the efforts of ODO, Archbishop of Canterbury (942). Odo was himself a Dane, and had been a soldier. After his conversion to Christianity he went to France, and became a Benedictine monk.

In 958, DUNSTAN was appointed Archbishop of Canterbury; and to him is due the credit of restoring Monasticism in England. He was of royal blood, and was born at Glastonbury. After spending some years in the French monastery of Fluery, he was ordered by King Edmund to rebuild the ancient monastery of Glastonbury, and to become its abbot. Many other abbeys were founded or restored, and the Benedictine Rule was established in all of them; among these were the important and great houses of Ely, Peterborough, Tewkesbury, Glastonbury, Evesham, Abingdon, Ramsay, and Tavistock.

When Edwy succeeded to the throne he quarrelled with Dunstan, and banished him from the kingdom. Not content with this, he attacked several of the monasteries which Dunstan had founded or restored, and turned out the monks. Dunstan was recalled by Edwy's successor, Edgar, who assisted his schemes for the revival of Monasticism, and himself built more than forty monasteries. Most of the Cathedral bodies were converted into congregations of monks; the Benedictine Rule was generally introduced, and the Church of England was brought more closely into union with the Church of Rome. After the death of Edgar (975) a period of disorder occurred, and many of the monasteries became the prey of marauding chiefs. A conference held at Calne (978) gave protection to the monks for a time; but the young King Edward having been murdered, the reign of violence once more prevailed, and the monasteries were again attacked.

Dunstan was succeeded by ÆLFRIC (995), who followed his steps in building and restoring monasteries. He was a man of piety and learning, and some of his writings have come down to us, which show how he laboured to purify the Church from abuses, and to stir up the bishops and abbots to promote the spiritual advancement of the institutions committed to their care.

Under Sweyne, and his son Canute (1016), the Danish power became paramount in England. Canute ultimately embraced Christianity, and restored some of the monasteries that had been destroyed by his ancestors, and founded the great abbey of St. Edmundsbury, in reparation for the cruel murder of King Edmund (870) by the Danes. The patient labour of the monks, during many generations, drained the land round the abbey, and made it fruitful and valuable; and this, added to many benefactions and grants of land, in course of time raised the monastery to a position of great wealth and importance.

ST. BENEDICT BISCOP was born of noble parents in 628. King Oswy attached him to his court, but at the age of twenty-five he determined to become a monk. He accompanied Wilfrid in his journey to Rome, and then assumed the monastic habit at

Lerins. Archbishop Theodore took Benedict with him to Canterbury, and made him Abbot of St. Augustine's. Benedict again made the toilsome journey to Rome, and returned laden with books, and was then entrusted by King Egfrid with the erection of the important monastery of Wearmouth, which was built of stone; and glass windows and pictures for the church were brought from France (674). Italian monks were introduced to instruct the English in music. In 682, Benedict began building another monastery at Jarrow, an imitation of St. Paul's-without-the-walls at Rome, as Wearmouth had been copied from St. Peter's.

In 1042 Edward the Confessor became King of England. He had been brought up in Normandy, and many French monks were introduced by him into monasteries which were cells of abbeys in Normandy; thus originating the system of "Alien Priories," which ultimately led to abuses and dissatisfaction; and when William, Duke of Normandy, became king, the Church of England was still further placed under the control of Norman bishops and abbots, and through them became, more than ever before, subject to the Pope.

The Conqueror was continually apprehensive of revolt among his Saxon subjects, and fear induced him to acts of cruelty and injustice. Many of the monasteries were seized by the King, and the monks ejected or slaughtered, and the revenues appropriated. A tax was levied upon all religious houses. Normans were substituted for Saxons in places of authority, and the French language was ordered to be used instead of Anglo-Saxon.

William was, however, on the whole a friend of the Church. During his reign the great abbey of Christ Church, Canterbury, was rebuilt on a grand scale, and also many other monasteries throughout the country.

After a period of terrorism, consequent upon the Conquest, order and quiet were restored, and the appointment of LANFRANC to the See of Canterbury greatly assisted the progress of the Church. Lanfranc, having himself been a monk, favoured in every way the growth of Monasticism, and he especially promoted the adoption of the Benedictine Rule.

During the reign of Rufus, the Church of England suffered, with the whole nation, from the tyranny and injustice of the King, and but for the strong hand and clear head of ST. ANSELM, Archbishop of Canterbury (1093), universal ruin would have prevailed.

"Throughout the reign of King John and his successor . . . the prelates and clergy of the Church of England displayed signs of secularization of temper and habits. The monastic orders had degenerated into wealthy landowners. The failure of the Church to keep pace with the moral needs of the nation was attested by the eager interest with which the coming of the Friars was welcomed by the people. For the revival of religion that followed, these devoted missionaries are no doubt entitled to the chief credit. Yet it is curious to contrast their condition in the first quarter of the thirteenth century with what it had become in the second half of the fourteenth, when Wyclif could with general applause denounce them as 'sturdy beggars.'"[1]

From this time monasteries were continually founded, and constant benefactions increased their wealth and importance, till there were nearly 200 houses for men or women which followed the Rule of St. Benedict, and whose revenues were estimated at nearly £20,000 a year, which represents more than ten times that amount in money of the present time. The cathedrals of Peterborough, Chester, Gloucester, Bath, Canterbury, Coventry, Durham, Ely, Norwich, Rochester, Winchester, and Worcester, and the great mitred abbeys of Glastonbury, St. Albans, Westminster, Reading, Thorney, Tavistock, Colchester, Tewkesbury, Winchelcombe, Hyde, Ramsey, Bardney, Croyland, Hulme, Shrewsbury, Bury St. Edmunds, Battle, Malmesbury, York, Evesham, and Selby, all belonged to the Benedictines, besides many smaller houses, and nunneries.

During the twelfth century a large number of monasteries were built in England. In the reign of William Rufus, and up to the end of the reign of King John, a period of about 100 years, 408 monasteries were founded. In the three following reigns, embracing 108 years, there were only 139 built; while in the fourteenth century there were only 23, and in the fifteenth century only three.

A great impetus to Monasticism was given by the introduction into England of the reformed branches

[1] H. D. Traill, *Social England* (Cassell).

of the Benedictine Order. The Cluniacs arrived in 1078. They were, however, never popular. The abbots and most of the monks were Frenchmen, and the Order was entirely under the direction of the abbot of Cluny. On this account the communities were always reckoned as "Alien Priories," and during the wars with France they were seized, and their revenues appropriated by the English kings. Wolsey dissolved four Cluniac monasteries in 1525, and appropriated their property for the endowment of his colleges.

The Cistercians came to England about 1128, and rapidly gained favour. Many large and important abbeys were founded for the Order, among which were Woburn, Furness, Tintern, Fountains, Kirkstall, Jervaux, Netley, Boxley, Whalley, and Byland. At the Dissolution there were thirty-six greater and thirty-nine smaller monasteries of the Order in the kingdom, besides twenty-three nunneries; and its total revenue was estimated to be £18,691.

Besides the monks of the Benedictine Order, and its branches, there were Orders entirely distinct from it. The Rule of St. Augustine was followed by a considerable number of communities, and the members were called Canons.

The Premonstratensians came to England in 1146, and they ultimately had thirty-five houses. There were also two nunneries of this Order. Another Order, which was founded in England in 1148, and never spread to other countries, was that of GILBERT OF SEMPRINGHAM. Like some of the early Saxon communities, each convent was double, and had a house for monks and another for nuns. There were twenty-five houses of the Order, chiefly in Lincolnshire and Yorkshire.

The Augustine Canons had 170 houses in England, some of which were large and important. Waltham, Cirencester, and Canterbury sent their abbots to Parliament.

There were also some communities dependent upon foreign Orders, the Bonhommes, the Nuns of Fontevrault, and those of St. Bridget.

The Templars had their principal house in London, the Church of which still remains. They had also Commanderies and Preceptories in different parts of England. Through the influence of Philip, King of France, this Order was suppressed in England in 1312; part of its property was appropriated by King Edward, and the rest was made over to the Hospitallers.

The Hospitallers, or Knights of St. John, came to England in the reign of King Henry I. (1103). Their principal convent was at Clerkenwell, in London, and they had twenty-seven others in different parts of England.

The Dominican Friars first settled in England in 1221, at Oxford. Their central house was a very large one in London, the site of which still bears the name of "Blackfriars." Besides this they had forty-two establishments in the country.

The Franciscans, or Grey Friars, came to England in 1224, and their first settlement was at Canterbury; they had sixty-five other houses.

The Carthusians first settled in England in 1180, but never became very numerous. Their principal house was in London, and was known as the Charterhouse.

The Trinitarians, Maturines, or Friars of the Holy Trinity, for the redemption of captives, came to England in 1224, and they had eleven houses.

The Carmelites, or White Friars, whose Rule is that of St. Basil, came to England in 1240, and they had forty houses.

The Order of the Crutched or Crossed Friars came to England in 1244, and they had seven houses.

The Austin Friars, or Friars Eremites of St. Augustine, came to England about 1250, and they had forty-one houses.

The Friars of Penance, or of the Sack, had nine houses.

The Bethlemite Friars came in 1257, and had but one house.

The Friars de Pica, and the Friars de Areno, had one house each.

The Friars de Domina, or of Our Lady, followed the Rule of St. Augustine. They had three houses.

The order of Grandmont came to England in the reign of Henry I. They had three houses.

There were also scattered over England a large number of Hospitals, where the old were sheltered and cared for, or where lepers and other sick persons were received. These admirable institutions were often placed under the care of some monastery, and a clerical monk acted as master or chaplain. Most of these charitable foundations were spared by Henry VIII., but they were suppressed, and their endowments appropriated by the avaricious advisers of Edward VI. The Hospital of St. Cross, at Winchester, has survived, and some idea of what these houses were may still be obtained by visiting it. That these charitable foundations were very numerous may be concluded from the entries in Leland's *Itinerary*, which was an account of an antiquarian journey through a great part of England, during the reign of Henry VIII., and commenced in 1538, at the King's own command. There is continual mention of some Hospital, or Hospitals, in the places visited by Leland, which no longer exist.

The principal persons in a monastery in England were as follows—

The Abbot was the head and ruler of the monastery. He was often appointed to his office by the king, but the Benedictine Rule required that he should be elected by the universal suffrage of the monks. He wore episcopal robes in the church, and conferred minor orders.

The Prior was the lieutenant of the abbot.

The Sub-Prior in larger abbeys acted for the prior in his absence.

The Precentor was next in rank to the prior. He had the charge of the services of the church.

The Cellarer had in his hands the management of the domestic affairs of the monastery, the cellar, the kitchen, and the refectory.

The Treasurer received the rents of the estates of the monastery, and kept the accounts.

The Sacristan had the care of the sacred vessels, the elements for the Holy Communion, the vestments, and other articles used in the church services. In the larger monasteries he had under him a sub-sacristan.

The Almoner superintended the relief of the poor and the dependents of the monastery.

The Cook, with his assistants, provided the meals taken in the refectory, and also in the infirmary.

The Infirmarer, with Brethren under him, visited and waited upon the sick.

The Porter had the charge of the keys of the gate, and, with his assistant, attended to all those who came to the monastery from outside.

The Refectioner took care of the cups and other vessels used in the refectory, the tables, cloths, mats, and the rushes upon the floor.

The Chamberlain attended to the clothes, bedding, and shaving of the monks, and the baths.

The Hospitaller, or *Guest Master*, received and entertained the poor and travellers.

The Hebdomadaries were those who, week by week, waited at table, or read during meals.

There were several curious rites used in giving possession of donations to religious houses. The most common was to give a glove, a knife, the bough of a tree, or earth from the estate. Sometimes the bells were touched while the donation was recited. Mabillon says that sometimes a nail of the hand was pared till blood came; and that sometimes a slap on the cheek was given.

Mr. J. A. Froude's 'Annals of an English Abbey'[1] gives a picturesque history of the chequered experiences of one of the great abbeys, St. Albans; selecting, however, from its manifold records chiefly those events that were not creditable, and omitting the many benefits that such a great institution conferred upon the country and the Church, and ignoring the lives of the many godfearing men, whose merit

[1] *Short Studies*, vol. iii.

was that they left no annals. Mr. Froude himself says, "To be entirely just in our estimate of other ages is not difficult—it is impossible."

The following sketch will give a good idea of the daily life of the inmates of a Cistercian abbey, where the Rule was duly observed.[1]

Suppose the monks all lying on their beds of straw, ranged in order along the dormitory, the abbot in the midst. Each of them lay full dressed, with his cowl drawn over his head, with his cuculla and tunic, and even with his stockings on his feet. His scapular alone was dispensed with. The bed-clothes consisted only of a rough woollen cloth below and a woollen rug over. The dormitory had no fire, and currents of air had full play under the unceiled roof. A lamp burned all the night. At the proper hour (usually about two a.m.) the clock woke the sacristan, and he rang the great bell, and in a moment the whole of this little world is alive, and every hand is making the sign of the cross. One by one the white figures glided along the cloister into the church. Matins lasted for about two hours, the greater part of the service being recited by heart, so that there were hardly any lights in the church. After matins the monks remained in the church to pray, or sat in the cloister. In one part was the Cantor marking out the lessons, or a novice would be learning to recite the Psalter by heart. In another part the brethren would sit in unbroken silence reading, with their cowls so disposed that it might

[1] See *The Life of Stephen Harding*, by J. H. N.

be seen that they were not asleep. In another corner the boys of the monastery would be at school, under the master of the novices. Lauds followed close upon the first glimmer of morning light. After this an interval was allowed, during which the brethren might go to the dormitory to wash, and change portions of the dress in which they had slept. As soon as the day had fully dawned, prime was sung, and then they went into the chapter-house. Around it were ranged seats, the novices sitting on the lowest row; in the midst was the abbot's chair. The Chapter opened with the martyrology; then followed the commemorating of the faithful departed, and, in some cases, a sermon; after which a portion of St. Benedict's Rule was read. Then each brother, who had in the slightest way transgressed the Rule, came forward and confessed it aloud before the whole convent, and received a penance if it were necessary. Then a still more extraordinary scene followed: each monk accused his brother if he had seen or heard anything amiss in him; and the monk who had grievously offended, stripped himself to his waist, and on his knees received the discipline. After the Chapter was over, the brethren went out to manual labour. Each Cistercian took his turn to be cook, cellarer, infirmarian, master of the novices, or porter. The brethren left the fields and their other employments and returned to the church for Tierce, after which followed the Mass. Then there was again time for reading or meditation. Between eleven and twelve the bell rang for Sext, after which the convent assembled in the refectory for the first and principal meal of the day, except on fast days, when they had only one meal, and that after Nones. The food consisted of a pound of the coarsest bread, one-third of which was reserved for supper, if there were one, and two dishes of vegetables. The drink was the sour wine of the country, well diluted with water, or thin beer, or a decoction of herbs. Even fish and eggs were excluded from the Cistercian dietary. A strict silence was observed, and one of the brethren read aloud some religious book during the time they were in the refectory. After the meal they went to the dormitory for an hour's sleep, and a wash. Nones were said at half-past two, after which they were allowed a draught of water before they returned to manual labour, which lasted till half-past five, when they sang Vespers. If it were not a fast day, they partook of their second repast, after returning from work, consisting of the remainder of their pound of bread, with some raw fruit or vegetables. From this time breathless silence reigned in the convent till Compline, which was said in winter about seven and in summer an hour later; after which all went to the dormitory for the night's rest.

"Travellers are often struck with the picturesque situations of ancient abbeys. The fact is, that those parts which are now the most beautiful, were in former times the wildest and most solitary. Besides which, rocks and mountains may be very picturesque to look at, and yet very uncomfortable as dwelling-places; and many a stream, the banks of which are now visited for the sake of a beautiful ruin, at the time when the monastery was built flowed through pathless wilds and uninhabited forests."[1]

Bishop Creighton said in a recent lecture—"It was often said that monks had their eyes open, and built their monasteries on the best sites in the country. That was a perfectly shallow and absurd criticism. When kings and others in olden days wanted to be generous they rarely gave away anything that was worth something to them. They gave the monks the worst sites in England, but the monks made them the best sites by their industry."

In the fourteenth and fifteenth centuries Monasticism had become a great power in England. The land held by monasteries has been estimated to have been from one-tenth to one-fifth of the whole acreage of the country. In the great towns, in country villages, in the midst of lonely moorlands or valleys, among the marshy flats of the fens, upon breezy sea-washed cliffs, the noble church, and the substantial buildings of the abbey might be seen; and by night and by day the melodious bells were heard telling of prayer and worship.

Foreigners who visited England were greatly struck by the size, the beauty, and the wealth of the abbeys, and have left records of their admiration.

The Abbey of Glastonbury, for example, was almost a town in itself. It covered sixty acres of ground. The church was 415 feet in length. Cromwell's visitors wrote to him in admiration of the

[1] *The Life of Stephen Harding*, by J. H. N.

building—"The house is great, goodly; and so princely, as we have not seen the like." The abbot was a member of the House of Lords. The sons of the first gentlemen in the county were educated within the walls. The library was very large, and contained a great number of most valuable books and manuscripts; legal documents relating to property and titles were kept there. Boundless hospitality was given to all comers, gentle and simple. The other great abbeys had similar dimensions, and were conducted on the same princely scale. The abbot was a temporal and spiritual lord, exercising jurisdiction, not only over the monks of his monastery, but over a multitude of tenants, dependents, and retainers. The whole town that had grown up round the abbey was entirely subject to its abbot, who held courts, and inflicted punishments. Monastic cells at a distance, parish churches with their clergy, schools, colleges, and hospitals, were connected with and dependent upon the abbey. Roads and bridges were made to connect distant farms and villages with it, and to facilitate travelling to the other great monasteries, towns, and the coast. The abbot was bound to visit other superiors, and to go to Rome, or to the mother-house to attend chapters, or to consult with the Pope, and the General of his Order. Each abbey was self-supporting and independent, having its own mills, breweries, fisheries, laundries, tailors', carpenters', and blacksmiths' shops. Horses, cattle, sheep, pigs, and poultry were bred, and every kind of agricultural operation was carried on, either by the monks themselves, or by their tenants and hired servants. There were but few inns, and yet travellers could go from one end of England to the other, and always find food and shelter in the guest-house of some abbey.

Mr. J. A. Froude thus speaks of the religious houses of England—

"Originally, and for many hundred years after their foundation, the regular clergy were the finest body of men of which mankind in their chequered history can boast. They lived to illustrate, in systematic simplicity, the universal law of sacrifice. In their three vows of poverty, chastity, and obedience, they surrendered everything that makes life delightful. Their business on earth was to labour and to pray; to labour for other men's bodies, to pray for other men's souls. Wealth flowed in upon them; the world, in its instinctive loyalty to greatness, laid its lands and its possessions at their feet; and for a time was seen the notable spectacle of property administered as a trust, from which the owners reaped no benefit, except increase of toil. Imperfect, perhaps, the monks always were; they were frail men, attempting prematurely to clothe themselves in a higher nature. But sacrifice was the principle of their Rule, which in England, for some eight centuries, they contrived tolerably to obey; and traces of the frail beauty of the monastic spirit we may yet see imaged in the sculptured figures which lie sleeping with folded hands upon the floors of our cathedrals."[1]

[1] *History of England*, vol. ii p. 407. Ed. 1856.

And again—"The abbeys which towered in the midst of the English towns ... were images of an inner spiritual sublimity, which had won the homage of grateful and admiring nations. Alike in the village and the city, amongst the unadorned walls and lowly roofs which closed in the humble dwellings of the laity, the majestic houses of the Father of Mankind and of His special servants rose up in sovereign beauty."[1]

Another writer says—"That the evils were great should not so much excite our wonder, as that they were not greater, considering the times in which they were founded, and the elements of which they were composed—the times, those of newly-found religious fervour—the elements, men tired of perpetual warfare, who vainly supposed that a life of restraint and comparative inactivity would not pall upon natures and tastes that had known no limit but the individual will. The social life of England really commences at the threshold of the monasteries. Canterbury, York, Peterborough, Ely, Beverley, Winchester, and Whitby, with many another, looked over hill and dale, river and fen, their towers signifying landmarks and light in a material and spiritual wilderness. New clearings in the woods were made; lands were reclaimed, and roads were made across hitherto impassable morasses and trackless forests."[2]

Bede, however, even in the seventh century, complains of the abuses that had crept into Monasticism,

---
[1] *Short Studies*, vol. i. p. 416.
[2] Yorke Powell, *Social England*.

and advocates the conversion of the property of the ill-managed monasteries into endowments for bishoprics and secular clergy. Even in his day there seem to have been lay abbots, and a system of dispensation which was fatal to all good order among the monks.

> "For in this bad world below,
> Noblest things find vilest using."

Without crediting all we read, we can easily believe that the state of the clergy in England, in the tenth and eleventh centuries, was anything but satisfactory. Almost all the higher offices of the State were filled by clergy. The Popes gave them dispensations to hold several benefices, nay, even bishoprics, together. Many were foreigners ignorant of the English language; preaching had fallen into disuse. The old orders of monks had become effete and wealthy; and many of the abbeys being in secluded places, far from the busy haunts of men, could have no influence for good upon the growing population of the towns.

The creation of the Orders of Friars was an effort to remedy these evils, and to supply the deficiencies of the monks. Wickliff welcomed the coming of the Friars, and hoped for a new era of life and progress for the Church. The Friars themselves held up the monks to ridicule, and unsparingly dilated upon their shortcomings, and their relaxations of discipline, which had completely set aside the stringent provisions of their Rule.

Grostête, the large-minded Bishop of Lincoln, who had seen and lamented the faults and failings of the monks, greeted the first coming of the Friars into England with joy and hope, looking for a new era of spiritual revival, and saying, " The people that walked in darkness have seen a great light."

The Friars, unlike the monks, went into the world, identifying themselves with the poor and suffering, taking up their abode in the lowest slums of large towns, as, for instance, near the shambles of Newgate, on a spot appropriately called Stink Lane. They preached at the corners of the streets, or in the market-places, in plain, homely language such as the most ignorant could understand; they frequented hospitals and lazar-houses, where others were afraid to enter, tending the lepers, and giving them the kiss of peace. A great revival of religion took place; crowds hung upon their words, and in a few years they had acquired greater influence than the older Orders had obtained after two or three centuries.[1]

Nevertheless in spite of their short-comings the monks were on the whole popular. There were, indeed, disputes between them and their tenants, especially in the towns; but they were generally easy and generous landlords, and compared favourably with the secular nobles, who often treated their dependents with cruelty and grasping selfishness. Chaucer probably expresses the common feeling of his day with respect to the monks, when he describes with good-humoured candour the good and bad characteristics of one of the fraternity who was among his Canterbury pilgrims.

[1] Note J, p. 388.

> "This ilke monk lette olde things pace,
> And held after the newe world the trace,
> He yave not of the text a pulled hen,
> That saith, that hunters bee not holy men;
> In that a monk, whan he is rekkles,
> Is like to a fish that is waterles;
> This is to say, a monk out of his cloistre.
> This ilke text held he not worth an oistre. . . . .
> Therefore he was a prickasome a sight;
> Greihoundes he hadde as swift as foul of flight:
> Of pricking and of hunting for the hare
> Was all his lust, for no cost would he spare.
> I saw his sleves purfilled at the hond
> With gris, and that the finest of the lond.
> And for to fasten his hood under his chinne,
> He had of gold ywrought a curious pinne;
> A love-knotte in the greter end ther was.
> His hed was balled, and shone as any glas,
> And eke his face, as it hadde ben anoint.
> He was a lord ful fat and in good point.
> His eyen stepe, and rolling in his hed,
> That stemed as a forneis of a led.
> His bootes suple, his hors in gret estat,
> Now certainly he was a fayre prelat.
> He was not pale as a forpined gost.
> A fat swan loved he best of any rost."

"The idea that monastic institutions were essentially opposed to good morals, and a high tone of Christianity, is one of those foolish notions which got hold of the popular mind in days when partisan falsehoods and profligate ribaldry were looked up to as authoritative evidence; but it is one of those notions which must vanish away as soon as historical truth is brought to light."[1]

Even Hume has no hesitation in allowing that the suspicion of flagrant irregularities was propagated, in

[1] *The Reformation in England*, J. H. Blunt, p. 280.

the time of Henry VIII., upon the slenderest evidence, in order to give colour to the attack which was in contemplation.

"When the clergy are accused by contemporary writers of immorality, we must remember what that accusation means. Before the time of Dunstan, many of the clergy were married, and this was the case, not only amongst the 'secular,' but also the 'regular,' clergy; and afterwards when they are forbidden to marry, they were often married nevertheless, but their wives were called 'concubines,' and they were on that account accused of immorality, even down to the time of Elizabeth."[1]

The greatest fault of English Monasticism was that it did not develop and adapt itself to the wants of the times. The Benedictine monk, in the fourteenth and fifteenth centuries, was usually a member of some good family, and "his life was something between that of a Fellow of a college in the last century, and that of a country squire. He was rich, leisured, aristocratic, fond of field-sports, and saluted by the title of 'My Lord.' The vulgar idea of the immorality of the monks is erroneous."[2]

The monasteries retained the old-fashioned system of farming, and did not adopt modern improvements; many of the smaller houses therefore became impoverished, their members reduced in number, and their buildings ruinous.

[1] *Eighteen Centuries of the Church in England*, A. H. Hore (Parker).
[2] *A Book about the Clergy*, J. C. Jeaffreson (Sonnenschein). See Note K, p. 388.

There was undoubtedly an element of spiritual selfishness in the ideal of Monasticism. Even in the fourth century Basil of Cæsarea said—"The eremitical life conflicts with the essential character of Christian love, since here each individual is concerned only for what pertains to his own good; while the essence of Christian love prompts each to seek, not alone what serves to his own advantage, but also the good of others." The monk hoped to "save his soul alive," by "going out of the world," not by "keeping himself from evil in it." There were good excuses for this line of conduct in the early ages; but as time went on, and vast changes took place, the active, useful life in the midst of the world seemed to be more needed than the contemplative life of the ascetic; and the easy and leisured existence of the monk of the less strict and more wealthy Orders came to be regarded with irritation. The Friars made an attempt to remedy this anomaly. Wolsey was alive to the need of monastic development and adaptation to the wants of the times; and if he had not been cut off in the midst of his days, he would doubtless have effected wholesome reformation, of which his Colleges at Oxford and Ipswich were the beginning.

Long before the final dissolution of the monasteries came there had been a growing feeling in England that there were too many of them. Edward I. and Edward III. enacted Statutes of Mortmain to check the accumulation of landed property in the hands of the monks. Archbishops Morton and Warham and

Cardinal Wolsey made visitations of the monasteries, and the last suppressed several and applied their revenues to endow his colleges. Particular communities, such as the Alien Priories, were suppressed, on different pretexts; and it was a common practice for the King to delay appointing an abbot, and to appropriate the revenues of the house during the vacancy.

The Lollards inveighed against the wealth of the monks. In the reign of Henry IV. (1410) a Bill was introduced into Parliament, by Lord Cobham, by which the King was empowered to take possession of Church property; but nothing came of it. William of Wykeham, Archbishop Chicheley (1437), Bishop Waynfleet (1459), and Bishop Alcock (1496), endowed their colleges with the lands of suppressed monasteries.

The Wars of the Roses and the Black Death impoverished many of the religious houses, and diminished the number of their inmates. Wadding, the Franciscan annalist, writes thus respecting the effects of the pestilence—"This evil wrought great destruction to the houses of religion, carrying off the masters of regular discipline, and the seniors of experience. From this time the Monastic Orders began to grow tepid and negligent. The rigours of discipline could not be renewed by the youths received without the necessary training, rather to fill the empty houses." [1]

In the city of Winchester, the Prior of St. Swithun's

---

[1] *Annales Minorum*, viii.

and the Abbess of St. Mary's both died, and there is evidence that a large proportion of both these communities must have perished at the same time. At the cathedral, the usual number of monks, previous to 1349, was sixty. After that date they were reduced to thirty-five. In 1387, William of Wykeham exhorted the community to use every effort to get up their strength to the original sixty members, but, notwithstanding all their endeavours, they were on Wykeham's death, in 1404, only forty-two. In 1487, their number had fallen to thirty, at which figure it remained till the dissolution.

The Hospital of Sandown, in Surrey, was left without a single inmate, through the Black Death.

Of the Priory of Shireborne, the Bishop writes in 1350—"The buildings are falling to ruins, and its fruitful fields, now that the labourers have been carried off, are barren."

The Bishop of Hereford says, in 1351, respecting the Priory of Lanthony—"The rents, through the pestilence by which the people have been almost blotted out, are, for the greater part, irreparably lost."

It need hardly be said that the scourge must have been most demoralizing to discipline, and fatal to observance.[1]

There was also in earnest and practical men's minds uneasiness at the evident inconsistency of the luxury of many of the tables of the monasteries with the simple and ascetic rule of life to which the

[1] See Gasquet's *Great Pestilence*.

monks had pledged themselves. Thus, at Tewkesbury, where there was an abbot and thirty-two monks, some records which have been preserved show that there were no less than one hundred and forty servants to wait upon them.

Giraldus Cambrensis gives this account of a dinner in the refectory of Christ Church, Canterbury, on Trinity Sunday, 1179—"Of the dishes, and the multitude of them, what shall I say? Sixteen or more, very sumptuous, were served in order, not to say against all order; and at last, moreover, vegetables were served upon every table, but were scarcely tasted. For you might see so many kinds of fish, roast and boiled, stuffed and fried, so many skilfully dressed with eggs and pepper, so many savours and salt things prepared by the art of the cooks in order to provoke gluttony and excite the appetite. Moreover, you might see here wine and strong drink, spiced cup and hipocras, must, and mead, and mulberry wine, and all that can intoxicate, in such profusion, that ale which is made of the best quality in Kent, had no place among the rest. What would Paul the hermit say to such doings? or Antony? or Benedict, the father and institutor of the monastic life?"[1]

Satirical poems, such as the *Land of Cockayne* and the *Supplication of Beggars*, held up the monks to ridicule, while others exhorted mothers not to put their daughters into convents.

There were therefore many causes operating for a

[1] *Chronicles of Great Britain*, J. S. Brewer.

considerable period, before the time of Henry VIII., which tended to wean people's affection and respect from the Religious Orders in England, and to make them calmly acquiesce in their suppression; while the Communities themselves were, in many cases, too weak to make any effectual resistance to their spoiler's attack. When Henry quarrelled with the Pope, and threw off his authority, he knew that the abbots, being closely allied with Rome, would find it more difficult than the secular clergy to accept the transfer of the Papal jurisdiction to the King, as Head of the Church in England; and he felt that if the monks were out of the way, he would more readily carry out his designs. There were twenty-six abbots and priors in Parliament, all more or less "Pope's men." Even in his early days, Henry had proposed to Francis I. to separate France and England from the Papacy, and to establish a separate Patriarchate, with Wolsey at its head.

The supposed revelations of Elizabeth Barton, called "the Holy Maid of Kent," were directed against the King, and excited much attention and gained wide credence. Sir Thomas More, Bishop Fisher, and even Archbishop Warham, were disposed to look upon the visions as true messages from God. Barton had been received as a nun into the Convent of St. Sepulchre's at Canterbury, and there she denounced the King's marriage with Anne Boleyn, and his rejection of the Pope's authority. This speedily led to an inquiry, and the nun and her friends were taken to London, tried, and finally executed in May 1534. Nor did the matter end here. Many of those who listened to the nun's revelations and prophecies were members of religious orders, and this fact was made a ground for attacks upon the Friars Observant, and for hostility to the monks in general, who were regarded as disloyal subjects and opponents of the policy of the King.

We may charitably suppose that there were, among the motives which led Henry to abolish Monasticism in England, that patriotic desire, which some writers have discerned in him, to make England a free and independent nation, and to remove all hindrances to the full development of her powers; just as his treatment of his wives may be regarded leniently, when his passionate anxiety to leave behind him a male heir to the throne is believed to have arisen from his foresight of the evils that would befall his kingdom, if, on his death, there should be a disputed succession, and all the national misfortunes that would be involved in a civil war. But it can hardly be doubted by the most devoted admirer of Henry, that the wealth of the abbeys excited his cupidity, and that he persuaded himself that the exigencies of the State justified him in appropriating funds which he believed to be applied to unworthy or useless purposes, and which he could, at that time, employ most opportunely and effectively to the benefit of his people both in Church and State. Thus he promised never again to ask for subsidies from Parliament, if he were authorized to appropriate the property of the monasteries to the use of the State. He gained the approval of many of the clergy by engaging to found several bishoprics and colleges, and to make the defences of the country more secure. But when the wealth touched his hands these promises were forgotten, or only partially fulfilled. At first he merely proposed to suppress the smaller foundations, stating that "in the great solemn and honourable monasteries of the realm, thanks be to God, religion is well kept and observed" (Act 27 Henry VIII., ch. 28); but the facility with which he became possessed of large sums of money speedily induced him to covet more; and his extravagant expenditure, both personally and for State purposes, was continually reducing his exchequer to penury. When he came to the throne he found himself the master of the great wealth which his father had amassed; but all was soon dissipated under his reckless disbursements. The fine which he inflicted upon the clergy to free them from the consequences of the *Act of Præmunire* is said to have given him £119,684 9s. 6d., a sum equivalent to more than a million at the present day. The annates and first-fruits which he received brought in a great amount of money. The income of the dissolved monasteries has been variously estimated from £150,000 to £200,000, or more, *i.e.* at least two millions per annum present value; and the sale of property, plate, jewellery, building materials, and live stock, realized an enormous sum of ready money; so that the property confiscated has been reckoned to have amounted to fifty millions of our money! But in a few years all was gone, and the King was needy and covetous once more; and it is said that, had not death prevented it, he would have made a raid upon the cathedrals and the universities.

That any Protestant convictions acted as inducements to spur on the King to the ruthless destruction of the monasteries is evidently an untenable assumption. He allowed a considerable number even of the smaller foundations to continue for a time after they had been condemned to dissolution, and even refounded some that had been suppressed; and he knew perfectly well that in them, and in the greater abbeys, which he pronounced blameless, all the old practices of "Popery" were being daily carried on. He had written against Luther, and although he cast off the jurisdiction of the Pope, he retained, and gloried in, the title of "Defender of the Faith," which the Pope had bestowed upon him for his attack upon Protestantism. The "Six Articles" which he caused to be enacted, and the execution of "heretics" during his reign, are proof enough that Henry was no Protestant, and that he had no doctrinal quarrel with the Church of Rome and its dogmas.

Henry having repudiated the authority and jurisdiction of the Pope in his kingdom, and having assumed to himself the Papal functions by claiming the title of "Supreme Head of the Church in England," was only exercising the prerogatives of his office when he appointed Cromwell to be his Vicar-General; and one of the first duties which the King imposed upon his representative was to visit and report upon the condition of certain smaller monasteries, of which unfavourable accounts had been received (1534). There was no public mention of suppression or confiscation. The visitation was ostensibly the due and proper act of the supreme ruler in Church and State, by which he was only doing his fatherly duty in seeking to promote the spiritual and temporal well-being of certain of his subjects and children, whose condition and circumstances demanded the interference of his authority. Some of the principal abbots received special commissions from the King to visit the monasteries of their own Order. The Cistercian abbeys in certain counties, and the Gilbertine convents, were thus visited. Such visitations had been made before by command of the Pope, and at the request of the rulers of the Church of England, and in other countries. But Cromwell had either received secret instructions of a different character, or he knew from other sources what was expected of him. The superiors of several monasteries speedily resigned, and placed their houses in the King's hand, and when this was not done, pressure was put upon the monks, threats were used, accusations were got up, and spies were quartered upon them, who impoverished the poorer establishments by the cost of their maintenance, till the only course that was open to the monks was to place themselves and their house at the King's disposal. Some of the lesser friaries were first dealt with. They were too poor to resist, and were without powerful friends; and, moreover, the Mendicant Orders were closely allied with the Pope, and their friars had gone about among the people preaching and speaking against the Royal Supremacy. In the meantime other steps were taken secretly to secure the attainment of the King's purposes. Preachers roused the cupidity of the people by declaring that if the monasteries were done away, their property would be divided among the laity, and that "no poor man would be hereafter in England."

A paper exists (MS. Cotton, Titus f. iii.) which seems to have been written in the reign of Queen Elizabeth by some one who had witnessed the dissolution of the monasteries, and who sets down his opinion as to the means by which so revolutionary a measure was carried out. He especially mentions the great share that Cromwell had in the matter, and specifies some of the steps which he took to prepare the country to accept the destruction of institutions that were so closely united with the history of the country, and were connected with the greatest families, and were valued by the poorest. He says— "Cromwell firste found meanes to perswade the King that it might lawfully be done . . . he caused preachers to goe abroade, and maintayned them to instruct the people . . . He caused to be placed in the Archbushopes place Cranmer, and in divers other bushoprickes and hier places in the clearge divers protestantes. . . . He placed abbottes and ffriers in divers great houses, divers learned men which were now readie to make surrender of their houses at the Kinges commandment. . . . He caused visitacions to be made of all the reeligious houses, whereuppon was retourned the booke called the Blacke Booke. . . . He caused the King of the abbes possessions to make suche dispersion, as it behoved infinite multitudes for their own intrest to joyne with the King in hollding them down ; by ffownding divers bushoprickes and Colleges with these possessions, selling many of them to many men four reasonable prices, exchainging many of them with the nobilitie and other for their ancient possession to their greate gaine with whome he exchainged, preferring many sufficient persons to the Kinges servis, who were some raised to nobilitie, and all indewed with maintenaunce out of the revenues of the abbyes."[1]

Henry proposed an oath to the members of the Religious Orders, which was evidently intended to be refused, and so to put them in his power for suppression. The Friars were first attacked. Some of them had told the King to his face in sermons at Greenwich that his second marriage was unlawful, and they would not be silenced by threats. This was declared to be an act of treason. The Friars were turned out of their houses, and many were imprisoned, and died through the cruel treatment which they endured. The monks of the Charterhouse were soon after dealt with, and again the charge of treason was pressed, because they declined to acknowledge the supremacy of the King. The Austin Friars at Brentford were also visited with similar results.

Parliament met (1534) and passed an Act acknowledging the King to be "Supreme Head of the Church

[1] Camden Society's *Transactions*, 1843.

of England," with power to "visit and reform all errors, heresies, and offences." Cromwell now sent Commissioners throughout the country to inquire into the condition of the cathedrals and monasteries. Shortly after this the execution of Friars and others who had refused to take the oath, began. They were hanged, drawn, and quartered at Tyburn. This visitation of the monasteries (1535) was made not with a view to exacting the Oath of Supremacy, but in order to get up accusations of immorality against the Religious Orders; and so great was the terror inspired by the unscrupulous visitors, that several monasteries was given up at once by their superiors, although no authority of Parliament, or otherwise, had as yet been given for such a proceeding. There was not time for the Commissioners to visit anything like all the monasteries, yet, when Parliament met, a report was presented as if all had been examined; and such a bad case was made out that the fall of all the lesser monasteries followed, almost as a matter of course; which was brought about by an Act of Parliament, which has disappeared. There are, however, in the Record Office certain papers (*comperta*) which appear to be reports of some of the visitors of the lesser monasteries, in which various charges are written down against the names of some of the inmates. There is nothing said as to evidence or proof; and as all the reports follow the same routine, there is the gravest suspicion that they were made to order as a justification of the subsequent suppression and plunder, and presented for signature by the monks unread. There are no authentic copies of the alleged "confessions" of the monks or nuns as to the irregularities which are said to disgrace their houses, and upon which subsequent writers dilate with such indignation. Even when grave accusations are made, it is often against but one or two members of the house; and there were many monasteries and convents of which the Commissioners themselves had no complaint to make. The "Black Book," said to have been read in Parliament impugning the monasteries, has never been found, and its existence is doubted. After considerable delay, and reluctance which only gave way under threats from the King, that he "would have some of their heads" if they did not speedily carry out his wishes, the Act (27 Hen. VIII. ch. 28) (1535) was passed, giving into the King's hands all "religious houses of monks, canons, and nuns," whose annual rental was not more than £200; and the Act was made retrospective, so as to secure possession of those houses that had been already surrendered to the visitors. Three hundred and seventy-six communities fell by this measure, although some were permitted to survive for a time, probably through "considerations" received by the Commissioners. At the same time, it was declared to be a cause of thankfulness to God, that "in divers great and solemn monasteries religion is well kept and observed;" which great monasteries were soon to be condemned and dissolved under charges of gross wickedness!

As soon as the Act was passed protests and petitions flowed in abundantly. The accusations were denied;

the representatives of the founders of abbeys remonstrated against the destruction of their ancestors' buildings, and the desecration of their tombs; even the Commissioners themselves asked for the preservation of certain Religious Houses which were in every respect well conducted. But all was in vain; no sooner were the monasteries threatened than Cromwell began to receive petitions that certain houses might be spared, together with offers of payment, or the sacrifice of part of the estates, in order that exception might be made in favour of some particular monastery. Some of these letters, especially those from the Superiors of the houses of women, are very touching in their simplicity and helpless distress. Even the Commissioners themselves pleaded in several instances with Cromwell for the exemption of some particular monastery from the general destruction. Thus George Giffard writes in favour of the Abbey of Woolstrope in Lincolnshire (MS. Cotton, Cleop. E iv.)—" The governour thereof is a vere good husbond for the howse, and welbeloved of all thenhabitantes thereunto adjoynyng, a right honest man, having viij religious persons beyng prestes of right good conversacion and lyvyng religiously, havyng such qualities of vertu as we have nott ffownd the like in no place; for ther ys nott oon religious person thear butt that the can and dothe use eyther inbrotheryng, wrytyng bookes, with verey ffayre haund, makyng ther own garnementes, karvyng, payntyng, or graffyng. The howse, without any sclandre or evyll ffame, stonds in a wast grownde verey solitarie, keepyng suche hospitalitie that, except by synguler good provision, itt cowld natt be meynteyned with halfe so muche landes more as they may spende, suche a nombre of the poure inhabitantes nye therunto dayly relevyd, that we have nott sene the like, having no more landes than they hawe. God be evyn my juge, as I do wright unto youe the trothe, and non otherwyse to my knowlege, which vere petie alloon causithe me to wright."[1]

A similar letter was written by the Commissioners to Cromwell on behalf of the Benedictine Nunnery of Polesworth in Warwickshire, "wherin ys an abbas namyd dame Alice Ffitzherbert, of the age of lx. yeres, a very sadde, discrete, and relygyous woman, and hath byn heed and governour their xxvij. yeres, and in the same howse under her rule ar xij. vertuous and religyous nonnes, as well by our examinacions as by the open ffame and report of all the countrey, and never one of the nonnes thar will leyve nor forsake their habite and relygyon."[2]

Lord de la Warr pleaded hard with Cromwell for the continued existence of Boxgrove Priory, saying that "his ancestors and his wife's mother rested there, and that he had made therein a poor chapel to be buried in." But all to no purpose.

"The smaller monasteries which were suppressed numbered 376, and their annual income was valued

[1] Camden Society's *Transactions*, 1843.
[2] Camden Society's *Transactions*, 1843. MS. Cotton, Cleop. E iv.

at £32,000, besides £100,000 worth of jewels and plate, sums which must be multiplied by ten at least to approximate to their amount at the present time. But what became of the servants? In one monastery, where there were only thirty monks, there were no fewer than fifty-four servants!—besides whom there were numerous outdoor labourers employed upon the farms. And what became of the dependents of these establishments? In one way or another, by the first Act of Dissolution, ten thousand persons were thrown upon the world, deprived of the means of existence, some at an advanced age. Then came the Vagrant Acts, by which begging was punished first by whipping and cutting off part of the right ear, and the third conviction was punished by death." (Hore.)

It is a curious fact, not generally known, and not quite easy of explanation, that soon after the first suppression of the monasteries, many of them were refounded by Henry himself. Some of those whose inmates had been most grossly denounced by the Visitors were restored, and the accused monks themselves were reinstated. Fifty-two religious houses were thus established, and were called "King Henry the Eighth's new monasteries." But their existence was shortlived, and they were in a few years again finally closed and ruined.

The suppression of the smaller monasteries, and the insolence and immoralities of some of the Visitors, caused great indignation throughout the country, and two armed risings took place in opposition to the unpopular and tyrannical measure. In Lincolnshire and in Yorkshire rebellion broke out in formidable proportions. "The Pilgrimage of Grace" was in reality a civil war on a small scale, and many noblemen, together with the Archbishop of York and several abbots, joined the cause, which was led by Mr. Aske. There were even some political schemes connected with, it which proposed the interference of the Kings of Scotland and France for the protection of the English people against the tyrannical acts of Henry. The rebellion, however, speedily collapsed, and a bloody reprisal was taken upon all connected with it, without mercy. A new excuse was also now found for the suppression of abbeys in Lincolnshire and Yorkshire, and some of the neighbouring counties, because their abbots had been more or less involved in the Rebellion, and having been convicted of treason, their houses were declared forfeited to the King.

By a variety of expedients several of the larger abbeys were taken possession of by the King's Commissioners; and in order to prevent further rebellions, many of the estates of the dissolved monasteries were given to the nobility and gentry; one mischievous result of which was the rise of lay-impropriations. Laymen received from the King, or at nominal prices bought the revenues of the benefices, and paid some cast-off monk the smallest pittance to discharge the duties of the Church; or some ignorant mechanic or labourer was actually ordained to take charge of the parish. Thus the Church was brought into contempt, and the foundation laid for the creation of numerous sects.

Another result of the lay appropriation of so much ecclesiastical property was the rise of a class of aristocracy, whose members were by self-interest committed to maintain the new state of things, and who therefore were ready to stand by the King, and to assist him in carrying out his schemes. The surrender of the mitred abbeys weakened the Church party in the House of Lords, and gave the King's adherents a majority. Thus in the Journals of the House of Lords we find that in the Parliament of 1536, twenty-eight abbots were present, or voted by proxy. In 1539, only twenty names occur, and most of these were represented by proxies. In 1540, all the abbots have disappeared.

Fuller says that in the reign of Henry III. sixty-four abbots and thirty-six priors had seats in Parliament. Edward III. reduced the number to twenty-five abbots and two priors; afterwards two more abbots were added.

In May 1539 an Act of Parliament (31 Henry VIII., ch. 13) was passed, confirming the King's possession of the estates, property, and buildings of the monasteries that had already been suppressed, and granting to him all other religious houses that might in the future be "surrendered" to him. This was of course intended to effect the confiscation of all the greater abbeys which had hitherto escaped. But the Act itself did not enjoin the suppression of Religious Houses, nor was one word contained in it impugning their order or discipline, or bringing any charges of immorality, neglect of duty, or treasonable designs, against the abbots. But Cromwell and his assistants, Leighton, Legh, Petre, London, and others, had their own methods to compel the monks to give up their houses to the King. Their instructions were—

To assemble every member of the Convent in the Chapter House;

To examine each individually;

That every one be compelled to give account of his fealty to the King, Queen Anne, and their issue;

To promise on oath to preach and teach the people the above;

To declare the King the Head of the Church of England;

To deny the supremacy of the Pope, and to speak of him only as Bishop of Rome;

Not to wrest Scripture to support any other doctrine;

To inquire how many preachers there are, and to examine their sermons;

To take an inventory of all plate, and other goods;

To take an oath of each for selves and successors to observe all this.

Such powers gave ample opportunity for high-handed measures. The Commissioners, on their arrival, took possession of all the keys of a convent, from those of the external gates to those of every locker and cupboard. They assumed the King's authority, and treated every one, from the abbot to the labourer, with arrogance and suspicion; and their retainers and servants made themselves still more disagreeable by their coarse insolence. Each monk was examined separately, and was encouraged to bring accusations against the rest, and to express a wish to be relieved from his vows. Many were thus got rid of; and all under twenty-four years of age were at once sent away. Inventories were made of all jewellery, plate, and movable property, and charges were brought against the abbot or some of the monks for concealing or conveying away valuables, which was declared to be a treasonable proceeding, and was actually made a sufficient reason for the deprivation or the execution of abbots who obstinately refused to resign their posts. The Commissioners received bribes and presents, and there are extant complaints against some of them of gross misconduct in the nunneries. "Henry's inspectors," says Mr. J. H. Blunt (*Reformation*), "were vile men, proved guilty of lies, oppression, robbery, and lust; while those whom they accused were often appointed to bishoprics, and other posts of trust and honour;" and Fuller says that "they were men who well understood the errand they went on, and would not come back without a satisfactory answer to him that sent them, knowing themselves were likely to be losers there." Thus Layton writes to Cromwell—"all monks be false, feigned, flattering, hypocrite knaves." Yet even these men reported of some monasteries, such as Bruton, Glastonbury, Godstow, and others, that there was nothing objectionable in them.

The grossest charges were brought against the prior and monks of Christ Church, Canterbury; but no sooner was the place surrendered, and the new cathedral body constituted, than these very vituperated monks were appointed to occupy stalls. The same course was followed in other places, and the men whose characters had been violently defamed were selected as worthy of honour and advancement, and were made bishops, deans, or canons of the new foundations. Mr. J. H. Blunt, having calmly reviewed all the evidence that can be collected on the subject, sums up his judgment thus—

"As it is quite certain beyond all manner of doubt that Henry VIII. was impelled to dissolve the monasteries by motives which had originally nothing whatever to do with their morality or immorality, so there is no trustworthy evidence whatever that their moral condition was greatly depraved." [1]

"The Visitors stuck at nothing that they thought would expose the monks, and would serve as an argument to the King for dissolving the abbeys and seizing the lands and revenues, and afterwards employing them to such purposes as himself, by the advice of those Visitors and other enemies to the monks, should judge proper." [2]

The so-called trials of abbots and monks were but a solemn farce. The death of the accused was determined beforehand. Some of Cromwell's private memoranda prove this. Thus—"Oct 26, 1539. The abbot of Redyng to be sent down to be tried, and executed at Redyng, with his complices; similarly the abbot of Glaston, at Glaston." [3]

[1] *History of Reformation*, p. 361 (Longmans).
[2] Letters of Thomas Hearne.   [3] *State Papers*, vol. xiv.

At this distance of time, and on account of the disappearance of all the original documents, it is impossible to form a just and unbiased judgment as to the real condition of the monasteries in England at the time of their dissolution. Human nature lives under the cowl quite as much as under the crown or the peasant's bonnet. Undoubted evidence shows that abuses have ever crept into the cloister, and there were doubtless black sheep in the time of Henry VIII. as there had been in every earlier period of Monasticism, and in every country where it existed. The spirit of Monasticism had waned, and the work of the religious houses had, in many cases, altogether fallen into abeyance. Many were poor, and all the consequent evils of poverty followed. The accusations against them must be received with caution, if not with suspicion, since they were got up by those who had an interest in destroying them, and by men who were of bad character themselves, and who knew that they must carry out their master's wishes by fair means or otherwise. "I am inclined to believe," says Mr. Dixon, "after an impartial consideration of all that can be said on the subject, that in the reign of Henry VIII. the monasteries were not worse but better than they had been previously, and that they were doing fairly the work for which they had been founded."[1]

In April 1536 instructions were issued to certain country gentlemen to make a survey of the religious houses. Wherever these reports exist they declare

[1] *History of the Church of England*, vol. i. p. 382.

the character of the inmates to be uniformly good, even in those houses of which the King's commissioners had quite recently made most damaging reports.

Viewed in the light of modern criticism, the evidence that charges the monks with immorality and other crimes absolutely breaks down, and the verdict of "not proven" is given by those best able to judge. A writer in the *Quarterly Review* (July 1895) says—"The accusations against the moral character of the monks were made in order that men might welcome the dissolution of the monasteries. But the charges were for the most part baseless. The evidence of the Visitors of Henry VIII. breaks down when carefully examined. The Visitors themselves were men of far from unblemished character. Their testimony, such as it was, only applied to a very small proportion of the houses accused. The so-called 'Confessions' they produced were infinitesimally few in number, and bore unmistakable signs of being simply cut-and-dried documents. No witnesses ever seem to have been produced, nor in any case do the monks appear to have been allowed to answer to the charges brought against them."[1]

But the end of the Monasteries had come. Gradually but surely every religious house fell into the King's hands; its revenue appropriated; its venerable buildings, stripped of roof and windows, left to fall into ruin, or their materials carted away to build

[1] For full details, see *Henry VIII. and the English Monasteries*, by F. A. Gasquet, and the *New Review*, February 1896.

houses or stables; their libraries sold for wastepaper; their inmates turned adrift, or, if obstinate, executed without pity. Some of the Carthusians of London, who refused to accept the King's supremacy, were hanged, drawn, and quartered at Tyburn; the rest were left to die slowly and miserably of starvation and prison-fever. The abbots of Colchester, Reading, and Glastonbury were ignominiously hanged, peers of the realm though they were, as common felons, on the charge of treasonable concealment of their abbey's treasures, which had become the property of the King. The barbarous execution of Whiting, the octogenarian abbot of the grand abbey of Glastonbury, raised a strong and lasting feeling of indignation in the west of England. Mr. Halliwell has published an old Somersetshire ballad of the seventeenth century which expresses the popular sentiment with respect to it, and which was still living and active more than a hundred years after the event. It runs thus—

> "'Tis an ominous thing how this Church is abused,
> Remember how poor Abbot Whiting was used."

A letter of his is preserved in the *State Papers*, written in April of the year in which he was executed, begging the King to excuse his absence from his place in the House of Lords, on account of his age and infirmities. It is said, too, that when he was brought into court to be tried as a prisoner, the poor old man began making his way to his usual seat upon the bench, where he had for many years presided, as judge, quite unable to realize his degraded position.

Every effort was made to stifle resentment. The nobility received manors; the people were often allowed to carry away furniture, fittings, hangings, and drapery from the churches and parlours of the monasteries; the live stock was sold cheaply, and land was let at a low rent. Many of the shrines had been popular objects of pilgrimage, but their contents were thrown upon dunghills and made contemptible or ridiculous. Becket's world-famed relics were burned; those of St. Edmund and St. Cuthbert shared a similar fate; the famous Rood of Boxley was carried to London and exhibited and burned at Paul's Cross; the Holy Blood of Hales was declared by Latimer to be a mixture of honey and saffron; and the mysterious treasure of Walsingham merely chalk and water.

An immense amount of misery was the immediate result of such a revolutionary catastrophe. Pensions were given to the superior officers of the monasteries if they yielded readily to the demands of the Commissioners; some of the monks, who were priests, found employment in the cathedrals and parish churches; but many of them, as well as the nuns, were sent into the world with "forty shillings and a gown," and those who had incurred the displeasure of the King's agents had to go as empty-handed beggars. The poor in towns and the country lost their dole; travellers, who could not afford to pay for their lodging, were no longer sheltered and fed;

pauperism increased by leaps and bounds; crime became prevalent; severe laws were enacted against vagrancy, and 80,000 persons are said to have died by the hand of the executioner in a population of three millions!

The French ambassador, Chapuys, wrote to his master—" It is a lamentable thing to see a legion of monks and nuns, who have been chased from their monasteries, wandering miserably hither and thither seeking means to live; and several honest men have told me that, what with monks, nuns, and persons dependent on the monasteries suppressed, there are over 20,000 who know not how to live."

Mr. Smiles says—" Large tracts of land relapsed into bogs, waste, and salt marsh, especially in the east of England." [1]

A large portion of the income of the monasteries was derived from the impropriation of parochial tithes; these were confiscated by the Crown, or by the laymen who obtained possession of the landed property, and so were entirely lost to the Church.

Much spiritual provision for the people was thus taken away; and the endowments of parish churches which had been made over to religious houses, on condition that the parochial services were maintained, were seized with the other revenues of the houses, and were not restored to the parish churches.

Another national misfortune was the injury done to education. Free schools were provided by most of the monasteries; and when the latter were destroyed,

[1] *Lives of the Engineers* (Murray).

the former perished with them. In many towns depopulation and decay followed the destruction of the monasteries, and an Act of Parliament (32 Henry VIII.) was passed to encourage people to migrate to the forsaken places.

"The abolition of the monasteries," says Macaulay, "deprived the Church at once of the greater part of her wealth, and of her predominance in the upper House of Parliament. There was no longer an abbot of Glastonbury or an abbot of Reading seated among the peers, and possessed of revenues equal to those of a powerful earl. . . . Those worldly motives, therefore, which had formerly induced so many able aspiring, and high-born youths to assume the ecclesiastical habit, ceased to exist. . . . During the century which followed the accession of Elizabeth, scarce a single person of noble descent took orders. The clergy were regarded as, on the whole, a plebeian class."[1]

Literature also was seriously injured. "Magnificent libraries were utterly destroyed. The fragments that remain at Durham give an idea of the dreadful loss which was sustained by the absolute destruction of the noble libraries of Glastonbury and other great abbeys" (Blunt). John Bale, Bishop of Ossory, wrote to Edward VI. in 1549—"I know a merchant-man that bought the contents of two noble libraries for forty shillings. This stuff hath he occupied in the stead of grey paper for the space of more than these ten years; and yet he hath store enough for as many

[1] *History of England*, vol. i. p. 325.

years to come." In other cases bakers' ovens were fed with MSS. and printed books; or the loose leaves were used as litter for cattle, and when rotten were scattered on the fields as manure.

In the library at Peterborough there were 1700 MSS. The library of the Grey Friars in London was 129 feet long and 31 broad, well filled with books. The abbey at Leicester and the priory at Dover had large libraries, the catalogues of which are still in the Bodleian at Oxford. At Croyland, even in 1091, there were 700 volumes. The library at Wells had twenty-five windows on each side of it.

Nine tons of gold and silver plate are accounted for in the receipts of the King's jewel-keeper, as coming from the dissolved monasteries; and their value has been estimated at £153,000, equal to a million and a half of our present money. No accurate returns can be found of the amount of jewellery, but it must have been very great. Erasmus, in his account of his visit to Becket's shrine at Canterbury, speaks of the gems that encrusted it as countless, and of great value. An eye-witness stated that the gold, silver, precious stones, and other valuables taken from the shrine filled twenty-six carts! One very large diamond, presented by Louis VII. of France, which had a wide notoriety for its size and purity, was set in a thumb-ring for the King. The other shrines, the reliquaries, crosses, chalices, mitres and robes, were, we know, richly ornamented with precious stones, and all were swept into the King's treasury, except some that clung to the hands of the Commissioners and their servants.

Stories are related of the King gambling away jewels, bells, and other monastic spoils. Henry had gained many Churchmen's reluctant acquiescence in his spoliation, by promising to found twenty-six new bishoprics and several colleges; but only six sees were actually created, and those with very inadequate endowments; and two colleges. Cranmer urged the King to convert many of the abbeys into colleges; Latimer prayed that one religious foundation at least might be allowed to remain in each county, and especially interceded for the continuance of the priory at Malvern. Strong representations were made in favour of the abbey of Hexham, as there was no other building of any kind for miles round. Similar common-sense reasons were given for allowing some of the monasteries in remote parts of the fens to remain. But all was in vain; the besom of destruction made a clean sweep; and Monasticism ceased to exist in England.

There is no doubt that the income of the abbeys was understated; yet taking the low estimate made at £141,000, then, in one hundred years, to say nothing of interest, £14,000,000 would have accrued to the Church. But besides this there was the value of the buildings, and the ornaments of the churches, underrated at £1,410,000. We have then in the first century after the dissolution a loss to the Church of £15,510,000.

"If one-half of the monasteries," says Canon Dixon, "if one-quarter, the sixth, the tenth part of them had been converted to colleges, schools, or hospitals, how much higher would the nation be now! If buildings had been spared because of their grandeur and beauty; if the libraries had been removed to convenient central places, with the same assiduous care with which the gold and silver were carted to London ; then would art and literature have had less cause to curse the names which bigotry has blessed. If a few of the monasteries had been kept as they were, and filled with those of the religious who desired of their own free will to keep that life, the revolution would have had a more honest appearance."

"If the results of the dissolution had been wholly good," says Mr. J. H. Blunt, "the manner in which those results were attained must still have been condemned as base, criminal, and sacrilegious ; and the character of the men by whom they were brought about could not have been redeemed from just odium and abhorrence by them."

Mr. Gasquet truly says—" It is impossible to read any account of the work done by the monasteries for the poor without perceiving in how many directions this present generation has been compelled by very necessity to devise some substitute for the consideration thus exercised. Our modern workhouses, our burial clubs, our hospitals and charities ever crying out for funds, much of which is swallowed up by paid organization and management, what are they but awkward and imperfect agencies for executing a portion of those duties to society which flowed naturally and unobtrusively from the religious communities in their ordinary practice of Christian charity ?"[1]

[1] *Henry VIII.*, vol. ii., chap. xiii.

The traditional English prejudice against Monasticism has, of late years, been removed to a great extent by a calm and unbiased consideration of its history and work, and by a clearer knowledge of the facts of its suppression by Henry VIII. Thus a recent writer says—" A great wrong has been done, knowingly or unknowingly, to the memory of a multitude of men who, with rare exceptions, according to their lights, seem on the whole to have done their duty well and faithfully. . . . Several centuries have elapsed since the monk was forcibly ejected from his home, and until recent years he has found no defender chivalrous enough to speak a word in his defence. . . . It is only fair—now that the real story is better known—that we should teach our children to look on the large majority of these helpless men and women as victims deserving our pity and respect, rather than as guilty culprits who met with a righteous doom. . . . Nothing can ever obliterate, or even dull, the memory of the splendour of the work done by the monastic orders."[1]

Southey, after pathetic lamentation over the ruthless destruction of the abbeys as "noblest works of architecture, most venerable monuments of antiquity, each a blessing to the surrounding country, and collectively the glory of their land," adds—" The persons into whose hands the abbey lands had passed, used the property as ill as they had acquired it. The tenants were compelled to surrender the writings by which they held estates for two or three lives, at an

[1] *Quarterly Review*, July 1895.

easy rent, payable chiefly in produce ; the rents were trebled and quadrupled, and the fines raised in even more enormous proportion, sometimes even twenty-fold. . ." William of Malmsbury observed that no person who appropriated monastic property escaped disgrace and the judgment of God ; and Feckenham, the last abbot of Westminster, wrote his *Caveat Emptor*, warning the possessors of abbey lands of the certainty of trouble for themselves and their children. Spelman, in his *History and Fate of Sacrilege*, published in 1632, enters seriously and fully into the same subject, and gives particulars of the misfortunes of the families who received the property of the religious houses—showing how commonly the race became extinct for want of heirs, and how violent death and disgrace and calamity became chronic in the few families that survived. The editor of the reprint of Spelman's book, says—"Out of the forty-one noblemen who were enriched by the spoils of the abbeys, eight only have, at the present time (1846), representatives in the male line. And the families that do exist, have experienced, with scarcely an exception, fearful judgments." In the present day, through lapse of centuries, and the frequent change of owners, it is difficult to trace rightly the effects of sacrilege. But in the time of Spelman the task was easy, and the statistics were striking. Thus he describes how he takes a circle with a radius of twelve miles about his own house. In this there were twenty-five abbey sites and twenty-seven gentlemen's parks. In the eighty years that had elapsed since the dissolution of the monasteries in 1535, he found that the latter had not changed families at all, whereas all the former, except two, had changed them twice at least, and some five or six times.

Another authority gives the following instance—" A. was the owner of a house of Austin Canons; he lived in adultery, and had one illegitimate son, B. B. has issue, C., a son, who, living in adultery, had two illegitimate daughters ; one of these was married into a family afflicted with insanity ; D., a son, who is blind and childless ; E., a daughter, who has left her husband, and is living in adultery."

Reyner gives another example — Henry VIII. divided the Church spoils in one part of England among two hundred and sixty gentlemen, and at the same time the Duke of Norfolk rewarded twenty of his gentlemen with £40 a year out of his own inheritance. Not sixty of the King's donées had a son owning his father's estate, while every one of the Duke's had a son of his own enjoying his father's inheritance.[1]

Monasticism in Ireland

The early history of Christianity in Ireland is uncertain and confused. The most probable conclusion is that St. Patrick commenced his mission there at the beginning of the fifth century. He

[1] *History and Fate of Sacrilege:* Introduction.

had passed his early years in Gaul, where he became acquainted with the Christian faith as it was taught in that region. In later times St. Patrick's name and mission were confounded with those of Palladius, a missionary monk sent from Rome, who appears not to have had much success. There is, however, no reasonable doubt that St. Patrick was first in the field, and that Palladius was unacceptable to the Irish Christians on account of the difference of his Roman usages from those taught by St. Patrick, and that the fact that the Romans never had possession of Ireland took away any influence that a Roman apostle would have had among the heathen population. According to the custom of the times, St. Patrick founded monasteries, and the Church in Ireland was during the whole of its early history governed and propagated almost entirely by monks. The invasions of the Saxons caused many of the British to seek refuge in Ireland. Towards the close of the fifth century ST. BRIDGET founded a nunnery at Kildare, and became a kind of female apostle of Monasticism. Abbeys were established at Armagh by Benignus, at Clonard by Finnian, at Clonfert by Brendan, at Clonmacrois by Keiran, at Bangor by Comghall; besides many others by less famous founders. Among the monks of Bangor was the celebrated ST. COLUMBA, whose mission and settlement at Iona has already been noticed. In the seventh century Ireland had attained the title of the *Island of Saints*, and was covered with monasteries. The number of monks is said to have been equal to half the population, and at the great abbey of Bangor three thousand monks were sometimes resident. The primitive Irish monasteries seem to have been, sometimes at least, the capital of a clan. The chief was the abbot, lay and clerical superior at the same time. Some of the men and women practised celibacy, and passed their time in prayer; but the rest followed their usual avocations. Ireland was at this time free from the invasions of barbarous tribes, who were desolating Britain and the continental provinces of the Roman Empire; and scholars from many countries retired to the monasteries there and pursued their studies in safety; so that learning as well as religion flourished in Ireland while they were being trampled down and destroyed elsewhere. The Irish monks were also the chief missionaries of the time. ST. COLUMBANUS about 589 set out on his journey to the continent, where he established many monasteries, bringing with him the oriental rites and practices which afterwards brought the so-called *Culdee* monks into collision with the Roman clergy. St. Gall, Kilian, Fursy, and Fridolin were also Irish missionary monks in different countries. In 629, Pope Honorius wrote to the authorities of the Church in Ireland respecting the time of keeping Easter, and the other points of difference which distinguished it from the Western Church. In consequence of this a Synod was held, and Cummian and some other monks were sent to Rome to study the question. On their return they succeeded in persuading the majority of the Irish clergy to adopt the Roman usages, but Iona and some other monasteries still held aloof. The intercourse between Rome and Ireland gradually became more intimate, and the great monastery of Armagh took the first place in rank and influence. In the eighth and ninth centuries the invasions of the Danes and the Vikings ruined many of the ancient monasteries, which remained for longer or shorter periods without inhabitants; and the constant wars between the kings and chiefs, from time to time, involved the destruction or the serious impoverishment of others; and the monks themselves not unfrequently armed themselves and joined in the faction fights. Some of the northern invaders settled in Ireland, and married native ladies, and ultimately became Christians; and their intercourse with their brethren in Normandy, who had become closely connected with the Church of Rome, led to a more complete union of Ireland with the Church on the continent, especially after the conquest of England by William the Conqueror. The Synod of Rathbreasil (1110) cemented the union of the Irish Church with the Pope, and firmly established the Roman system, but not without opposition, and even bloodshed.

Early in the twelfth century, ST. MALACHY lived and laboured in Ireland. He rebuilt and presided over the monastery of Bangor, and was afterwards Archbishop of Armagh. He visited St. Bernard at Clairvaux, who afterwards wrote his life. He introduced the Cistercians into Ireland, and founded a monastery for them at Mellifont (1142), and five others in succeeding years. He visited Rome to obtain the pall for the Irish primates; and was canonized by the Pope in 1190.

In 1171, Henry II. of England, on various pretexts, one of which was the instigation of Pope Adrian, an Englishman, landed in Ireland, and very soon obtained the sovereignty of the whole kingdom. This was rendered possible, if not easy, by the perpetual wars that were waged between the native kings and princes; in which, it was said, that more churches and monasteries were reduced to ruins than in all the invasions of the Danes and Northmen. Henry's army, under Strongbow, perpetrated similar outrages, and treated the Irish with great cruelty and injustice. Englishmen took possession of tracts of country much as they pleased; and by building magnificent abbeys hoped to atone for their rapacity. The Benedictines, Cistercians, Canons Regular, Knights Templars, and other Orders were thus firmly established in Ireland; and most of their members were foreigners. The Dominicans settled in Ireland in 1224, and very soon had several houses. The Franciscans came in 1230, and the Carmelites not long after. The Templars were suppressed in Ireland by Edward II. in 1307, under circumstances of great cruelty. When the Irish Parliament was established, twenty-four of the abbots and priors had their seats there; but many of these, either on account of distance, poverty, or local wars, seldom sat in them. When Henry VIII. commenced his attack upon the monasteries in England, he also contemplated a similar policy in Ireland. Through the influence of Cromwell, Dr. Browne was made Archbishop of Dublin (1535), and he at once took steps to prepare the way for his master's schemes. Some of the religious houses had already been suppressed on the ground that they were ruinous, and too impoverished to maintain themselves. In 1542, an Act of Parliament (33 Henry VIII., ch. 5) placed the property of all monasteries (500) in the hands of the King; and as grants of it were made to the principal nobles, the opposition was weakened, and confined chiefly to the Jesuits and the Friars. In Ireland, as in England, the endowments of many parish churches had been given to monasteries, on condition that the monks should provide for the services, and when the monasteries were secularized, these endowments went with the rest, and the parishes were left destitute, and the churches fell into ruin. Some of the abbots conformed to the King's supremacy, and were pensioned, or appointed to other offices; charges of treason and evil living were brought against many of the monks, and they were executed, or turned adrift penniless; but some of the monasteries of the Friars seem to have escaped the general ruin, and their inmates still begged about the country even in the reign of Elizabeth.

Monasticism in Scotland.

THERE are various legends respecting the early introduction of Christianity into Scotland. A Greek monk, St. Regulus or St. Rule, is said to have landed at the spot where St. Andrews now stands, bringing with him part of the bones of St. Andrew (369), and to have built a monastery there. The Ven. Bede asserts that ST. NINIAN, who had been a disciple of St. Martin of Tours, built a monastery at Whithorn, which, on account of its stone church, was called *Candida Casa* (400). The names of other missionaries are given by monkish historians, but no reliable record occurs till the time of ST. COLUMBA, who came from Ireland, and established himself with a few other monks at Iona (563); and whose life was written by his successor St. Adamnan. St. Columba spent the rest of his life at Iona, and laid the foundation of the establishment of Christianity in Scotland. For nearly three hundred years Iona was the source of light and spiritual progress to the whole country. MSS. were laboriously written or copied, and in the midst of savage nature and more savage men learning and piety flourished. The Vikings and the Danes destroyed the monastery several times, but it was always rebuilt. ST. MUNGO, or Kentigern, was another missionary monk, contemporary with St. Columba, but it is difficult to learn any certain facts respecting him and his work from the legendary accounts that have been handed down. ST. CUTHBERT, Abbot of

Lindisfarne (664), and his successors were also founders of monasteries, some of which were in Scotland. After the Synod of Whitby (664) the Roman tonsure and other continental usages were gradually, and not without resistance, introduced into northern monasteries; but many monks and hermits continued to follow the traditions of Iona, and were called Culdees; and are mentioned as existing up to the fourteenth century. ST. MARGARET, Queen of Malcolm III. (eleventh century), was a strenuous advocate of Roman customs, and opposed the variations of the Culdees. The sons of St. Margaret were energetic founders of monasteries, and most of the then existing Orders, both for men and for women, had houses in Scotland. Dunfermline, Coldingham, Scone, Jedburgh, Kelso, Melrose, Holyrood, Dryburgh, Cambuskenneth, and others, were established in the twelfth and thirteenth centuries, and were well endowed, often, unfortunately, with the tithes of the parish churches, till James III. (1471) caused the practice to be discontinued. At the time of the Reformation there were in Scotland nearly two hundred convents for men or women; of these thirty-two were Benedictine, forty-eight Augustinian, fifteen Dominican, seventeen Franciscan, and nine Carmelite (Spottiswoode). There was also a Carthusian abbey at Perth, and there were houses of Templars at Edinburgh, Leith, and Southesk, and the Hospitallers were settled at Torphichen, Edinburgh, and some other places. The mitred abbots sat in Parliament, and held important offices in the kingdom. There were flourishing schools attached to the principal abbeys; and the monks were the pioneers in the introduction of improvements in agriculture, building, and the fine arts; and they were the chief friends and protectors of the poor. By the lavish gifts of kings and nobles, the Scotch monasteries became wealthy, till, as some authorities declare, half the property of the kingdom was in the possession of the Church. The usual evil consequences of wealth followed—luxury, the neglect of the Rule, the intrusion of foreigners into important benefices, simony, traffic in appointments, pluralities, and the impropriation of revenues by laymen, and even children. When the University of Glasgow was founded in 1450, many of the professors and students were monks, as was also the case with the subsequent foundations of St. Andrews and Aberdeen. The building of monasteries had already become less frequent, and the Lollards were propagating their opinions in opposition to the tenets of the Church. The Lutheran Reformation in Germany speedily influenced Scotland. Those who embraced Protestant opinions were at first harshly treated; Hamilton, the lay Abbot of Ferne, was burned; Seaton, a Dominican friar, was exiled; Forest, a Benedictine monk, was condemned to the flames; and many more were arrested, put to death, or driven from the country, or forced to recant and conform.

When Henry VIII. dissolved the English monasteries he tried to persuade his nephew, James, the King of Scotland, to follow his example, sending Sir Ralph Sadler as his envoy, whose letters to his master may be found among the State Papers. James was poor, and the short and easy way to wealth proposed to him was tempting; and a further inducement was held out by Henry, who offered him his daughter Mary, with right of succession to the throne of England. But James refused both offers, and said with respect to the charges against the religious houses made by Sadler—"God forbid that if a few be not good, for them all the rest should be destroyed. Though some be not, there be a great many good; and the good may be suffered, and the evil must be reformed, as ye shall hear that I shall see it redressed in Scotland, by God's grace, if I brook life." Later, Henry again made proposals to Scotland, wishing to marry his son Edward to James's infant daughter Mary, afterwards the unfortunate "Queen of Scots." But the Scottish Parliament rejected Henry's offer; and soon after war broke out between the two kingdoms. The English army not only attacked the Scottish forces, and the towns, but seemed to take especial pleasure in falling upon the defenceless monks. Kelso, Dryburgh, Melrose, Jedburgh, and other monasteries were sacked, and burned to the ground (1545). Meanwhile religious controversy ran high. Wishart, the Protestant reformer, was burned (1546), on one side, and Cardinal Beaton was assassinated, in the same year, on the other; John Knox began his preaching; while ballads and lampoons held up the clergy and the monks to ridicule, or charged them with crimes. Mobs began to attack the monasteries, and to destroy all the "popish ornaments" in the churches. In 1559 some of the Scotch nobility met, and consulted how the Reformation might be promoted in the Church, and they presented a petition to the Queen Regent, expressing their wishes. After a sermon by Knox, at Perth (1559), every convent in the town was sacked and reduced to ruins. Soon after the historical and beautiful abbey of Scone shared the same fate. Then the religious houses in Stirling, the abbeys of Cambuskenneth, Paisley, and Dunfermline, and others were destroyed. In 1560 the Parliament suppressed all surviving monasteries, finally abolished Romanism, and established Presbyterianism as the State religion. The greater part of the monastic property passed into lay hands, and brought not only wealth, but secular titles and dignities to many families. In other cases the abbots themselves became Protestants, and were allowed to retain the estates of their abbeys, and the temporal lordships that went with them.

CHAPTER V

THE CORRUPTIONS OF MONASTICISM; ITS ABUSES, DECAY, AND SUPPRESSION

> Thou hast brought a vine out of Egypt; Thou hast cast out the heather, and planted it. Thou madest room for it; and when it had taken root it filled the land. The hills were covered with the shadow of it; and the boughs thereof were like the goodly cedar-trees. She stretched out her branches unto the sea, and her boughs unto the river. Why hast Thou broken down her hedge, that all they that go by pluck off her grapes? The wild boar out of the wood doth root it up, and the wild beasts of the field devour it.—*Psa.* lxxx. 8—13.

Humanum est errare. There is a mysterious innate corruption in human nature that sooner or later breaks out and causes ruin. The body inherits or is impregnated with the germs of disease; the mind displays strange aberrations; the moral nature falls under internal or external temptation. Bodies of men and institutions display the same downward tendency as the individual; systems and schemes flourish for a time and then decay, fail, and perish. If man comes up like a flower, and like the flower fades, loses all use and beauty, and dies; so man's works and creations have but a short time to live, and then come to an end. The world is strewed with ruins. When explorers first traversed the new-found continent of the west, they were amazed to discover there, as in the old continents, vast mysterious ruins, without name, without history. In the desolate and lonely islands of the ocean there are strange erections, huge figures, illegible inscriptions, the work of some past generation of men of whom we know nothing. Empires, dynasties, deep-laid plans of government, noble theories of moral reformation, high principles of philosophy, social advancement, beneficent plans for healing the ills of life, scientific discoveries or guesses, statesmen, poets, famous men and queenly women—all have their little day, and then pass away and are done with, and forgotten.

We might have supposed that there would be a limit to this law of decay, and that those things upon which God had laid His hand and His blessing would be eternal and unchangeable like Himself. But it has not been so. Adam, "the son of God," yielded to temptation, and forfeited his high vocation. Abraham's seed was multiplied, as had been promised, and had a marvellous history; but then came the destruction of the Temple of God, and the scattering of the chosen people; Jerusalem a second Babel. Then came the Christ. His claims to empire were boundless; His kingdom was, He said, to be world-wide and everlasting; His Spirit, He promised, would abide with His Church, and lead it to all truth. We might have expected visible unity, undoubted infallibility, a never-failing oracle to settle all difficulties, to reply to all questions, to remedy all human frailties.

But no. The first disciples of Christ looked for a visible earthly kingdom which should overthrow the Roman Empire, and more than restore the dominion of Solomon. They were mistaken. Since their day Christians have dreamed of a spiritual kingdom of Christ upon earth, and have thought that the words of their Lord justified their theory and their hopes. If Peter was so very wrong in his ideas of his Lord's will and plans, that he was denounced as Satan-led and deceived, repeating the satanic temptation on the "exceeding high mountain," we may well believe that the vast scheme of temporal and spiritual dominion, gradually evolved by those who claimed to be the successors and representatives of Peter, was a grand mistake; a radically-wrong reading of our Lord's words; a terrible evil, tricked out with promises of good; an earthly and material rendering of spiritual and heavenly words which God alone in His own way will fulfil and realize.

Our Lord Himself warned His narrow-minded disciples beforehand of inevitable coming evil even in His Church. He spoke of "the mysteries of the kingdom of heaven"; and then by parables foretold division, the successful evil-working of human passion and frailty, and destroyed the fond hope that the Church on earth should be "without spot or wrinkle, or any such thing."

The hard logic of facts teaches the same strange, sad truth. If Christ was rejected and put to death, what must His nearest and most-like disciples expect? If one of the Twelve sold his Lord for money, and another denied Him for fear of a sneer or the Cross, and all forsook Him in the day of His humiliation, need we be surprised at any inconsistency among Christians, or any failure in the work of the Church? If St. John, fresh from the bosom of his Lord, slept in the garden, "the spirit willing, but the flesh weak," and was rebuked, "What! could ye not watch with Me one hour?" is it wonderful that the long routine of prayer and worship was sometimes found tedious and wearisome by monks and nuns? If Ananias and Simon appeared in the infant Church while the Holy Ghost visibly lived and worked in it and by it; if Demas found St. Paul intolerable, and loved the world much better; if the Corinthian Church "turned aside like a broken bow," as soon as its apostolic founder left it to itself; if the Churches of Asia, in the very hands of Christ, fell as we read, and displayed such human faults and depravities—are we not prepared beforehand for any lapse into unspiritual living, any degeneracy in Church institutions, any disappointment of high hopes, any apostasy, and any number of prodigal sons in the household of God?

What is all Church history but the record of a continued series of lapse and reformation, of ceaseless conflict between the flesh and the spirit, between Christ and the world? Just as the nations of Canaan, which were doomed to destruction by God's command, were allowed to exist side by side, and even in the midst of the people of God, and so led Israel into idolatry and its attendant vices; so the world, which should have been converted by the Church, entered into the Church and corrupted it. As soon as persecution ceased, and Christianity became respectable, and then was made fashionable, fine ladies and worldly-minded men made a profession of the new religion, and were Christians in name, but not in heart and life. Even in earlier times, we are told that there were many who outwardly conformed to the Church in times of toleration, but that when persecution broke out, they went in droves to the Prefect either to sacrifice to the gods, or to obtain a certificate that they had done so; lightly and readily denying Christ and apostatizing from the faith to save their lives or their possessions. Just as the Old Testament prophets, one and all, cry aloud against the sins and the inconsistencies of their people, their lapse from their high calling, their becoming "like the heathen round about them," so Christian writers lament and denounce the wickedness of professing Christians, and the abuses that had arisen and become chronic in the Church. When Bishops became rich and powerful, greedy and ambitious men coveted episcopacy; and instead of being shepherds of Christ's sheep and lambs, they were rather wolves to devour; following the example of the priests of the Jewish Church, whom Ezekiel charges with the same crimes.

Monasticism could not escape degeneracy when corruption and evil-living prevailed in the Church.

Cucullus non facit Monachum. Augustine, when he retired into the desert, and mortified his body by fasts and austerities, nevertheless lamented that his thoughts sometimes wandered back to the sights of the circus, and lived in the memory of sensual indulgences. "Out of the heart of man proceed evil thoughts." "Narrowing nunnery walls" will not keep out temptation. Rules and systems cannot compel the wanton will. If Satan followed our Lord into the wilderness, and there tried Him with every form of seduction that appeals to the natural passions and desires of the human body and mind, can we wonder that evil spirits tormented even the early solitaries, and sometimes prevailed in their attempts to lead them back to the evil of the world which they had forsaken, or to the sins of the flesh which they hoped was crucified and dead? And if this could not be done, the instilled poison worked other results. Fanaticism, cruel intolerance, party hatred and violence, narrow bigotry, and even bloody persecution of those who opposed them, these terrible and unchristian vices were seen among monks, even in very early times, and stain the records of Monasticism in its palmiest days, so that a fear and distrust of it has taken possession of men's minds.

"A melancholy, leading to desperation, known to theologians under the name of 'Acedia,' was not uncommon in monasteries. The frequent suicides of monks, sometimes to escape the world, sometimes through despair at their inability to quell the propensities of the body, sometimes through insanity produced by their mode of life, and by their dread of surrounding demons, were noticed by the early Church."[1]

"St. Augustine reckoned eighty-six sects as existing in his time.... The followers of St. Cyril of Alexandria, who were chiefly monks, dragged the pure and gifted Hypatia into one of their churches, murdered her, tore her flesh from her bones with sharp shells, and having stripped her body naked, flung her mangled remains into the flames."[2]

"Prolonged celibacy tends to insanity and moral perversion. No physiologist can read the records of Roman Catholic saints, especially females, without discerning the domination of a passion, unconscious indeed and distorted, but the more powerful and all-pervading, because denied its rightful place and play."[3]

"Vast societies living in enforced celibacy, exercising an unbounded influence, and possessing enormous wealth, must necessarily have become hotbeds of corruption, when the enthusiasm that created them expired. The services they rendered to agriculture, the refuge for travellers, the sanctuaries in war, the counterpoise of the baronial castle, were no longer required when the convulsions of invasion had ceased, and when civil society was definitely organized."[4]

Jerome complains that even in his day many persons of low origin and habits became monks,

---

[1] Lecky, *Morals*, vol. ii. [2] *Ibid.*, vol. ii.
[3] *Devil's Advocate*, Percy Greg.
[4] Lecky, *Morals*, vol. ii. p. 184.

esteeming the life comparatively easy, and so brought scandals, and injured the reputation of Monasticism by their inconsistent lives, and even by notorious crimes. Some wandered about the country begging, or selling sham relics, and extorting money from the credulous or the compassionate by their stories and pretensions.

"A tumult broke out at the funeral of Blessilla, who had succumbed under the austerities imposed upon her by Jerome, and there was a loud cry, 'Why do we tolerate these accursed monks? Away with them; stone them; cast them into the Tiber.' ... Hosts of monks encounter in Syria, meet in the field of battle, consider that zeal divine with which they strive, not to instruct and enlighten, but to compel each other to subscribe the same confession; each slaying and dying in unshaken confidence that eternal salvation depended upon the acceptance or rejection of the Council of Chalcedon."[1]

St. Chrysostom in his sermons combated the excessive adulation of Monasticism, and defended the adoption of the ordinary Christian life in the world.

The Emperor Valens was hostile to Monasticism, accusing the monks of idleness, cowardice, and want of patriotism, and by an edict (373) insisted that they should serve in the army. Similar complaints are made in the ensuing centuries when men were sorely needed to resist the incursions of the Barbarians. St. Augustine speaks in condemnation of the errors and abuses that had arisen among the monks, some of

[1] Milman, *Latin Christianity*, vol. ix.

whom had lapsed into Manichæan heresies, decrying marriage as sinful, deserting their families, and speaking with contempt of all those who lived in the world. Jovinian and Vigilantius attacked the fundamental principles of Monasticism on philosophical grounds.

"When the Monophysite controversy was at its height, the palace of the Emperor at Constantinople was blockaded, the churches were besieged, and the streets commanded by furious bands of contending monks. Repressed for a time, the riots broke out two years after with an increased ferocity, and almost every trading city of the East was filled by the monks with bloodshed and with outrage."[1]

The Emperor Constantine Copronymus shut up many monasteries, and slaughtered a great number of monks, making various charges against them, but chiefly because they opposed his Iconoclasm.

In later times the unedifying spectacle was seen of one Order vilifying another, and charging its members with neglect of duty, or actual moral transgressions. Thus Bernard wrote a series of letters against the Abbot of Clugny, accusing him and his monks of luxury. The Cistercians fell into schism, and rival Generals used violent language against one another and their adherents. The Dominicans and Franciscans were frequently in conflict; and the older Orders complained of the conduct of the Friars, while the latter were utterly unscrupulous in their denunciation of the wealth and useless lives of the former. Pope Innocent III. issued a Bull (1215) forbidding the

[1] Lecky, *Morals*, vol. ii. p. 196.

formation of any new Order. The Synod of Constance (1417) set about the reform of the Benedictine foundations in Germany. The Council of Basle followed the same course with respect to the houses of Canons Regular. Cardinal Nicholas of Corsa, Papal Legate (1450), instituted a general visitation and reformation of the monasteries, and met with much opposition.

In 1343, Pope Clement VI. wrote to Elyan de Villeneuf, Grand Master of the Knights Hospitallers, rebuking him for the luxury which prevailed in the Order. The Pope complains that in spite of the vow of poverty, "equos magnos et pulcros equitant; cibis vacant delectabilibus; pomposis vestibus, vasis aureis et argenteis, et pretiosis aliis ornamentis utantur; aves et canes tenent et nutriunt venaticos; pecunias congregant et conservant innumeras, et raras vel modicas eleemosynas largiuntur."

There are numerous instances of bishops attempting the reformation of the monasteries in their dioceses, but as it was common for founders to obtain the exemption of their houses from episcopal jurisdiction, it was exceedingly difficult to effect the desired ends. Arnulf, Bishop of Lisieux, appealed to Pope Alexander II. for authority to visit the monasteries of his diocese. The Archbishop of Rouen made a visitation of his diocese from 1248 to 1269, and found many disorders in the religious houses. Carlo Borromeo, Scipio de Ricci, Fenelon, Archbishop Morton, Wolsey, and many other prelates followed the same plan, and with similar results. In 1538, the Pope was urged to forbid all the Orders to receive any more novices. The Venetian ambassadors to Pope Alexander VII. petitioned for and obtained leave to suppress several convents in Venice, on account of their unsatisfactory condition. For similar reasons Francis I. closed many monasteries in Florence in 1751. Blanco White made great complaints respecting the condition of the Religious Orders in Spain.

The Visitations of the Order of Clugny (Sir G. F. Duckett) show that great abuses existed in their monasteries, but also that they were constantly inquired into, and punished by the authorities.

Even Pope Pius IX. said with reference to the wholesale confiscation of monastic property by the Sardinian Government in Italy, "It is devil's work, but the good God will turn it into a blessing, since their destruction was the only possible reform for them."

An unbroken catena of authorities, from Chrysostom to Erasmus, can be produced to show how abuses and corruptions have arisen in the bosom of Monasticism. All along its history a goodly series of reformers may be traced, who have shamed its professors into consistency, and re-established primitive purity and the practice of the original high aims and principles. Antony was a reformer; Basil, Benedict, Bernard, Theresa, and a host of other godly and vigorous men and women performed the hard and thankless task of sweeping out the Augæan stable, and letting in sweetness and light to the dark and fouled cells of degraded religious houses. Clugny, Citeaux, Camaldoli, were the seats of reforms of the Benedictine Order; and the creation of the Order of Friars was a protest against the wealth and worldliness of the monks. There have always been wise and prudent minds who could see the good foundation of "gold and precious stone" beneath the superstructure of "wood and hay and stubble," and who understood that reformation and not destruction was the true remedy for the abuses that they lamented. They could say, "Take away the battlements, for they are not the Lord's"; while they protested against those narrow and cruel bigots who cried against the city of God, "Down with it, even to the ground." There were always good physicians and surgeons who knew how to probe and amputate, how to administer purging and healing remedies; and who declined to cut off the head to cure a toothache, or to leave the wounded man by the wayside to die, when a little patient and loving ministration would save a valuable life.

"It was this wonderful attribute of the monastic system to renew its youth, which was the life of mediæval Christianity; it was ever reverting of itself to the first principles of its construction. In France, in Italy, in England, in Germany Monasticism renewed its youth, either by restoring austere devotion within the old convents, or by the institution of new Orders."[1]

Whenever a reformed Order was instituted hosts of youthful zealots were ready and eager to join it.

[1] Milman's *Latin Christianity*, vol. iv.

The second Benedict reconstructed the Benedictine Order on the original lines. Molêsme, Citeaux, Clairvaux, Assisi, were centres of renewed life for Monasticism, the revival of its first principles, when they had been forgotten, or had been invaded by the world-spirit, or had been superseded by dispensations and indulgences. In the midst of modern French atheism Lacordaire inspired again the Dominican preaching Order with its pristine vigour, and commanded the attention and admiration of frivolous Paris.

It is an unpleasing task to rake among the records of the past in order to gather up the sad and shameful facts respecting the sins of our fellow-men. There are those who delight in the pursuit, but they are not true reformers. From Juvenal to Voltaire, from Henry's Commissioners to the writers in the "Society Papers" of to-day, there have always been those who have made a reputation and a personal profit by showing up abuses; but they have no real abhorrence of them, no intention or desire to remove them. "The satirical literature of our age, and perhaps all writing directed against prevalent wrong-doing exaggerates the evils which it criticizes. It is very seldom that men, who care much for the truth, write satire; and popular castigators of vice are usually men of indifferent character, who gratify bad passions by making it a trade. There never was a society sunk so low that it would not pay some one to come forward and pretend to be dissatisfied with its morality." [1]

The true reformer, like Jeremiah, suffers himself

[1] Matthew Browne.

while he lashes the betrayers and enemies of his country. He cries, "O that my head were waters, and mine eyes a fountain of tears, that I might weep for the transgressions of my people." The true reformer, like our Lord, denounces abuses, and laments with heart-breaking sobs the shameful degradation of Jerusalem, but then He gives Himself a sacrifice to atone for man's sin, and brings in a larger and nobler kingdom, and lays the foundation of a "city which shall not be moved." Thus St. Bernard set himself fearlessly to denounce the errors of his time. He spoke without respect of persons, and told the Pope himself that the sword of Phinehas was needed to take vengeance upon members of the Roman Curia, who were not only foul and venal themselves, but made themselves the defenders of those who transgressed every law of God and man, and who found at Rome sanction for their crimes and immunity from their just punishment. But at the same time he provided a remedy for the evils which he lamented and condemned, and by his own example, and by the austere and holy lives of the reformed Order of Citeaux, he did much to bring back Monasticism to its primitive principles and practices.

It must not be forgotten that even in the worst times there were still godly men and women, devoted and saintly bishops, and religious houses where the service of God was duly and faithfully carried on, and where works of mercy and charity were unceasingly performed.

Even Voltaire could say—"There is scarcely a monastery which does not contain admirable souls who do honour to human nature. Too many writers take pleasure in searching out the disorders and vices by which those sanctuaries of piety are sometimes profaned. It is certain that secular life has always been more vicious, and that great crimes have not been committed in monasteries, but they have been more remarked by their contrast to the rule; no state has always been pure."[1]

Archbishop Fenelon, in a sermon on St. Theresa, said—"Behold the daughters of Theresa; they lament for all sinners who do not lament for themselves, and arrest the vengeance which is ready to fall. They have no longer eyes for the world, nor the world for them. Their mouths open only for sacred songs. Tender and delicate frames bear, even in extreme age, the burden of labour. Here is my faith consoled. Lord, smite not the earth, whilst Thou findest there this precious remnant of Thine election! . . . The imperfections of the cloister which meet with such contempt, are more innocent before God than the most shining virtues to which the world does honour."

The decrees of the Council of Trent (Session XXV.) made great reforms in all religious houses, which have never since fallen into their former disorder.

"It has been asserted with such iteration that the very frequency of the assertion has been accepted as evidence of its substantial truth, that the clergy of

[1] *Essai sur les Mœurs*, c. 139.

the Catholic Church of Germany before the Reformation, and the monks and nuns, were utterly and irremediably demoralized. But, on the contrary, the flaunting, the audacious vice, and the defiance of all that the Church had held sacred, which took place at the Renaissance, is rather to be taken as a proof that the Church had done her duty, had impressed the sacred obligation of the Decalogue and of decency on men. The Renaissance was a revolt against these restraints, by men who were pagans at heart, and would not endure them. The Renaissance will never be understood unless it is looked upon in this light. It was a new birth in every particular, in religion, in the laws; it was a revolt of the individual man against society, which had, perhaps—which had undoubtedly—exacted from him more than was its due. The Reformation is not to be considered apart from the Renaissance. It was but the same spirit of revolt, the revolt of the individual against society in another department. It was the casting away of bonds and restraints, here of more, there of less—it went so far in extreme cases as to cast away even the moral law."

"It has been asserted that the Mediæval Church was a sink of corruption. All that was corrupt came as scum to the surface, was talked of, and chronicled; but the humble annals of the poor parish-priests, their steady continuance in well-doing, their diligent discharge of their duties, all these were unrecorded. If, four or five hundred years hence, writers desired to discover what manner of men we were at the close of the nineteenth century, and were to measure us by the records of the police-courts and the gossip of the Society papers,—they would describe us as it pleases those who glorify the Reformation to describe the Church before that revolution."[1]

"In one sense, indeed, what is gained by any great religious movement? What are all reforms, remedies, restorations, victories of truth, but protests of a minority—efforts, clogged and incomplete, of the good and brave, just enough in their own day to stop instant ruin,—the appointed means to save what is to be saved, but in themselves failures? Good men work and suffer, and bad men enjoy their labours, and spoil them; a step is made in advance,—evil rolled back and kept in check for a while, only to return, perhaps, the stronger. But thus, and thus only, is truth passed on, and the world preserved from utter corruption."[2]

The first cause then of the abuses that arose in Monasticism was THE FRAILTY OF HUMAN NATURE. The monks and nuns were, after all, but men and women; and when corrupt living was common in castle and palace, in bishops' houses, and in the homes of the great and powerful laity, it is not wonderful that the cloister caught the infection, and that in spite of vows and rule, the lusts of the flesh and of the mind made themselves felt, and finally gained the upper hand. Those writers who speak of the "Ages of Faith" as times of universal godliness

---

[1] S. Baring-Gould, *History of the Church in Germany* (Gardner, Darton & Co.).

[2] Dean Church quoted by Dean Boyle in his *Recollections*.

are writing romance, not history. With every desire to believe the best of those whose profession bound them to a high standard of Christian life, it is impossible to doubt that there was all through the existence of Monasticism a constant relapse into laxity and even gross indulgence, and that the inconsistencies and open violation of all godly principles, was a scandal to many devout minds, and a lasting injury to the Church and to the welfare of religion.

"The dissolution of the morals of the clergy surpassed everything that can be conceived. Not only did some of the wealthy prelates have concubines, but some whole harems. The best prelates struggled hard to stem the tide of irreligion, but they met with the most bitter opposition; and abbots who attempted to reform their monks were frequently poisoned, stabbed, or expelled by them."[1]

"When Charles the Great began to reign (768), he found that in the thirteen years since the death of St. Boniface, matters ecclesiastical in Germany had fallen back greatly from the high position to which that great reformer, supported by Carlmann, had brought them. The majority of the episcopal sees and abbeys were occupied by men who were drunkards, roysterers, turbulent warriors, and passionate hunters, who had neither the will nor the faculty to fulfil decently the obligations of their sacred calling."[2]

"By degrees the Church had become the greatest

---

[1] S. Baring-Gould, *History of the Church in Germany* (Gardner, Darton & Co.). [2] *Ibid.*

possessor of land in the realm of the Franks. The kings had given the bishoprics to whom they would, men unscrupulous and thirsty for power. . . . Disorders broke out in the monasteries. The monks of Rebais revolted against their abbot, and drove him away. The Abbot Berchar was murdered by his monks because he rebuked them. Bishoprics were given by the kings and the mayors of the palace to young men not thirty years old. They were bought openly. Bishops regarded their dioceses as their private estates, and bequeathed them away. Bishops and abbots not only neglected their duties, but deserted their palaces and abbeys to live as laymen, and donning helmet and breast-plate to go to war, or else spend their time in hunting and revelry."[1]

"The end of the twelfth century was a dark and foul period in the Church. No wonder the coming of Antichrist was believed at hand. Then God raised up two marvellous saints,—Francis, to teach the merit of poverty; Dominic, to show that learning must be subjected to the service of the Cross. . . For a generation, the fervour of these Orders was marvellous. The wonderful conversions . . . put one in mind of St. Peter's sermons. . . Pass three hundred years, and we find the Franciscans—what? a set of jovial, popular, well-fed beggars, despised and yet liked, first-rate boon companions; and that all. . . Take another instance. If there is one pattern of a virgin saint since the Church passed from her period of persecution, it is the dear spiritual daughter of

[1] S. Baring-Gould, *History of the Church in Germany.*

St. Francis, St. Clare. Pass four hundred years; and in a reform of the Clarissines in Holland, we find the Rule forbidding sins as not uncommon among them, which God forbid you sisters should meet with in the purlieus of Crown Street!"[1]

"The wattled hut, the rock-hewn hermitage, is now the stately cloister; the lowly church of wood, the lofty and gorgeous abbey; the wild forest or heath, the pleasant and umbrageous grove; the marsh, a domain of intermingling meadow and corn-field; the brawling stream, or mountain torrent, a succession of quiet tanks or pools, fattening innumerable fish. The Superior, once a man bowed to the earth with humility, careworn, pale, emaciated, with a coarse habit bound with a cord, with naked feet, is become an abbot on his curvetting palfrey, in rich attire, with his silver cross borne before him, travelling to take his place amidst the lordliest of the realm."[2]

Bishop Anngerville (1334) addresses the friars of his day thus, little more than a century after Francis of Assisi had preached—"Now base Thersites handles the arms of Achilles; the choicest trappings are thrown away upon lazy asses; blinking night-birds lord it in the nest of eagles; and the silly kite sits upon the perch of the hawk. Liber Bacchus is respected, and passes daily and nightly into the belly; Liber Codex is rejected, out of reach. Flocks and fleeces, crops and barns, gardens and olive-yards, drink and cups, are now the lessons and studies

[1] Dr. J. M. Neale's *Sermons to the Sisterhood*, East Grinstead.
[2] Milman's *Latin Christianity*, vol. iv.

of monks, except of some chosen few, in whom not the image, but a slight vestige, of their forefathers remains."[1]

St. Theresa did not hesitate to describe the conventual life as she had known it unreformed, as "a short cut to hell"! "Rather let fathers," she said, "marry their daughters basely, than allow them to face the dangers of ten worlds rolled into one, where youth, sensuality, and the devil invite and incline them to follow things worldly of the worldly. Where is that spirit and fervour, that holy madness, which in past ages shed so strange a radiance over the early struggles of the Orders, now delivered over to a stupid and deadening routine? Those who should have been examples for the improvement of others in virtue have completely blotted out the labour left by the spirits of the saints of other times. . . . We have an instance of how thoroughly secularized convents had become in the case of that at Cordova, where the nuns divested themselves of their habits to take part in a comedy, which they acted before a large assembly of gentlemen and ladies of the town, the convent church being thronged to witness the spectacle. The discipline was not severe. Nearly a hundred merry, noisy, squabbling, sometimes hungry, chattering, and scandal-loving women, made the best of a life forced upon them by the exigencies of a society, two-thirds of which were either monks or nuns. The convent parlours were open to all comers, and thronged with visitors, brought thither by pleasure

[1] *Philobiblon.*

or business. Nor was the jingling of swords an unfrequent sound. The gay and idle young gallants of the town, who had nothing better to do on the long summer afternoons, loitered down to the convent, to visit some sister or relation who happened to be among its members. The nuns themselves enjoyed an amount of liberty altogether at variance with our modern ideas of the strictness and repose of monastic life. They went and came, and mingled freely and without restriction among the visitors, with whom they were closely connected either by ties of relationship or of a life-long intimacy."[1]

Towards the end of the sixteenth century, Cardinal Ximenes, who had himself been a friar, and who when he was raised to the Primacy of Spain, continued to live a most severe and ascetic life, commenced a vigorous reform of his Church, and especially of the Religious Orders. As has always happened, he met with opposition and resistance, but Queen Isabella supported him, and finally all those who attempted to thwart the good work, from Pope Alexander VI. down to the monks and friars, who vainly endeavoured to defend and to maintain their lax conduct and the neglect of their Rule, were overcome; and it was said that Luther's movement did not spread to Spain, because the Church had already been so thoroughly reformed by Ximenes.[2]

Nigel Wireker wrote a burlesque on the monks of his day under the title of the *Story of Burnellus, the*

[1] *Life of St. Teresa*, by G. Cunningham Graham.
[2] See *History of Spain*, by A. R. Burke, 1895.

Ass, something in the style of Apuleius. This ass had ambitions, and desired to become a man. He studied and matriculated at Paris, but still found himself an ass. In despair he seeks advice, and is recommended to found an abbey, "where the monks may gossip as at Grandmont, leave fasting alone as at Cluny, dress well like the Premonstratensians, and have a female friend like the Canons."

Erasmus brought grievous charges against the monks of his day, and that not only in his own country, but against the religious orders in Germany, Spain, England, and elsewhere. He had an especial hatred against them because they criticized his books, and did not go with him in his admiration for pagan literature. His language is so violent and coarse, and his accusations are so gross, that they somewhat arouse our suspicions, and lead us to attribute some, at least, of his rancour to the *odium theologicum*. The following extract from one of his letters to an English bishop will give an idea of his style and his accusations—

"The monastic profession may be honourable in itself. Genuine monks we can respect; but where are they? What monastic character have those we see except the dress and the tonsure? It would be wrong to say there are no exceptions; but I beseech you—you who are a good pure man—go round the religious houses in your own diocese; how much will you find of Christian piety? The mendicant orders are the worst . . . they are hated, and they know why; but they will not mend their lives, and think to bear down opposition with insolence and force. Augustine says that there are nowhere better men than in the monasteries, and nowhere worse. What would he say now, if he saw so many of these houses both of men and women little better than brothels? I speak of these places as they exist now among ourselves. Immortal gods! how small is the number where you will find Christianity of any kind! To abolish them is a rude remedy. It has been done in some places, but they ought to be brought back to their original purpose as schools of piety, and it will be a good day for the monks when they are reformed. They must not be allowed to live in idleness. Their exemptions must be cancelled, and they must be placed under the bishops; and as to their images, the people must be taught that they are no more than signs. It would be better if there were none at all, and if prayer were only addressed to Christ. But in all things let there be moderation." [1]

In the sixteenth century the world was scandalized with the spectacle of the Jesuits and the Carmelites vilifying each other, and degrading themselves in volumes of rancorous abuse!

Later an indignant eye-witness writes thus (1776) —" Many monasteries have been established there (Madeira). The monks are a lot of hypocrites, greedy of domination, and lead a life of debauchery within their walls, while making an outward display of devotion. I was a guest at some of their evening meals, which were anything but characteristic of

[1] *Ep.* dccclxxiv. quoted by J. A. Froude.

anchorite sobriety." And again (1786)—" I set off in the direction of Picardy (France) with a prelate held in high esteem by the monks of all the convents situated on the road to Abbeville. We were eagerly welcomed in them ; joy and pleasure presided over the meals ; those which they spread for us were sumptuous, and repeatedly ended in orgies."[1]

Hospinian quotes an epigram of his time which runs:—

> Vos Monachi vestri stomachi sunt amphora Bacchi ;
> Vos estis, Deus est testis, deterrima pestis.[2]

Another potent cause in effecting the degeneration of Monasticism was THE ACQUISITION OF WEALTH by the convents. All moral writers, of every age and country, speak of the manifold danger of riches. All history, whether of nations or of individuals, gives examples of the marvellous corrupting power of wealth. Our Lord's teaching is most emphatic on this subject. "A rich man shall hardly enter into the kingdom of God." "Except a man forsake all that he hath, he cannot be My disciple." The parable of the rich man and Lazarus ; our Lord's interview with the young ruler who "had great possessions" ; His praise of poverty, and His own choice of it for His human life, all prove that He impressed upon His disciples the inevitable evils that accompany the possession of wealth ; and the words of His apostles, and their own and their followers' adoption of poverty and the renunciation of their property, show how they

---

[1] *Memoirs of Barras* (1895), vol. i.
[2] *Hospinian de Orig. Mon.*, l. 1. c. 1.

understood their Master's teaching. In the early ages the first act of the convert to Christianity was commonly his selling all his property, and distributing the proceeds to the poor. All the early recluses practised absolute poverty. Stories and legends give startling examples of the way in which the lust of money died hard even in the bosoms of the ascetics of the desert, and of the ruin that came to devout souls through the cropping up of the sin of Achan and of Ananias among those who had formally renounced mammon, and whom other temptations could not affect.

The acquisition of wealth by the monks was not originally their own act. Possessions came to them unsought. The miserable land that surrounded the hermit's hut, or the poverty-stricken monastery, was gradually improved by the never-ceasing labour of many generations of toiling monks, till it became productive and valuable. Famous vineyards, rich corn-lands, wide tracts of forest abounding with game, fisheries, special breeds of cattle, these sources of wealth came into existence in the course of time in the hands of the abbots, who one after another received and wisely ruled their houses, and ever added to their prosperity. In other cases towns grew up through natural causes around the once lonely convent, and the abbot became the lord of the place, and the receiver of much of the productions of the industry of his tenants. The records of most of the great abbeys contain accounts of disputes between the abbot and the townspeople who lived upon the abbey lands, and there are constant complaints that the abbey was wealthy, and that the tenantry were hardly dealt with by money-loving abbots.

Beside this, there were donations of money and of land made to monasteries with various motives. Rich men, moved with pious impulses, sought admission into the ranks of the monks, and giving up all they had, made the abbey their heir. At the time of the Crusades, those who took the Cross often mortgaged their estates to raise money for their equipment, and dying on the battle-field, their property remained in the hands of the abbot who had granted the mortgage. When the doctrine of Purgatory gained credence, it was a very common practice for a dying man to leave money or land to endow a chapel or an altar in the monastery church, where masses should be daily and for ever said for the repose of his soul. In other cases the penitent was clothed upon his death-bed with the robes of a monk, and was thus admitted into the Society, and gave up his property, or some of it, into its possession. The monastic churches became the favourite burial-places of kings and nobles, and the privilege of interment in them was well paid for. The tithes and endowments of parish churches were frequently alienated and bestowed upon some abbey, whose priest-monks then undertook the performance of the services, or supplied some ill-paid vicar to minister to the parishioners.

"The monasteries acquired legitimate riches by the culture of deserted tracts, and by the prudent management of their revenues, which were less exposed to the ordinary means of dissipation than those of the laity. Their wealth, continually accumulated, enabled them to become the regular purchasers of landed estates, especially in the time of the Crusades, when the fiefs of the nobility were constantly in the market for sale or mortgage. But other sources of wealth were less pure. . . . The canonical penances imposed on repentant offenders were commuted for money. . . . The monkish confessors inculcated upon the wealthy sinner that no atonement could be so acceptable to heaven as liberal presents to its earthly delegates. To die without allotting a portion of worldly wealth to pious uses was accounted almost like suicide, or the refusal of the sacraments."[1] .

In these, and in other ways, wealth flowed in upon the monasteries, and brought with it the inevitable evils. Greedy and worldly-minded men coveted the position of abbot, which conferred upon them riches and power; and those who obtained appointments with unworthy motives did not fail to make a bad use of their opportunities for further aggrandisement. "Much would have more." Dispensations were obtained which made the provisions of the Rule of none effect, and encouraged the acquisition of riches by many indirect means. Bribery and simony followed. Preferments were bought and sold, and the dignitary who had paid a heavy price for his post made it h's first thought to get as good a return for his investment as was possible during his incumbency.

[1] Hallam's *Middle Ages*.

"My vow of poverty," boasted a lordly monk, "has given me a hundred thousand crowns a year; my vow of obedience has raised me to the rank of a sovereign prince."

Roth maintains that under the Merovingian princes, two-thirds of the land of France was possessed by the Church.

"The estates of forty German bishoprics and countless abbeys in the twelfth century, composed one-third of the whole territory of the realm, and the revenues of the Church, including the tithes, one-half of the national income."[1]

In the eighteenth century, the Abbot of Citeaux, the successor of the saintly and ascetic St. Bernard, had an income of £20,000 a year, and maintained the state of a prince. The abbots of many of the great monasteries were endowed with the rank and prerogatives of temporal sovereigns, and exercised all the functions of royalty, levying taxes, carrying on wars, and making treaties, besides holding courts and tribunals, and inflicting capital and other punishments.

Even the abbesses of the more important convents became temporal sovereigns, and maintained armed forces to defend their rights.

"The bishops, occupying the ranks of princes, affected the dress and sports of laymen. The worldly life of the bishops was speedily copied by the canons. The stalls were filled with the younger sons of princely houses. The Chapter of Liège at one

[1] S. Baring-Gould, *History of the Church in Germany*.

time consisted of twenty sons of kings and princes. When Conrad II. ascended the throne he found his exchequer empty, and he adopted the fatal expedient of making the offices of the Church disposable for money. It was an old custom for every one who came before the emperor to make him a present. —By degrees those presents were formulated into a table of fees, and each bishopric and abbey cost so much, according to its value. Matters of this sort were, however, far worse in France and Italy, where the sale of benefices and orders was carried on with unblushing effrontery, and nowhere worse than in the Papal Court, where every office had its price."

Here is a picture of a wealthy convent in Spain in the sixteenth century. "Men-at-arms and dependents fill the outside courts with animation and life; the poor throng round the gates, waiting for the evening dole; as evening steals over Burgos, and the last gleam of the setting sun flushes its lace-work spire, pilgrims and travellers find food and shelter for the night in its hospitable guest-house. . . . The nuns are all daughters of the nobility; each is served by her own waiting-woman. The perpetual Abbess of Las Huelgas exercises civil and criminal jurisdiction over sixty towns and villages. No one from the king downwards can muster or bring into the field so many vassals. She can convoke synods and make synodical constitutions and laws, binding not only her ecclesiastical but her secular subjects. The abbesses of seventeen affiliated convents attend the great and solemn chapter held every year on St. Martin's Day. On those occasions when the Abbess of Las Huelgas goes forth in solemn state to assist at the election of an abbess in one of the convents subject to her authority, surrounded by nuns and servants, her journey is little less than a royal progress. . . . From the altars of the church requiem masses ascended day and night for the souls of the kings and queens who slept before them. Twenty-one chaplains celebrated the services, no less solemn and stately than those of a cathedral." [1]

Fierce contests for prerogative, jealous resistance of encroachments, the sort of *esprit de corps* that leads to haughtiness, ambition, and uncharitableness, would seem to be the temptations to which these sisters were liable when the riches of the world flowed into their treasury.

The creation of the Orders of Friars was, among other things, a protest against the wealth and worldly grandeur of the monks. Absolute poverty was insisted upon by St. Francis, who professed to have taken sacred Poverty as his bride. His Friars were to beg for their daily bread, and were to have no shelter but that which charity offered them. But it is a remarkable and grievous fact that the evils which did not come upon the old Orders generally for centuries, broke out among the mendicant Orders very soon after their inauguration.

While Francis was still alive, evasions of the strictness of his Rule, forbidding even a corporate posses-

[1] *Life of St. Teresa*, p. 41, by G. C. Graham.

sion of worldly goods, began to find favour with many, and much more after his death; and ere long, with the boast of poverty, his Order became the richest in Christendom.

"Bonaventura, himself the head of the Order, and writing not fifty years after the death of Francis, does not scruple to say that already in his time the sight of a begging friar in the distance was more dreaded than that of a robber."[1]

"The vow of poverty was evaded by the Friars. They said they were not allowed to possess property, but that they might enjoy the use of it. The wealth that grateful people poured in upon them was therefore vested in the hands of the Pope, to be applied by him for the benefit of the Order. Thus, by the middle of the thirteenth century the mendicant Orders possessed magnificent buildings all over Europe. In the same way Francis had contemned all learning except the reading of the Bible; but after a few years his followers collected libraries, and filled professors' chairs in the Universities. The Pope exempted their houses from episcopal jurisdiction, and gave them leave to preach in the churches, to administer the sacraments, and to bury the dead, without the permission of the incumbents of parishes, or the licence of bishops. If the friar was refused the use of the church, he would erect his pulpit at some cross-way, and would rail at the sloth and ignorance of the secular and regular clergy, calling them 'dumb dogs,' and 'cursed hirelings.' By the time of Erasmus the

---

[1] Trench, *Med. Ch. Hist.*

friars were the butt of every tavern; they were exhibited in pot-house pictures as friars preaching, with the neck of a stolen goose peeping out of the hood behind; as wolves giving absolution, with a dead sheep muffled up in their cloaks; as apes sitting by a sick man's bed, with a crucifix in one hand, and the other in the sufferer's pocket."[1]

"If I knew," said Lacordaire, "that our house would grow rich, even by your savings, I should rise to-night and set fire to it at its four corners." "Fatal wealth!" writes Montalambert; "the daughter of charity, of faith, of a generous and spontaneous virtue, but the mother of covetousness, envy, robbery, and ruin! But who will not regret with me that the Church, which alone has the necessary discernment and authority, should not herself have set limits, at a suitable moment, to the unlimited increase of wealth in the monastic corporations? The increase was lawful, natural, often was involuntary, but dangerous and exorbitant. . . . No man can say from what evils and crimes the world might have been spared if the Church, which was destined to be the chief victim, had arrested with a prudent and steady hand the rising tide of ecclesiastical wealth, saying, 'Hitherto shalt thou come, but no further; and here shall thy proud course be stayed.'"

Another fatal cause of the decay of Monasticism was the miserable system of COMMENDAM. This was indeed one of the indirect evil results of excessive wealth. When monasteries became rich, and their

[1] Blunt.

abbots were temporal lords and princes, the eyes of covetous and ambitious men of the world were attracted by the glittering prizes of the Church, and in order to enjoy them they entered the ranks of the priesthood, not to labour for Christ and His Church, but that they might enjoy the good things of this life. Many of the abuses and scandals that are recorded against Monasticism arose from the worldly and voluptuous lives of abbots, who cared nothing for their duties, who absented themselves from their houses, and winked at, or were actually ignorant of, the relaxed discipline, the petty squabbles, and the entire neglect of the Rule which prevailed in the monasteries of which they were nominally the heads. The monks found themselves virtually free and irresponsible, and those who were so disposed lived as they pleased, and the whole tone of the place degenerated. The abbot needed money to keep up his state at Court, or even to furnish him with military equipments, and he caused the property of his abbey to be burdened with mortgage or debt, or irritated the tenants by exactions and monopolies. Many greedy and unscrupulous men, not satisfied with one rich appointment, sought and obtained others, which they held as pluralists, altogether ignoring the responsibilities of their office, and caring nothing for the terrible consequences that arose from their shameless conduct, and treating with lordly contempt the remonstrances and entreaties of godly men who grieved for the dishonour that fell upon the cause of religion. Bribery and simony followed hard upon all this. Valuable appointments were paid for, and patrons appointed the buyer *in commendam*, without any idea of his fitness for his place, or even with the least expectation that he would attempt to fulfil its duties and responsibilities. Indeed it was often impossible that he could undertake them at all. Lay abbots were common, who never even set foot in their abbeys. Young men, under the canonical age for ordination, and even children, were nominated to ecclesiastical dignities. The Popes, with their assumed powers of dispensation, were great offenders in this respect. The new-born children of those whom it was desirable to conciliate, were endowed with gifts of Church preferment, and it was said that sometimes there was so little care bestowed that it was doubtful whether the infant abbot was a boy or a girl!

Giovanni di Medicis, afterwards Leo X., was made Abbot of Monte Cassino and of several other abbeys while still in his cradle. Some of the better Popes fulminated against these abuses, and sovereigns were sometimes made to swear at their coronation that they would not give any abbey *in commendam;* but the evil constantly broke out again. The Church in France was especially wealthy, and it was in that country that this vicious and fatal practice most widely prevailed. The King had the right of nominating the heads of all the religious houses. The post of abbot became a sinecure, bestowed upon courtiers and royal favourites, the price often of some disgraceful act. Cardinals Richelieu and Mazarin each held the nominal rank of abbot of several of the largest monasteries in France, and received their revenues, while the number of the monks was reduced to a minimum, and the abbeys became little more than farms managed for the benefit of their impropriators. Junior and illegitimate members of the royal family were provided with incomes in this way, and the infamous Abbé Dubois enjoyed an income of 204,000 livres supplied entirely from the endowments of several religious houses.

Montalembert says—"Of the many thousand monasteries founded in France during thirteen centuries, there remained, in 1789, only 120 which were *en règle*—that is to say, which retained the right to elect their abbot and dispose of their incomes." "The last Abbot of Bec—the house founded by Hérlwin, and made glorious by Lanfranc and Anselm—was M. de Talleyrand!" (*Church*).

It could not fail that such perversions of the object of religious foundations would render Monasticism contemptible, and sooner or later ensure its ruin. But it is not just to impute to the system the faults and abuses that were forced upon it by a godless world, and by debauched and unscrupulous men.

There were other causes that led to the decay of Monasticism that are not so well known. The frequent wars that desolated Europe involved the burning of many religious houses which were never rebuilt; and in other instances their property was wasted or actually alienated; the number of inmates was reduced, and the remnant in abject poverty relapsed into relaxed and undisciplined living. The BLACK DEATH had not only a fatal effect upon the monasteries during the time of its prevalence, but it produced lasting results from which many of them never recovered, and which were the direct causes of some of those defects and irregularities which were complained of in subsequent visitations, and which were used as justification for suppression. In 1350, Europe was not only decimated of its inhabitants, but men's hearts were prostrated with terror. We are told that the world gave itself up to riot and vice, maddened by horror and despair; and that the physical plague resulted in a moral degeneracy which invaded the cloister as well as the palace and the cottage. Great numbers of monks and nuns died. In the Abbey of Fleur-Champs, 80 fell victims to the disease; at Foswert, 207. The Superior was often carried off, and the remaining members of the community, without a guiding hand, gave up the observance of their Rule, and even left their house. In some cases every one within the walls died, and the monastery lay deserted and open to any one who liked to rob or take possession of it. Nor was this all. When the pestilence abated, there was not only a deficiency of clergy, but of monks and nuns. The consequence was that persons were received under age, and without the usual term of probation, who, having no real vocation for the religious life, demanded relaxation of the Rules, and gave cause for complaint by the lax and careless lives which they led. When these monasteries were inspected by their Visitors, it was found that the number of inmates was far below that which the terms of the foundation provided ; and this was made a ground sometimes for suppression, sometimes for the amalgamation of several communities, a course which often ended in jealousies and confusion.

Such were some of the causes that led to the decay, and finally to the general suppression of monasteries. In the fifteenth and sixteenth centuries hardly any new foundations were made, and schools and colleges began to be built instead of abbeys and nunneries. Fewer men and women sought admission to the Religious Orders, and the spread of the theories and principles of the Renaissance and of Protestantism paved the way to their discredit and abolition.

The suppression of the great Order of the Templars (1307) was really the first step for the general attack upon Monasticism. There can be no doubt that the great wealth of the Order attracted the covetousness of the King of France, and the charges that were brought against the Knights have been regarded with increasing suspicion, as it has been made clear that they were necessary to defend and justify the ruthless spoliation and the relentless cruelty which accompanied the destruction of such a powerful and long-respected institution.

The final loss of the Holy Land, and the abandonment of the Crusades had, to a great extent, done away with the *raison d'être* of an Order of fighting monks ; and with the loss of their occupation it would not improbably happen that pride and the other accompaniments of wealthy idleness would make themselves felt in the barracks of these lordly soldiers. We must, however, correct the romance of *Ivanhoe* by the tragic and pathetic records of the protestations of the tortured Grand Master and his veteran and noble comrades during their trial in Paris, and by the horror which the recital of the barbarous treatment of those unfortunate men excited in other countries, and by the reluctance with which the King of England and other monarchs followed the lead of the King of France.

Dr. Döllinger says—"At this day in England, so far as I am aware, almost every authority on English history regards the acts of the trial of the Templars, which have been fully preserved, as bearing weighty testimony to the innocence of the whole Order. Previously to October 13, 1307, the day on which the great blow was dealt, no mention had been made of the assumed corruption and degeneracy of the Society. I find, on the contrary, in the literature of the time and of the period immediately following, even as late as the beginning of the fourteenth century, that authors who sharply condemn the degeneracy of the ecclesiastical communities of the day, give evidence in favour of the Order of Knights Templars, either negatively, by omitting any mention of them in the enumeration of degenerate orders and monastic bodies, or positively, by holding them up as a pattern to others."[1]

It was through the preaching of Luther, and still more by the violent denunciations of his disciples

---

[1] *Addresses on Historical Subjects* (Murray).

and successors, that the abolition of Monasticism throughout Europe commenced. There was a revolt in men's minds, first against the abuses and superstitions of Romanism, and then against all Catholic doctrines and practices. So Mr. Lecky says, "The suppression of monasteries has been, for the most part, elicited by no scandals on the part of the monks, but was simply the expression of a public opinion which regarded the monastic life as essentially contemptible and disgraceful."[1]

The beginnings of the Reformation must be sought in the principles of the Renaissance. Paganism, which men thought had been ended by the decrees of Constantine, revived and found favour even in the Court of the Popes. The deadly wound of the Beast was healed. "The world," which seemed to have been "overcome" and converted by Christ, once more fascinated men, and commanded their allegiance. Mortification of the body was exchanged for passionate admiration of the beauty of its form, and for the gratification of its natural desires. Painters and sculptors revelled in their delineation of the nude, and in copying the triumphs of Greek art. The Oriental interpretation of the prophet's words, "He hath no beauty, that we should desire Him; no form or comeliness," was rejected, and Michael Angelo depicted Christ on the wall of the Sistine Chapel as a magnificent Jupiter hurling his thunderbolts upon the damned. The Virgin Mother and her Child displayed the perfection of human loveliness; the

[1] *Rationalism*, vol. ii.

Magdalen's penitence gave opportunity for exquisite delineations of the female form; St. Sebastian and a host of martyrs became merely the lay-figures for studies in flesh painting; and the lives of the saints and the incidents in Gospel story, furnished the skilful imagination with subjects that brought out all the marvellous displays of human passions, and the manifold and picturesque events of daily life.[1]

"That great movement," says Mr. Mallock, "which goes by the name of the Renaissance, was the return of human nature to a lost part of itself, or the welcoming back to itself of a part that had been long banished. For centuries men had aimed at the purification of the mind merely, now they aimed at its cultivation. That part of themselves which for centuries they had despised and suppressed, they began to educate and adorn. The beauty of the human form, the glories of colour and light, which were regarded by Augustine as so many temptations of the devil, changed their aspect, and seemed part of man's noblest heritage. The mediæval sense of the beauty of holiness was supplemented by a sense of the nobility and holiness of beauty; and along with this—or rather as the subjective side of this—reappeared a sense that had slept or been in hiding for centuries—a sense of the beauty, we might almost say, the duty, of pleasure. In spite of Christ's words, and all the traditional interpretations of them, in spite of all the machinery of the Church for emphasizing and confirming their meaning, human nature, after some

[1] See *Renaissance Fancies and Studies*, by Vernon Lee, p. 106 etc.

fourteen centuries, could be no longer restrained within the strict Christian limits, but insisted at all costs on again appropriating and enjoying those pleasures and perfections, physical, intellectual, and emotional, which the Pagan worlds of Greece and Rome had cultivated, and from which it had so long debarred itself. This movement has during the present century been, year by year, receiving some fresh stimulus, as science has fixed man's attention on the things of the present life, and has been, step by step, discrediting the teaching of the Gospels as to another."[1]

The capture of Constantinople by the Turks (1453) drove into Italy a multitude of fugitive Greeks and Jews, and with them came the study of the Greek language, and a taste for Greek and pagan literature. Asceticism had been carried to extremes; there was a swinging back of the pendulum; and men began to worship what they had burned, and to burn what they had worshipped. Rationalism developed into rejection of Christian dogma, and a Pope was heard to sneer against religion as a "popular superstition," which he nevertheless outwardly professed because he found it "profitable."

In Germany Luther translated and circulated the Bible, and in his interpretation of St. Paul's Epistles proclaimed "justification by faith" as a final and complete substitute for all the traditional system for the pardon of sin, both in this world and the next. Many of the monasteries had been founded, or

[1] *Studies of Contemporary Superstition*, 1895 (Black).

subsequently endowed, that masses might be for ever said for the repose of the souls of the departed; Luther and his fellow-reformers denied the efficacy of such prayers. The doctrine of the Mass itself was controverted; fasting, and watching, and the repetition of long offices of devotion were argued against, and so the occupations of monks and nuns were gone. Luther declared that once, when he was at Rome, he heard a priest who was celebrating mass, say, instead of the formula of consecration, "Panis es; et panis manebis—Vinum es; et vinum manebis."

The strange theory was propounded that the elect might and ought to commit sin as an act of defiance of the devil, and to show their confidence in the boundless power of faith in Christ to free them from the guilt and consequences of sin, and as a protest against the Roman system of penance with its complicated and tedious regulations, and the necessary mediation of the priest.

"Pecca fortiter" was advocated in the pulpit, and that which had been merely a theological phrase, became a new gospel of licence to the people, which natural propensities only too gladly welcomed and acted upon. Those whom Luther taught soon went far beyond their master, and in his later years he vainly endeavoured to stem the torrent which he had let loose. He, a professed monk, had married a professed nun, and such an act did more even than his violent sermons to discredit Monasticism, and to bring about its total abolition in Germany. Protestant mobs besieged the convents, and led or drove out the inmates. Sometimes the release was welcomed; for there were monks and nuns who had embraced the new doctrine, and others, who had never had any vocation, but for various unworthy causes had "entered religion"; but in many cases the professed "liberty" was not desired, and devout souls went forth regretfully from their peaceful cloisters, and as soon as possible sought elsewhere the resumption of the life of retirement and prayer which was their unalterable choice. The property of the monasteries was soon appropriated by willing hands, and the revival of dissolved communities was effectually prevented. "Pull down the nests, and the black birds will not be able to return," was the advice of the leaders, and their followers carried out the suggestion thoroughly. Bucer said, "The great bulk of those who joined the Reform, proposed to themselves freedom from the Pope and the bishops, and gave themselves up to all carnal passions. 'We are justified by faith,' said they; 'good works, which are not to our taste, are useless.'" Erasmus, Justus Jonas, Weller, and others make the same complaints. "Look at Germany," said Luther, in one of his times of despondency and remorse, "in a moral point of view, it has fallen into a condition a hundred times more hideous than war could produce."

In the Peasants' War that followed Luther's triumph, 100,000 men perished. In 1527 Rome was taken and sacked by an army of Lutherans under Frunsberg and the most awful slaughter, cruelties, and sacrilege were perpetrated. The Thirty Years'

War cost Germany half its population; and it was simply a conflict of Protestant against Catholic. Dr. Döllinger writes, "John Faure, a Jesuit, acknowledged, in 1750, that the only cause of the separation of the northern nations was not their love of Protestant doctrines, but their hatred of the Pope and the Court of Rome, increased by the profligacy, pride, and domineering and covetousness of the clergy, and especially of the Religious Orders."

Mr. H. N. Oxenham says—"The Reformers undermined Catholicism; the deistical writers of the last century have undermined orthodox Protestantism; Rationalism and Unitarianism have made an end of Bible infallibility."[1] Bishop Watson defined Protestantism, as "the right of saying what you think, and thinking what you please." A writer in the *Spectator* of July 14, 1883, says with respect to the state of religious thought in Switzerland—"The older Protestant ministers still preserve some remnants of orthodoxy, but nearly every minister elected since 1874 is either an avowed Agnostic, or a declared opponent of Christianity. The Protestant Church is a chaos of doctrines. The old and the new pastors have nothing in common, not even a belief in God. That which one man builds up, another pulls down. The people are sinking into a condition of cynical indifferentism. They not only believe that there is no truth in religion, but they doubt if there be truth in anything. The Church of Basle has abolished baptism. Swiss Protestantism is transformed into pure Rationalism. . . . The Catholic

[1] *Short Studies, Ethical and Religious* (Murray).

Church was more persecuted in Switzerland than in Prussia, but the Catholics in Geneva are more numerous and powerful than at any time since the Reformation."

"The Church of Luther does not exist. It escaped from the authority of Rome, to fall under the complete subjection of temporal princes, and has been jangled down to Voltaireism itself";[1] Pastor Kuntze said at the Berlin Protestant Diet in 1853, that 400,000 people never attended any place of worship. In 1872 the official statistics stated that less than two per cent. of the population of Berlin professed any religion. In 1869, out of 23,070 burials, only 3612 had religious services. In the same year, at a meeting of the Dresden Protestant Verein, it was decided that the doctrine of Christ's Atonement was an exploded superstition.

Calvin's rule at Geneva began in 1541; he established a quasi-religious republic. Everything was regulated by law—dress, the arrangement of the hair, the dishes to be served at meals. The most relentless system of espionage and cruelty prevailed. The gaols were crowded with offenders against the moral regulations; fifty-eight persons were executed in four years, in a small community, and seventy-eight were exiled. At Münster a fanatic set up a still more tyrannical theocracy, which speedily lapsed into such a chaos of debauchery and crime that the neighbouring towns rose up in indignant rage, and making war upon the place, took terrible revenge upon the leaders of a system that outraged every law of God and man.

[1] *German Home Life.*

Germany has never recovered from the effects of those religious revolts. Lutheranism lapsed into Calvinism; and Calvinism into Rationalism. It was said with satisfaction by "advanced thinkers" in the sixteenth century,

> "Tota jacet Babylon; destruxit tecta Lutherus,
> Calvinus muros, et fundamenta Socinus."

"The Protestant revolution," says F. Seebohm, "was the beginning of a great revolutionary wave which broke in the French Revolution. It was quite as much a political as a religious revolution,"[1] and Mr. Lecky and Mr. J. F. Stephen acknowledge that the Reformation was everywhere brought about by force.

"The reason of these changes," says L. Eckenstein, "lay not altogether with those who professed religion in convents, they were part of a wider change which remoulded society on an altered basis. For the system of association, the groundwork of mediæval strength and achievement, was altogether giving way at the time of the Reformation. The socialistic temper was superseded by individualistic tendencies which were opposed to the prerogatives conferred on the older associations."

In the *Genevois*, the semi-official organ at Geneva, during the election of the Council in 1883, it was said—"Most people happily trouble themselves very little with what the Church calls the salvation of souls. The first thought of every man of well-

[1] *The Era of the Protestant Revolution* (Longmans).

balanced mind is to make the best of this world. Aspirations after the infinite are confined to delicate natures and exceptional organizations. The mass of ordinary mortals know nothing of these. Among the multitudes religious belief is fast disappearing. Faith has had its time."

"By their fruits ye shall know them." *Experientia docet.* The principles that have thus developed hardly commend themselves to devout and sober minds. The opinion of such leaders of thought with respect to Monasticism does not compel the respect, or command the credence of those who have the New Testament in their hands, and the lives and words of saintly monks and nuns in their memories. *Non tali auxilio.*

Monasticism then was not judged and condemned at the Reformation period on its fundamental principles, or on account of the faults of its members, but because there was a wave of revolt against the ancient system of government in Church and State; because there was an outburst of mental and spiritual liberalism; and because the rulers of the time lusted after the temporal possessions of the monasteries. Christianity remains true, and worthy to be venerated and accepted as the one best guide of faith and practice, notwithstanding the frightful abuses and errors that have disgraced its professors, and which by some are mistaken for its real principles. The doctrinal novelties of Rome, the popular superstitions that are held by many who call themselves Christians, the conflicting dogmas of the numerous sects, the erroneous imputations of the enemies of religion, all these leave the essence of Christianity untouched. The most earnest reformers may rightly denounce them, as our Lord denounced the traditions of the Scribes and Pharisees. The lost piece of money may be cleansed from its dust and accretions; the ship may be freed from the animal and vegetable growth that foul its hull; the street Arab's dirty face may be washed; so religion may be reformed without being destroyed; and the fundamental principles of Monasticism may remain true, and blessed, and fit to be embraced and practised by those who possess a vocation, although monks and nuns have lived unworthy lives, and their profession has been made contemptible and hateful in the eyes of some godly and consistent Christians. If the tree has been barren; if the vine has brought forth only wild grapes, the Master says not, "cut them down," but "prune, dig about, and dung them." If the woman has sinned with lovers, He holds the hands of those who would cast the death-giving stone, and says to her, "Go; and sin no more." When the unclean spirits are cast out, the saved victim sits at the feet of Jesus "clothed and in his right mind," and is presently sent by Him a missioner of glad tidings. Peter denied His Lord, but is pardoned, and is commissioned to feed His sheep and His lambs.

In 1523 Magdeburg, Weimar, Rostock, Stettin, Danzig, and Riga expelled the monks and nuns from their houses. In 1526 the Landgrave of Hesse confiscated all the monasteries in his dominions by the advice of Luther.

Many of the inmates of the monasteries left them most unwillingly. A curious record exists of one Caritas Prickheimer, the abbess of a convent in Nuremberg, who successfully resisted the efforts which were made to suppress her house.[1]

In 1527 Gustavus Vasa forced the Reformation upon Sweden, and confiscated the property of the Church, suppressing the religious corporations, and appropriating their property to the State, or bestowing it upon the nobility, who were by this means prevailed upon to favour a step which they viewed at first with disapprobation. A similar course was adopted in Denmark in 1534; in Norway in 1537; and in Iceland in 1550. In England the lesser monasteries were seized in 1535 by Henry VIII.; and in 1539 the great abbeys were plundered and destroyed. In Scotland in 1559 the preaching of John Knox stirred up the people, and a raid was made upon the monasteries in Perth, and those in other parts of the kingdom were soon after sacked and confiscated one after the other.

In 1791 a decree of the Directory abolished all corporations civil and religious in France, and declared all their property to belong to the State.

Eighty-two abbeys and 255 convents for women, besides colleges and other establishments, were suppressed, and their revenues, reckoned at 95,000,000 livres, were appropriated by the Government.

[1] See L. Eckenstein's *Woman under Monasticism*.

In 1790 Joseph II. abolished the Mendicant Orders in the countries under his rule, and soon after, by his own autocratic will, and in opposition to the wishes of his people, he closed 624 monasteries.

In 1830 after the Revolution in France, a fresh attack was made upon Monasticism, and it is said that 300 were suppressed in different parts of Europe between 1830 and 1835.

In 1834 the Crown seized upon the possessions of 500 monasteries in Portugal, and a contemporary writer speaks of "the tears of the people who had always found there succour in their illnesses and bread in their old age." In 1835 the monasteries in Spain were confiscated. In 1847 many religious houses were abolished in Switzerland.

In 1859 the revolutionary government of Mexico, under the presidency of Juarez, confiscated the whole of the Church property of the country, suppressing 150 monasteries and convents, and turning out 2000 nuns and 1700 monks. The value of the Church endowments thus secularized was estimated at £100,000,000, and was probably more; yet two years after this enormous sum had been appropriated by the State, the Public Treasury was absolutely empty![1]

In 1875 Prussia decreed the suppression of all Orders except those devoted to sick-nursing. In 1887 this law was abrogated, as it had been found to be most unpopular, and Religious Orders of all kinds were sanctioned.

[1] Vide *Life of Benito Juarez*, by U. R. Burke.

In 1866 the Kingdom of Sardinia practically destroyed the monastic system in its dominions; and finally, in 1872, the Government of United Italy at Rome decreed the suppression of the convents throughout the whole country, without regard to the historical interest of many ancient foundations, the religious needs of some remote districts, and the cruel results that the step inflicted upon many helpless women; and in spite of the indignant protests of men of all shades of religious opinion, and of every civilized European nation.

"The abolition of the religious institutions has been grievously felt throughout the country, and there are few, even among the friends of Italian unity, who have not had personal reason to experience its injustice. The convents and monasteries were richly endowed; they supported the needy, the sick, the helpless, and the blind among the people, who received their daily dole of bread and soup from the convent charities. When the marriage-portions of the nuns were stolen by the Government, there was scarcely any family of the upper classes throughout Central Italy which did not suffer; for almost all had a sister, aunt, or cousin 'in religion,' upon whom a portion of £1000, £5000, or £10,000 had been bestowed, and who was thrown back helpless upon their hands, her fortune confiscated, and with an irregularly paid pension of a few pence a day, quite insufficient for the most miserable subsistence."[1]

[1] A. J. C. Hare, *Cities of Northern Italy*.

CHAPTER VI

THE REVIVAL OF MONASTICISM IN THE CHURCH OF ENGLAND

> They that shall be of thee shall build the old waste places: thou shalt raise up the foundations of many generations; and thou shalt be called, The Repairer of the breach, The Restorer of paths to dwell in.—*Isaiah* lviii. 12.

THE practical question arises, after we have considered the fundamental principles and the history of Monasticism, "Is it possible to revive it?" and then there follows another equally important question, "If it were possible to revive Monasticism, is it desirable to do so?" When we see from history what a mighty power Monasticism has been in the life of the Church throughout the world, and in all periods of her existence, the question seems to be answered at once, and we feel compelled to say, "Monasticism must be revived; the Church cannot do without it; her present enfeebled condition is the result of the loss of this essential element in her constitution and her work."

But a little inquiry will speedily convince us that such an opinion is not held universally, and that the direct contrary is maintained very strongly by many whose judgment is respected and influential. "Monk," said Voltaire, "what is that profession of thine? It is that of having none, of engaging oneself by an inviolable oath to be a fool and a slave, and to live at the expense of others." "The principles of Monasticism," said Joseph II. of Austria, "from Pacôme to our own days, are entirely contrary to the light of reason." Lamartine spoke of "the beatified aberrations and ignorance of monkish asceticism"; and Le Semeur adds, "The monks and nuns are but sluggards, fattened at the expense of the people." "I cannot praise," said Milton, "a fugitive and cloistered virtue unexercised and unbreathed, that never sallies out and sees her adversary, but slinks out of the race, where that immortal garland is to be run for, not without dust and heat. Assuredly we bring not innocence into the world; we bring impurity much rather: that which purifies us is trial, and trial is by what is contrary. That virtue, therefore, which is but a youngling in the contemplation of evil, and knows not the utmost that vice promises to her followers, and rejects it, is but a blank virtue, not a pure."

Byron's idea of monks was that they were men who,

"In hope to merit heaven,
Were making earth a hell."

Madame Roland exclaimed, "Let us sell the ecclesiastical possessions; we shall never be freed from these ferocious beasts till we have destroyed their dens."

So Mr. Lecky writes, "Political liberty is almost impossible when the monastic system is supreme, not merely because the monasteries divert the energies of the nation from civic to ecclesiastical channels, but also because the monastic ideal is the very apotheosis of servitude. When men have learnt to reverence a life of passive, unreasoning obedience as the highest type of perfection, the enthusiasm and passion of freedom necessarily decline. In this respect there is an analogy between the monastic and the military spirit, both of which promote and glorify passive obedience, and therefore prepare the minds of men for despotic rule; but on the whole the monastic spirit is probably more hostile to freedom than the military spirit, for the obedience of the monk is based upon humility, while the obedience of the soldier coexists with pride. Now a considerable measure of pride, or self-assertion, is an invariable characteristic of free communities. . . . The peculiar vigour with which the feeling of self-respect has been developed in Protestant countries may be attributed to the suppression of monastic institutions and habits."[1] He further describes the monk as "a hideous, sordid, and emaciated maniac, without knowledge, without patriotism, without natural affection, passing his life in a long routine of useless and atrocious self-torture, and quailing before the ghastly phantoms of his delirious brain, who had become the ideal of nations which had known the writings of Plato and Cicero, and the lives of Socrates and Cato." And again, "The monasteries in Spain, in numbers and wealth, had reached a point that had scarcely been equalled,

[1] Lecky, *Morals*, vol. ii. p. 187.

and besides subtracting many thousand men, and a vast amount of wealth from the productive resources of the country, they produced habits of mind altogether incompatible with industry. The spirit that makes men devote themselves in vast numbers to a monotonous life of asceticism and poverty is so essentially opposed to the spirit that creates the energy and enthusiasm of industry, that their continued co-existence may be regarded as impossible."[1]

In the same spirit Mr. J. A. Froude says—" Cursed be he who rebuildeth Jericho. Never were any institutions brought to a more deserved judgment than the monastic orders of England; and a deeper irreverence than the Puritan lies in the spurious devotionalism of an age which has lost its faith, and with its faith has lost the power to recognize the visible working of the ineffable Being by whose breath we are allowed to exist."[2]

Similar quotations might be almost indefinitely multiplied; and if it be objected that the words of these men bear little weight with Churchmen, there would still be obtainable an array of calm conclusions that might be gathered from the writings of consistent and able English Churchmen, unanimously protesting against the revival of Monasticism among us. Thus one writes, "The day of monasticism has for ever set in England. There is no longer any need of its existence. More than Benedictine learning sheds a ray of glory upon our colleges. Our Poor

---

[1] Lecky, *Rationalism*, vol. ii. pp. 114, 331.
[2] *Short Studies*, vol. iii.

Laws render unnecessary the alms from the monastery wicket; and such doles would become a positive evil now as an encouragement to idleness and sloth. Our parochial clergy are welcome visitors at the cottage fireside, where the monk of later days was not with his sack for contributions for his house. There is more hope of recovering to life the carcase around which the eagles have gathered than of renovating monkdom."[1]

Bishop Creighton says—"Monasticism outlived its time, and the worst rubbish was the relics of what once was good, but had ceased to be so. Every reform became in its turn an abuse. There was nothing which the march of time did not make useless, and there came a time when Monasticism died down, not because it was bad, but because it had done its work. Nothing was bad in itself; but things were bad when they were not wanted. Thus it was with Monasticism. Englishmen, with their ordinary common sense, were the first to find out its uselessness, and Monasticism had only been useless about two hundred years when England discovered the fact."

Other writers express similar opinions. There is also the strong and plausible argument which practical and matter-of-fact Englishmen find convincing— the argument from experience. It is said, Monasticism has had every opportunity of commending itself to the judgment of mankind; it has possessed wealth, power, public favour, and a long existence; and the

[1] Theological Dictionary. Ed. J. H. Blunt.

world's verdict has been against it; it has everywhere been abolished. *Securus judicat orbis terrarum.* At various periods of its history, among peoples of totally different origin and characteristics, and for more than one crying fault, Monasticism has been scouted, execrated, and stamped out. It has been reformed from within, and from without, but it has always relapsed. It evidently possesses in itself incurable disease; the virus may be purged away partially, or for a time, but it invariably breaks out again sooner or later. There is no remedy but absolute extinction.

Let us see what may be said in reply to all this, and on the other side.

First, the argument from abuse may be set aside, because it attempts to prove too much. There is no human institution that has not suffered from abuse. There is nothing so venerable, so indispensable, that must not be rooted up and abolished, if abuse is to do away with use. Governments of every kind, learning, inventions, modern civilization, commerce, marriage, the Bible, the Church, Christianity itself, which of these has not been misused, corrupted, and made an instrument for evil? *Corruptio optimi pessima.* The real question is, not whether there has been corruption, but whether the thing corrupted is or is not in itself good originally.

We have seen what is the theory and innate principle of Monasticism, that it is the love of God; that the devout soul desires God above all things, God alone; that it seeks solitude that it may the better commune with God; that it finds many temptations and distractions in the world, and therefore flees from it and from them; that it experiences the down-drawing of the flesh, and therefore "keeps under the body and brings it into subjection"; that as it grows in likeness to Christ, it becomes imbued with His Spirit, and is forced to imitate His life of mercy and regard for the bodies and souls of men; that power is gained by this system of self-discipline which is not otherwise attained, and that results can thus be secured which are striven for in vain by other methods; and that the blessing of God, and the evident presence and beneficent operation of the Holy Spirit have always been seen and felt when Monasticism has been true to its original principles, and has carried out those principles to their logical consequences in action. We have seen that Monasticism is nothing else than the honest and literal acceptance and fulfilment of our Lord's precepts in the Sermon on the Mount and elsewhere, and that it can adapt itself to the requirements of all times and all environments. Why then is it unsuitable for the present day, and for the Church of England?

Notwithstanding its wholesale suppression, Monasticism still exists. "Monasticism increases most rapidly in France in spite of State opposition and the spread of atheism."[1]

Besides, as has been well said, "The argument which is derivable from past abuses is rather favourable than adverse to the establishment of Monasti-

[1] *Visits to French Monasteries*, A. Taylor.

cism, inasmuch as it diminishes the probability of their recurrence, by exciting a greater vigilance in the proceedings of such societies, and providing safeguards against those avenues through which corruption might be expected to advance . . . and the feeling that such an institution was contending with an unfriendly prejudice would almost necessarily lead to a correspondent policy; for wariness, circumspection, and an avoidance even of the semblance of evil, usually mark the conduct of men who are conscious that all their actions are scrutinized by invidious judges."

"There are in France at the present time about 1200 male and female congregations, comprising about 160,000 'religious,' of whom 6000 only are of the 'contemplative' orders. As regards the missionary associations, M. Louvet, in *Les Missions Catoliques au XIXe Siècle*, says that there are 13,300 missionary priests, 4500 brothers, and 42,000 sisters at work abroad, and about 10,000 native sisters."[1]

Mr. J. A. Froude says—"Among other strange phenomena of this waning century, we see once more rising among us, as if by enchantment, the religious orders of the Middle Ages: Benedictines, Carmelites, Dominicans, houses of monks and nuns, to which American and English ladies and gentlemen are once more gathering as of old, flying no longer from a world of violence or profligacy, but from a world of emptiness and spiritual death. . . . In England, where the past is obscured by sentimental passion;

[1] *Guardian*, June 12, 1895.

in America, where there is no past, and where the lessons of the old world are supposed to have no application; in France, where the entire nation is swimming in a sea of anarchy, and the vessel of the State is shattered, and the drowning wretches cling to each floating plank which the waves drift within their reach, conventual institutions are springing up as mushrooms after an autumn rain."[1]

Montalembert says (*Monks of the West*, vol. v.)—" Never since Christianity existed have such sacrifices been more numerous, more magnanimous, more spontaneous than now. Every day since the commencement of this century, hundreds of beloved creatures have come forth from castles and cottages, from palaces and workshops, to offer to God their heart and their life. This right is afforded to us everywhere, not only in our old and unhealthy Europe, but in that America which all generous spirits regard with hope and confidence."

In Italy, where the religious houses were ruthlessly suppressed by Victor Emmanuel's Government in 1871, there are still some that remain, being either too poor to tempt pillage, or too popular to be altogether destroyed, or which have been restored under another name. For instance, the Franciscans bought back their church and buildings at Tre Fontane, near Rome, and were recognized by the Government as an "Agricultural Society." The friars have planted eucalyptus in great numbers round their premises, and the result has been that

[1] *Short Studies*, vol. iii.

the air and the soil are so purified that it is now possible for the brothers to sleep in their house, without fear of malarial fever, which no one had ventured to do for many years.

"There is still a body of nearly a score of friars at Camaldoli who have part of the convent buildings. The Government has taken all their vast possessions, but has allowed the Order to go on and to recruit itself, as far as they are able to maintain themselves by their own resources, which are said to be considerable, as they have many friends. They now lease their buildings from the Government on a ten years' lease, paying no rent, but they are bound to keep up the buildings, and to spend twenty thousand lire in the ten years upon them. They are still the big people of the place, looked upon as ill-treated owners, who will one day get their own again. . . . At La Verna, the Franciscans have been let alone, and are quite masters of the situation. There are ninety of them (twenty-seven priests), and they collect alms enough to give food, on an average, to two hundred travellers and 'poveri' a day; while on any great festa they give to eat to over a thousand."[1]

In Switzerland, Germany, and Austria, several of the religious orders are flourishing; and where monks are banished, Sisters of Mercy go about in their habits, and carry on the traditions of the religious life in one or more of its characteristics. A very large Carthusian convent has been built at

[1] *Life of Dean Church* (Macmillan).

Parkminster, in the Parish of Cowfold, Sussex, with a fine church, and was completed and opened in 1886. There are thirty-six monks. This was founded when the religious orders were for the most part driven from France, and when it was feared that the Grande Chartreuse would be confiscated, from which many relics were brought hither. The Grand Chartreuse was, however, spared, because the French revenue would have lost the profits derived from the manufacture and sale of the liqueur at the abbey.

Most of the other Orders, both for men and women, are represented in different places in the United Kingdom, and are found to be adapted to the requirements of our own time, and are constantly supplied with applicants for admission. Some monasteries are said to have been secretly set up in England in the seventeenth century. James II. brought many monks to England. Mr. Wild established a branch of La Trappe at Lulworth in the eighteenth century, which received some orphans of the murdered French nobility.

In 1831 a Roman Catholic landowner gave some acres of barren ground for the establishment of a Cistercian monastery on his estates in Leicestershire. A few monks and lay brothers came from Ireland, and settled themselves in such poor hovels as they could build for themselves. Gradually the nave of the church has been erected, and considerable buildings for the monks, for guests, and for farm purposes. The Cistercian Rule is followed in all its strictness.' No meat is eaten, and there is but one meagre meal a day for the greater part of the year, but at certain times a second slight refection is taken. The monks rise at two in the morning to say the first offices in the church, and the other six offices, besides masses, are regularly recited by the monks, the lay brothers only attending twice, and saying short prayers at the other hours, while they are at their work. All the members, whether lay or clerical, do exactly the same work, which consists of farm labour, gardening, cattle breeding, and doing all the work of the establishment, washing, cooking, making clothes, gas-making, attending to the steam-engine, waiting upon guests and boarders, feeding the poor at the gates, and repairing the buildings. The clerical monks go out to conduct Retreats and Missions. Many priests retire to the abbey for a period of rest, or spiritual refreshment, and old and superannuated priests often spend the last years of their lives in the monastery.

Among the modern forms of Monasticism that have flourished in the Roman Church, there is none more practical and better adapted for introduction into the Church of England, than that of the Society of the "Christian Brothers." The founder of this most successful institution was Jean Baptiste de la Salle, who was born of a family of ancient and honourable lineage at Rheims, in 1651. By one of the bad customs that prevailed at that time, De la Salle was made a canon of the cathedral, when he was only sixteen years of age. He set himself at once to prepare for minor orders, and studied at Cambrai and at St. Sulpice in Paris, and was finally ordained priest in 1678. His first work outside his cathedral was the care of an orphanage in the town. A rich and pious lady at Rheims had founded a free school for boys, and De la Salle was persuaded to superintend its management; and soon afterwards a second school was commenced. The masters of these schools were provided with a house, and De la Salle drew up a code of regulations for their life, and finally he removed them to his own house, and lived entirely with them. The majority of the young men, however, soon found the rule of life required of them too severe, and all but two left. Others were presently found ready and willing to conform themselves to the semi-monastic regulations imposed upon them, and a larger and more commodious house was secured for their home, where the little community continued to reside till the Revolution of 1792, when in the name of liberty they were driven into the street, and their house was confiscated. In 1880 the society was enabled, by the contributions of religious people, to buy back its premises for 10,000 francs, and the brothers still occupy them, and conduct a school for four hundred poor children of the town of Rheims.

In 1683 De la Salle resigned his canonry, and actually gave away to the poor his own private fortune, that he might unite himself in poverty and dependence to his school-masters. He had great difficulty for some time in accustoming himself to the plain and scanty food that his funds could afford, and with little sleep and hard work he lived a most ascetic and mortified life. He now adopted the title of "Frères des Écoles Chrétiennes" for his brothers, and clothed them in a plain cassock and a long black cloak made of strong and coarse material. Several of the school-masters died, others retired at the end of a year or two, finding the work and life too hard for them, and other difficulties arose in the little community; but nothing daunted the devoted Superior, who ever found in earnest and long-continued prayer his solace and strength. To complete his self-abnegation, in 1686 he resigned his office of Superior, and caused one of the brothers to be elected in his place, while he himself became but one of the school-masters, rendering loyal obedience and respect to the newly-appointed Superior. This act brought the patience of his friends and relations to a crisis. They had been scandalized before that a man of birth and education, a doctor of divinity, and a Canon of Rheims, should stoop to the humble position and employment that he had chosen, but now they persuaded the Archbishop to interfere, and by his order De la Salle was once more re-instated as Superior.

The fame of his schools soon spread, and the country clergy began to beg him to provide them with devout and able school-masters. This led to an extension of the work, and a training college was commenced. All this time there was no endowment, and it is hard to say how money was found to support some fifty persons; but the venture of faith was approved by God, and money came in, not in abundance, but in sufficiency for the modest wants of the little society.

In 1688 De la Salle was urgently entreated by the Curé of St. Sulpice in Paris, to undertake the charge of the parish schools, which had fallen into a most disorganized condition; and with considerable reluctance, and not without opposition from the Archbishop of Rheims, he at last, with two brothers, commenced the difficult task which was demanded of him. Jealousy and slander hindered his work as soon as it began to prosper, and a serious illness prostrated him for a time. Death again thinned the number of his workers; legal proceedings were taken against him; and a variety of troubles fell upon him, but did not crush him, or deter him from pushing on his labour of love.

In 1691 a house was taken at Vaugirard as a place of rest for the brothers who broke down under the pressure of hard work and poor food and lodging, and as a home for the training of novices. Here unstinting hospitality was given to all who claimed it; and the charity that offered it was often abused. Passing clergy used the house as a free hotel, and many young men came out of curiosity, or under the mistaken idea that they were fitted for the work of the Society, and after staying for a time, left without joining it, and without making any return for their maintenance.

In 1694 the regulations that had already governed the Community were formulated into a Rule, and it became a regular religious order. Young men were not to be received under the age of sixteen. No one was allowed to take the vows for more than three years till he was of the age of twenty-five years. After that period life-vows might be taken. The vows were five in number. Besides the ordinary three vows of Poverty, Chastity, and Obedience, there was the vow of steadfastness to continue in the Society for the time agreed upon, and the vow by which a promise was made to teach children the Christian religion without payment or remuneration of any kind. The Superior must not be a priest. The daily routine of the brothers' life was as follows. Rise at 4.30 all the year round. Devotions till six. Mass and study till 7.15. Breakfast, followed by prayer in preparation for the day's work. School at eight till eleven, the children being taken to church during the morning. Self-examination at 11.30, then dinner, then recreation till one. Prayer in the oratory. School at 1.30 till five. After school the brothers return to the oratory, and at 5.30 there is spiritual reading till six, when half-an-hour is occupied in mental prayer; after which the brothers confess to one another the faults they have committed during the day. Supper at 6.30, with reading aloud from the Bible, or some devotional book. Recreation till eight. Then study of the Catechism till 8.30; then evening prayers in the oratory. Bed at nine.

De la Salle wrote several books on different branches of education, and in his manuals instruction is given as to time-tables, subjects of lessons, classing of children, their various dispositions, and the best methods of dealing with each, the furniture of the school-room, lighting, heating, &c.

In 1688 a school of a higher class was commenced, especially for the sons of English and Irish refugees after the Revolution in England in that year; and shortly afterwards a Sunday-school for elder lads was also opened in Paris. In 1703 the unattached school-masters of Paris, alarmed at the success of the free schools of the brothers, got up a violent attack upon the Community, and persuaded the municipality of Paris to espouse their cause. The schools of the brothers were closed, and they themselves were treated with personal violence. De la Salle retired to Rouen, and many new schools were opened in other parts of France, to which he himself travelled on foot.

In 1717 De la Salle once more resigned the office of Superior, and Frère Barthelémy became the second Superior of the Society; in 1719 the saintly founder died.

At this time the Christian Brothers possessed twenty-seven houses, and there were 274 brothers and 9885 children in their schools. In 1720 the Pope confirmed the Rule, and gave the institute the rank of a religious order.

In 1792 the National Assembly abolished the Order, with all other civil and religious corporations. In 1802 Napoleon, as First Consul, endeavoured to collect the scattered members of the institute who still survived, and remained in France, and several houses were reopened. At the Revolution of 1830 all Government grants were withdrawn from the schools, and the brothers were attacked by the Press; but private benevolence and Christian feeling gave them assistance, and in 1833 M. Guizot, then Minister of Public Instruction, recognized the good work they had done, and, Protestant as he was, he persuaded his Government to make them an annual grant of 8400 francs.

When Frère Philippe was Superior, the Society made great advances, and extended its labours into several new channels, and the number of boys under instruction was several thousands.

During the siege of Paris in 1871, one of the houses was struck by a shell which killed five boys and mutilated many more. On account of the famine price of provisions, it was found most difficult to feed the children; some were sent home, but food never actually failed for those who remained, who for safety were lodged in the college. The brothers then volunteered to receive the wounded into their houses, and to act as an ambulance corps in the battle-fields, and to bury the dead. Small-pox and fever broke out in the army; the brothers fearlessly nursed the sufferers. During the Commune "every single individual who pronounces the name of God" was doomed to be shot; the houses of the brothers were looted by the mob, and any who were found were imprisoned as "hostages." After the restoration of order, the brothers reopened their houses, and recommenced all their good works. In 1878 their numbers had increased to 11,640; they had 1249 establishments, and 390,607 scholars. The efficiency of the schools was proved by the large number of open scholarships and exhibitions gained by the pupils. Notwithstanding the Government favour and assistance of the secular schools, out of 490 exhibitions, 364 were adjudged to the boys of the Christian Brothers' schools, by examiners whose inclination and interest it was to favour the secular schools.

The French Government has done everything possible to hinder the work of the Christian Brothers, and to put an end to their schools. They have withdrawn all grants of public money, and have taxed the country to support the secular schools, and to make them efficient and attractive, and even to give food to the children. But the noble efforts of godly people have maintained the Christian schools, and raised the number of scholars in them in Paris alone from 50,000 to 60,000.[1]

A report (1896) by M. Thureau-Daugni, of the French Academy, states that from 1879 to 1892 the pupils of the Christian Brothers' schools had nearly doubled, and that in the latter year they were educating 1,365,886 children. About a quarter of a million of children had been withdrawn from the secular State schools, and sent to those of the Brothers. This is the more remarkable, because the State had all this time been making great efforts to improve the attractions of the secular schools. The

[1] This sketch has been made from the book of Mrs. R. F. Wilson on *The Christian Brothers*. Kegan Paul, 1883.

Education Grant, which amounted to 94,000,000 francs in 1877, had grown to 185,000,000 in 1892.

In the United States of America the growth of Monasticism is rapid and extensive.

In the East the ancient monasteries remain wherever the Turk has, for one reason or another, abstained from his usual policy of destruction. These monasteries seem to be deficient in activity and adaptation to the changed circumstances of the times, but they appear to be free from the imputation of immorality which has often been brought against Western monks. Thus Mr. O. H. Parry writes, "The Syrian Patriarch, who has two hundred thousand subjects of the Porte who acknowledge him as their head, besides three hundred thousand subjects of the Queen on the Malabar coast and in Ceylon, recently declared that he would not believe a charge made against a monk, because during all his ninety-five years such a charge had never occurred."[1]

Mr. Curzon, in his *Visits to the Monasteries of the Levant*, gives an interesting account of the convents at Mount Athos, in Syria, the islands of Cyprus, and in Bulgaria, Asia Minor, and Persia. Some of these are very ancient, dating even back to the fifth century. Many are built upon the summit of rocks, and are only accessible by ladders, or by baskets drawn up by ropes. The monks are very ignorant, but there are no reports of scandals or immorality against them. Their discipline is very severe ; they never eat meat ; they have above a hundred fast days in

[1] *Six Months in a Syrian Monastery.*

the year; their prayers occupy eight hours in the day and about two in the night.

Miss F. P. Cobbe thus describes a visit to Mar Saba, "Through the arid burning rocks a profound and sharply-cut chasm suddenly opens and winds, forming a hideous valley, such as may exist in the unpeopled moon. Barren, burning, glaring rocks alone are to be seen on every side. Along the ravine in an almost inaccessible gorge of the hills, are the caves and holes half-way down the precipice, the dwellings of the hermits. We could see some of them, as we passed, sitting at the mouth of their caverns, or walking on the little ledges of rock which they had smoothed for terraces. Their food (such as it is) is sent from the convent, and let down from the cliffs at needful intervals. Otherwise they live absolutely alone in this hideous desolation of nature, with the lurid, blasted desert for their sole share in God's beautiful universe. There are many such hermits still in the Greek Church. I have seen their eyries perched where only vultures should have their nests, on the cliffs of Caramania, and among the caverns of the Cyclades."[1]

In the dark forests of Muscovy, by the frozen waters of Archangel, is carried out the same rigid system, at least in outward form, that was born and nurtured in the burning desert of Thebaïd. There is no variety of monastic order in Russia. The one name of Black Clergy is applied to all alike. The one Rule of St. Basil governs them all. Hermits still exist, and display the wild asceticism of Stylites and Antony.

[1] *Life of Miss F. P. Cobbe*, vol. i.

The Monastery of the Troitzka (Holy Trinity) (1338) is an immense pile, containing university, palace, and cathedral. The Donskoi is another vast fortress monastery, and the Simonoff Convent is similar. From the walls of the Kremlin the eye rests on the towers of enormous monasteries, which at regular intervals encircle the whole city, each encompassed with embattled walls. The same may be said of Novgorod.

Visitors give interesting accounts of the convents, and in not a few cases show how even the unchanging Greek Church can feel the pressure of the times, and adapt monastic life to the circumstances and requirements of the age and of the particular country where it is flourishing. Thus, for example, Mr. W. Hepworth Dixon writes in his book on *Free Russia*, "The steamer that conveyed pilgrims to the monastery of Solovetsk was manned by monks in cowl and frock, captain, mate, steward, engineer, and cook. As we start every head bows, and every hand makes the sign of the cross ; and the same whenever a church is passed. As the wind rises, all join in hymns for protection. . . At the monastery are crane and dock and tramway, not found generally in Russian ports ; the monks, as of old, being the pioneers of science. . . In the monastery is every sort of work, ship-building, fishing, farming, painting, photography, &c. &c. The charities are boundless. Boys are educated ; pilgrims and the poor far and wide are fed and helped. The convent is a hive of industry—forges, dairies, salting-rooms, studies, ship-yards, bakehouses, weaving-sheds, rope-walks, sewing-rooms, fruit-stores, breweries, boot-shops, &c. &c., all carried on by monks, on an islet locked up by ice eight months in the year. A steamer was entirely planned and built there. Her captain is a monk and a priest."

Professor Bryce thus describes a visit in 1876 to the principal monastery of the Armenian Church, at Etchmiadzin,[1] "The monastery of Etchmiadzin (here, as in Russia, it is at monasteries that Episcopal sees are fixed; every Russian prelate lives in one) has frequently been destroyed or injured by the numerous invaders that have swept over the country, and as often restored. The present church is supposed to contain some bits of wall as old as the fourth century, the main body of it being ascribed to the seventh or eighth. . . . Within the lofty and embattled walls that enclose the monastery, which has in its day repelled many a band of Tartar or Persian marauders, and may perhaps even have stood sieges before the days of cannon, there lies a great mass of buildings of different kinds, as well as some gardens and open spaces. Besides the cells of the monks, who number from twenty to thirty, there are apartments for the Patriarch and for the archbishops, bishops, and archimandrites from other monasteries, who are frequently to be found here, consulting him on the affairs of their churches, or attending the general and supreme synod, which sits, almost in permanence, under his presidency. There are many subsidiary buildings, and among them a sort of bazaar, where some trade

[1] *Transcaucasia and Ararat* (Macmillan).

is done, chiefly in hay and corn produced by the monastic lands ; in fact, one has almost a little town within the walls of this fortress-convent, a mile in circuit. Finally, there is a seminary for the education of young Armenians chiefly, but not exclusively, with a view to their entering the priestly office. The school is supported by the monastic revenues, which, as they are said to amount to nearly £10,000 a year, arising partly from landed property here and in Georgia, but mainly from the contributions of the loyal Armenian churches throughout the world, can well afford this charge, in addition to the sum paid to the Patriarch, and the maintenance of the monks in their establishment. There are about eighty boys or young men there attending, who are lodged in the monastery, and for the most part remain in it from the beginning to the end of their education, coming often from great distances. A magazine, called *Ararat*, has recently been established, and is printed at the monastery ; nor is the press of Etchmiadzin idle in producing educational manuals. . . . The dress of the monks consists of a long black robe of thin serge, and a peaked cap, from which a sort of veil falls over the neck and shoulders. On the whole, they impress the traveller more favourably than the inmates of convents generally do; inferior as they are in learning and polish to the brethren of the famous Western foundation, the mother of all Western monastic houses, which is perhaps the chief rival of Etchmiadzin 'in antiquity and historical fame—the great Benedictine abbey of Monte Casino."

Nor is the Church of England altogether without examples of revived Monasticism in one or other of its forms. The Society of Mission Priests of St. John, founded in 1865, at Cowley, aims at the practice of both the active and contemplative religious life. Thus, in the preface to the Statutes, it is laid down, that "The Society of the Mission Priests of St. John the Evangelist has been formed for the cultivation of a life dedicated to God, according to the principles of Poverty, Chastity, and Obedience, and will occupy itself in works both missionary and educational, both at home and abroad, for the advancement of the Kingdom of Christ, as God in His good providence may seem to call." The Society has done good work in various parts of Great Britain, in India, at Cape Town, and at Boston in America, where a branch house was established in 1872.

The Pusey House at Oxford, and the Bethnal Green Mission are also foundations of a similar character.

In 1877 a Missionary Brotherhood was formed at Cambridge, which has been working ever since in India.

In 1879 a Missionary Brotherhood undertook work in Tokyo, Japan.

In 1890 a Brotherhood was formed in Trinity College, Dublin, and in 1891 the members commenced work at Chota Nagpur in India, under the Bishop of Calcutta.

In the *Church Times* of August 23, 1895, it is reported—" The Society of St. Paul, consisting of ' priests and laymen separated and consecrated to the service of God, and our sailors in holy religion,' originally founded at Calcutta under Father Hopkins, and now removed to England, with its headquarters at Barry, near Cardiff, is the beginning of a movement which is sure to be watched with genuine interest, and, what is still more certain, will receive the criticism of friends and foes alike, neither of which should affect it injuriously.

"A friend has presented to the society some thirteen acres of land in one of the most beautiful parts of Hampshire, and a wing of the temporary Abbey building has already been erected. The present accommodation consists of three rooms, an entrance hall and a kitchen, and here some of the Brothers are in possession, and before the winter sets in it is hoped that sufficient progress in building will be made to enable the postulants and novices to settle down to quiet study and training during the long winter evenings. All these particulars we learn from Father Hopkins' monthly letter in the *Messenger*, and also the fact that an additional £250 will be needed if the building is to go on. The Brothers are building the outhouses with their own hands, their skill in the craft evidently not being such as to justify them in dealing with the main building. Father Hopkins anticipates that these temporary buildings will last for quite a century, and by then 'we all anticipate that the Order will be firmly established, and in a position to build a real and goodly abbey proper.' Father Hopkins also explains the object of this new development of the work. He says—' The Brothers in India, as well as clerical and other friends at home, have constantly urged upon me the advisability of separating the Novitiate from direct contact with active work amongst seamen; and for the last eight years I myself have seen the necessity of it; but not until now have I seen my way clear to the accomplishment of it. Around our quiet home here we hope also to gather a few of our aged seamen, and two are with us now helping in the house and garden work. Thus our Abbey Camp will be threefold in its usefulness to us. It will be (1) the Mother house for the centralization of direction and control of the other houses at home and abroad; (2) it will be the training home of the young members of the Order; and (3) a home of rest and refuge for the aged and infirm, be they Fathers, Brothers, or seamen.'"

Other Brotherhoods have been formed, or are in course of formation, at Radley, under Canon Gore; at Plaistow, by Rev. Hon. J. Adderley; at Wolverhampton, by Mr. Colville;[1] at Barking, by Canon Mason; at Gloucester, by Canon Bowers; in South London, by Bishop Yeatman; besides numerous Guilds which partake more or less of the character of religious communities.

Among the numerous philanthropic efforts to help the victims of crime and misfortune, and the sufferers from the weak points of our modern civilization, there is none more practical and successful than the

[1] Note L, p. 389.

CHURCH ARMY. It is not a monastic institution, but its principles and the motives of its founder and its active members are the same as those that, as we have seen, are the root and the moving impulse of Monasticism, love of God and love of man, a desire to imitate Christ, and to follow Him literally in His precepts and practice. There is a band of lay evangelists, whose work is not unlike that of the preaching Friars in their early and purer days. These are regularly trained in well-ordered houses, and are then sent out into the low parts of great cities and the remote districts of the country to hold personal intercourse especially with men, to teach them the elements of godliness, and to be their friends in every way. Women are trained as nurses. There are homes, refuges, and workshops for those who are out of employment, laundries, food depôts, emigration offices, dispensaries, registries for providing situations, second-hand clothes sale-rooms, coffee taverns, and other institutions. Mission vans are sent round with preachers and distributors of books; lantern services and lectures are given. Large numbers of publications are issued. Sympathy and external assistance are obtained by associations, working parties, collectors, and prayer unions.

A very remarkable instance of the revival of an old Order, and its adaptation to the requirements of the times, is seen in the case of the Order of the Hospitallers of St. John of Jerusalem. This Order was originally founded in 1104 for housing pilgrims at Jerusalem, and for protecting them on their way. It was suppressed in England, with the other religious orders, by Henry VIII., but has been revived, and in 1871 a code of statutes was adopted, and officers appointed. The Order assists the patients of the London Hospitals; it has established a hospital at Ashford, in Kent; it gives medals for saving life, &c.; it has provided and maintains a complete ambulance service for use at mining and colliery districts; and has founded *The National Society for the Aid of the Sick and Wounded in War.*

There are now (1896) 6500 members, besides 700 nursing sisters, and 146 surgeons, in the Ambulance Brigade.

There are also many Brotherhoods in the United States. *The Living Church*, Dec. 1893, gives the following account of some of these—

The Order of the Holy Cross, Westminster, Md. U.S.A. Founded, 1881. A Religious Order for Priests and Laymen. Objects: The discipline of the spiritual life in prayer and good works, especially in giving missions and retreats.

The Order of Brothers of Nazareth (Incorporated), U.S.A. Founded, 1886. A Religious Order for Laymen. Objects: Prayer and manual work. Persons living in the world desiring to further the objects of the Brotherhood are admitted as Associates. The works of the Community are: All Saints Convalescent Home for men and boys; De Peyster Home for consumptive boys and young men; industrial training on the farm for boys; St. Andrew's Cottage; "Fresh Air Work." Rahberg, a Clergy House of Rest. The Mother House is at Verbank, Dutchess Co., N.Y.

The Brotherhood of St. Andrew.—An organization for the spread of Christ's kingdom among young men. There are now 911 Chapters, and about 11,000 members. Central Office, New York.

At the Church Congress at Norwich (1895), Mr. A. Giles said respecting this society—

"I cannot speak of it without regarding it as a world-wide order, bound by and interlaced with two rules, in the logical application of which the Brotherhood of St. Andrew has been the only means by which the earnestness and enthusiasm of young men have been called out in the Church of the United States.

"The rule of prayer is to pray daily for the spread of Christ's kingdom among young men, and for God's blessing upon the labours of the brotherhood. The rule of service is to make an earnest effort each week to bring at least one young man within hearing of the Gospel of Jesus Christ, as set forth in the service of the Church and young men's Bible-classes. What the American Church has seen, and that in the colonies is observing, is, that to get at men the Church must use the young men to move among them, that it must deliver unto these a message, clothe them with a holy consciousness that they have a work to perform, and send them forth as messengers of Christ to deal with men in prayer and with tact.

"While some are busy around drawing friends and acquaintances in the direction of the house of God, special are the plans in aisle and pew for caring for strangers and welcoming young men. Bringing the unbaptized to baptism, others to confirmation and Holy Communion, which 500 chapters particularize, is another effort. Six hundred emphasize bringing some to Church services and Bible-classes. Of 400 Bible-classes clergy conduct 162, laymen 238, and ladies eight. At boarding-houses and on the streets attractive cards of welcome to services and classes are distributed in hundreds of parishes; while visiting young men in their homes is the work of most, and certainly of 400, chapters. About 200 chapters carry on Missions, and 300 engage in visitation of hotels to direct men to or induce them to go to church. Sick and poor, those in hospitals and prisons, are extensively visited. Fifty chapters manage rescue Missions. Seven-hundred Brotherhood men are lay-readers, and 184 are preparing for holy orders. Special men's services, men's clubs, and work among sailors have largely occupied the attention of many, as have also meetings for various purposes. The training of boys for the Brotherhood has been a speciality of 160 chapters. But I may say that the methods of work are multifarious, nothing being done without the knowledge of the rector. Lay co-operation, not lay rivalry or lay interference, is essential to a chapter's usefulness and continuance. Bazaars, concerts, and other entertainments, and likewise financial schemes, are excluded from the Brotherhood idea. Members who engage in such do so as individuals apart from Brotherhood obligations.

"Under due licence, lay-readers have gone about with their chapter members to outlying or to populous districts, and held services, simple but sufficient to touch hearts and awake consciences. Churches and Mission stations have been the result of new ground thus broken. Similar efforts have also drawn many to regular Church ordinances, for there are numbers who will only respond to unconventional services, who yet afterwards are induced to tread regular paths. The coldness and rigidity which characterize too many of our present congregations do not give a salutary first impression. It is the province of the Brotherhood to introduce and supply a felt warmth into every aisle, and a heartiness of worship into every pew, and to miss no opportunity of bridging the way to the church porch. Nor have home Missions satisfied the young Americans; their branch has now a missionary in Japan and another in China, and the Church has formally declared the Brotherhood one of its missionary auxiliaries. (To Japan the Scottish Brotherhood has twice contributed.)

"You will understand that a society pledged to seek must take care not to lose. A chapter's home responsibility therefore lies to a degree in not letting a single man leave home without commendation mailed to where he is going, and by his own hand delivered to a church or chapter when he reaches his destination.

"I hope it is plain to every one that the Brotherhood is an effort to awake the zeal of the laity, much of whose work, to quote from Bishop Westcott, has in the past been added by the clergy to their own, to their mutual and grievous loss. It is more. The embodiment of the ministry of laymen, indeed, a fellowship after St. Francis d'Assisi, who never received the priesthood, is in it presented to men. . . . In political and commercial life an astounding abundance of youthful lay energy is displayed, and the Church claims a rightful portion of enthusiasts, so that in the ingredients of the world's freshest life there may be a fair amount of salt that has its savour to preserve noble souls for the world to come. The first Brotherhood members at St. James's, Chicago, had no idea of a society. In three years they increased the men at church from a handful to 300. Their example was copied; the success of simplicity spread. It passed from West to East, went South and North, crossed the boundaries of states, territories and oceans, to be known in Britain, and to appear at the Antipodes. It has touched India, Germany, Japan, and Brazil, and now numbers about 20,000 men."[1]

There is moreover throughout the Anglican communion a deep and widespread desire for the revival of the religious life in all its forms, especially for men. A large amount of literature has been published dealing with the question in all its bearings; for example: A paper on Religious Life for Men, by Fr. Benson, in the *Literary Churchman*, April 5, 1889; another by the same, read at the Church Congress, at Manchester, 1888; also papers by the Dean of Lincoln, Rev. C. J. Ridgeway, Rev. Dr. Maclear, and others; an address by Fr. Goreh, in the Sheldonian Theatre, Oxford;[2] a Defence of Religious Vows, by Fr. Convers, *Eclectic Review* (American), Sept. 1892; a paper by Fr. Page, at the Missionary Conference;

[1] See Note L, p. 389.   [2] See Note M, p. 390.

another by Mr. Kenward, on the need of a "Preaching Order," at the Church Congress, at Birmingham, 1893, and many others.

The subject of the formation of Brotherhoods, both for home and foreign mission work, has constantly occupied the attention of Convocation, and of various Diocesan Conferences. Thus—

Norwich D.C. 1888.—Resolved: "That an extension of the system of community of life among her clergy and her lay workers is greatly needed by the Church in her mission work at home and abroad, and that a committee be formed to inquire and report how such a scheme may best be carried out."

Canterbury Convocation U.H. 1888.—Resolved: "That a joint committee of both Houses be appointed to consider and report as to any organization that may be found to be required for enabling the Church to reach those classes of the population which are now, from a variety of causes, outside religious ministrations."

Southwell D.C. 1889.—Resolved: "That it is desirable to meet the needs of our rapidly-growing population by forming Clergy Brotherhoods in aid of and in consensual union with the parochial clergy."

Norwich D.C. 1889.—Resolved: "That this Conference recommends the adoption and extension of the principle of community of life in the mission work of the Church at home and abroad."

Canterbury Convocation L.H. 1889.—Resolved: "That, in the opinion of this House, the time has come when the Church can, with advantage, avail herself of the voluntary self-devotion of Brotherhoods, both clerical and lay, the members of which are willing to labour in the service of the Church, without appealing for funds to any form of public support."

Exeter D.C. 1890.—Resolved: "That this Conference approves of the establishment of Brotherhoods as a means of reaching the masses of the people who are beyond the present organizations of the Church."

Lichfield D.C. 1890.—Resolved: "That this Conference

approves, on the whole, of the recommendations of the Lower House of Convocation and commends the same to the prayerful consideration of the Church."

Oxford D.C. 1890.—Resolved: "That this Conference feels that the masses of population accumulating in our urban centres can only be met satisfactorily by the organization of communities of men living lives of dedication for prayer and missionary effort in the midst of them."

Winchester D.C. 1890.—Resolved: "That it is desirable to establish Communities of both clergy and laity for the purpose of mission work in the Diocese, and that such Brotherhoods should work in strict subordination to the Bishop of each Diocese in which they are established, and only on the invitation and under the sanction of the parochial clergy."

St. Albans D.C. 1891.—Resolved: "To strengthen her work the Church may with advantage, among other agencies, avail herself of the voluntary self-devotion of Brotherhoods, clerical and lay, the members of which are willing to labour in the service of the Church under the sanction and control of Diocesan Bishops."

York D.C. 1891.—Resolved: "That it is desirable in many parishes to supplement the existing parochial system by the help of Brotherhoods, or other evangelistic agencies under the control of the Bishop, and in every case (save for very grave and exceptional reasons) on the invitation and with the co-operation of the parish priest."

Canterbury Convocation L.H. 1890.—Resolved: (2) "That a wide elasticity is desirable as to the rules and system of such Brotherhoods as may be formed in the several dioceses." (3) "That the members of such Brotherhoods should be allowed to bind themselves by dispensable vows of celibacy, poverty, and obedience." (4) "That such Brotherhoods should work in strict subordination to the authority of the Bishop of each Diocese in which they are established, and only on the invitation and under the sanction of the parochial clergy."

Canterbury Convocation U.H. 1891.—Resolved: (1) "That this House, recognizing the value of sisterhoods and of deaconesses and the importance of their work, considers that the Church ought definitely to extend to them her care and guidance." (2) "That those who enter a sisterhood shall be permitted, after an adequate term of probation, and being not less than thirty years of age, to undertake lifelong engagements to the work of the community, provided that such engagements be liable to release by competent authority." (3) "That the form of such engagements should be a promise made at the time of admission, before the Bishop or his commissary, from which, if the Bishop think fit, upon cause shown, he might subsequently release the sister." (4) "That the statutes of the community should be sanctioned by the Bishop under his hand, and not be changed without his approval, signified in like manner." (5) "That no statutes should contain any provision which would interfere with the freedom of any individual sister to dispose of her property as she may think fit." (6) "That no branch house of a sisterhood should be established or any branch work undertaken in any Diocese without the written consent of the Bishop of such Diocese." (7) "That no work external to the community should be undertaken by the sisters in any parish without the written consent of the incumbent of such parish, subject, if that be refused, to an appeal to the Bishop." (8) "That deaconesses having, according to the best authorities, formed an order of ministry in the early Church, and having proved their efficiency in the Anglican Church wherever the order has been revived, it is desirable to encourage the formation of deaconesses' institutions, and the work of deaconesses in our Dioceses and parishes." (9) "That a deaconess should be admitted in solemn form by the Bishop, with benediction by the laying-on of hands." (10) "That there should be an adequate term of preparation and probation." (11) "That a deaconess so admitted may be released from her obligations by the Bishop, if he think fit, on cause shown." (12) "That a licence to serve in any parish should be given by the Bishop of the Diocese, at the request of the incumbent, to any deaconess employed therein." (13) "That the dress of a deaconess should be simple, but distinctive." (14) "That a deaconess should not pass from one Diocese to another without the written permission of the Bishop." (15) "That special care should be taken to provide for every deaconess sufficient time and opportunity for the strengthening of her own spiritual life."

House of Laymen, 1890.—Resolved : (1) "That this House is of opinion that the sanction of the Church should be given to such communities or brotherhoods, whether lay or clerical, as shall undertake to labour for the salvation of souls and the service of the Church : provided always (*a*) that their rules be approved by the Bishop of the Diocese, and (*b*) that they work in strict subordination to the Bishop of the Diocese, and on the invitation and under the sanction of the incumbent of the parish." (2) "That the members of such communities or brotherhoods should be allowed to bind themselves by vows of celibacy, poverty, and obedience, the Bishop of the Diocese having the power at any time to release any member from such vows."

Canterbury Convocation, U.H. & L.H. 1891.—Resolved: (*a*) "That those who enter a brotherhood should be permitted, after an adequate term of probation, and being not less than thirty years of age, to undertake lifelong engagements to the life and work of the community, provided that such engagements be subject, on cause shown, to release by the Bishop of the Diocese in which the brotherhood is established." (*b*) "That the statutes of the community should be sanctioned by the Bishop under his hand, and not be changed without his approval signified in like manner." (*c*) "In every body of statutes it is desirable that provision should be made for the exclusion of unworthy or inefficient members of the brotherhood, with the assent of the Bishop."

Hertford D.C. 1892.—Resolved: "That the spiritual work of the Church, both in town and country, might be furthered by the existence and aid of brotherhoods."

Canterbury D.C. 1892.—Resolved: "That the plans for the formation of Brotherhoods and the increase of lay ministrations deserve all possible consideration in view of the pressing spiritual needs of the times."

London D.C. 1892.—Resolved: "That in view of the increasing demand for trained women in Church work, it is expedient that the primitive order of deaconesses be more fully developed as one of the authorized organizations of the Church of England."[1]

The following passage in Rev. S. Kettlewell's *Thomas à Kempis, and the Brothers of the Common Life*, expresses that which seems to be a general and growing belief among Anglican Churchmen: "It is a question well worth considering and think-

[1] *The Official Year Book*, 1892—1895.

ing out by leading men, who are anxious for the spread of true religion, whether or not institutions might not yet be made to some extent a blessing to this country, if fashioned with care, carried on wisely, and somewhat associated with the common life, after the pattern of those with which Thomas à Kempis was connected; where by plain living and constant work of a suitable character, a high tone of religionship might be maintained. Places—call them monasteries or not, or Brotherhoods, Sisterhoods, or with a simpler title, Christian settlements—where the members might live together in an unostentatious manner, with vows or without, or under agreement for a certain time, wearing simple clothing, not of too distinctive a character; where, nevertheless, a rigid discipline might be carried out, more time given to the service of God, to devout meditation, prayer, reading, and the self-culture of the mind and spirit; not that they should live to themselves, or seclude themselves from their fellow-men, but trying to imitate the life of Christ after the manner of the primitive Christians, 'who had all things common,' and were 'of one heart and one mind'; they should be most diligent in all good works, going in and out among men with this very purpose, not having a thought of their own advancement, interests, or credit, but having the welfare of their fellow-creatures near them constantly in view; they should constantly endeavour to draw those whom they could influence to think less of themselves and of the world, to live nearer to God, to prepare more for the life to come, and to heed less what should befall them in this present life, so long as they had food and clothing, so that they might gain at last the heavenly inheritance provided for them. Not only might such institutions be the means of raising up among us more saint-like characters than we have at present, but might be a refuge for many weary, forlorn souls, who have found the emptiness of all this world has to offer, and a help to them in attaining to that eternal rest for which they long; might largely conduce to lead many other Christians who have to engage in worldly business to strive after a higher life than they are wont; and might produce a class of men and women better fitted from their habits of simplicity, order, obedience, self-denial, and devotion, to do much effective work among the spiritually destitute, who want some one to speak to them about their souls, and to care for them. We are not all constituted alike, any more than we are all in like circumstances, or alike of one height; and there is no reason why the Christian life should be always cut after one pattern and to one measure after some procrustean idea. Some persons are capable of higher attainments of grace and of the divine life than others; they have stronger desires than others to give themselves wholly to God and the good of their fellow-men, which others have not, and are not capable of attaining in the same degree. Why should they not be permitted and encouraged to do this? The world around us suffers from not having a higher standard kept before it of the Christian life. The rule of our

Saviour on such matters is, 'He that is able to receive it, let him receive it.'"

In Lent, 1895, the Bishop of Argyle invited the clergy and laity of his Diocese to join him in a Retreat at Iona, "to consider whether they have a call from God to work out their salvation in what is generally known among us as the Religious Life."

But if the revival of the religious life for men, while it is so earnestly and generally desired, has after all at present been only partially obtained, it must not be supposed that on this account it is impossible of attainment. A devoted celibate priest thus writes on this subject—"You cannot create religious communities by public opinion, or by Convocation resolutions. The call of God to a dedicated life of special sacrifice makes a Religious; and however much we may want him, we cannot manufacture him. The Rule, the money, the habit, the convent may all be found, but it takes a Divine call, and years of spiritual training to make a well-established Religious. Probably our sisterhoods have had such a remarkable development, first, because the Bishops frowned upon them, or ignored them, and the newspapers published scandals about them, and they were mobbed by Protestant zealots (as the East Grinstead Sisters were). There was no popularity or romance about them to make them attractive; and religious dedication was nourished by neglect and obscurity. I think it would do good to emphasize this—the supernatural, *i.e.* the real side of the Religious Life, which is the least realized, and generally not at all understood. It is often thought to be little more than a matter of organization, costume, and a general desire to do good."

It must be remembered that the great Religious Orders of old began most modestly and obscurely, with the absolutely sacrificed life of one Christ-like man, and that they grew slowly and with many checks, and even failures. All life that we are acquainted with has this history and experience. "The husbandman has long patience" while the buried seed is germinating. "Rome was not built in one day." It is not the wise, and the devout, and the men whom God chooses for His work, who presumptuously cry in the face of the Almighty, "Let Him make speed, and hasten His work, that we may see it; and let the counsel of the Holy One draw nigh and come that we may know it."

But if patience and hope are needed while we desire and pray for and labour to re-establish brotherhoods, we are wonderfully encouraged and filled with thankfulness when we contemplate what has already been accomplished by the will of God in the foundation and marvellous growth of sisterhoods.

"We often hear it objected that the communities of men do not grow as much as those of women. This perhaps is not so much the case as it seems to be. Many men are drafted off as priests in mission districts, living a life which externally is not very different from that of a religious community, and are living lives perhaps of even greater hardship than would be required of them under religious vows.

Then again we must bear in mind that the dedication of a daughter to the Religious Life is by no means the same difficulty to the family which a dedication of a son would be. In some cases a daughter would rather relieve the family difficulties by so doing."[1]

"The state of Christendom for many centuries hindered the formation of such Orders as that of Sisters of Charity. Women were affiliated to the great Monastic Orders, but they were invariably cloistered. It was the glory of St. Vincent of Paul to found, in 1633, the Society of the 'Filles de la Charité,' and, by doing so, to lay the foundation of all modern religious communities leading an active life of charity. This Order now numbers some 40,000 Sisters, and has 2000 houses all over the world."

"There are now ten important Anglican Sisterhoods, namely, at Ascot; Clewer; St. Peter's, Kilburn; All Saints; East Grinstead; Wantage; St. Raphael's, Bristol; Lloyd Square, Clerkenwell; Hayward's Heath; and Randolph Gardens, Kilburn; with hundreds of houses all over England, and many in India, America, Australia, and China. Besides these, there are eleven smaller Sisterhoods, those at Ditchingham; St. Peter's, Vauxhall; Fulham; Belper; Birmingham; Brighton; Bussage; Horbury; North Ormesby; Oxford; Warminster; St. Mary and St. John, Aberdeen; Malling Abbey (contemplative and enclosed)."

The beginning of this great movement was made in 1845, when a small house near Christ Church,

[1] R. M. Benson, *Literary Churchman*, April 5, 1889.

Albany St., London, was taken for a few ladies by Dr. Pusey and the present Duke of Rutland.

In 1849 Miss Sellon began a Sisterhood in Plymouth. In the same year the Sisterhood at Clewer originated in small beginnings through Mrs. Tennant.

The following particulars respecting the Anglican Sisterhoods at present existing in the several dioceses are given in *The Official Year Book*—

    Chichester.—**Sisterhood of St. Margaret**, The Convent, East Grinstead : To provide sisters to visit and attend the sick in their own homes, in hospitals, and infirmaries. (1) St. Margaret's Orphanage : Orphanage for girls, about eighty in number ; charge for each, £14 a year, but about thirty are received free. (2) St. Agnes' School : School for the daughters of professional men : Middle Class Day-school. (3) St. Katherine's, 32 Queen Square, Bloomsbury, W.C. : School of ecclesiastical embroidery. (4) St. Saviour's, Hitchin : Orphanage and Mission work. (5) St. Margaret's, Cardiff : Government Schools ; Middle Class Day-schools ; parochial work in six parishes. (6) St. Katherine's Hospital, Ventnor, Isle of Wight : Incurable cases of consumption. (7) St. Thomas's, Regent Street : Mission work, Golden Square. (8) Holy Trinity, Stirling : Mission work. (9) St. Margaret of Scotland, Aberdeen : Nursing, Mission, Schools, and Penitentiary work. (10) St. Saviour's Priory, 18 Great Cambridge Street, Hackney Road, E. : Nursing, Mission, and Schools in Haggerston and St. Paul's, Knightsbridge. (11) St. Margaret's, Boston, U.S.A. : Mission work : Industrial School ; and charge of hospitals. (12) Roath, Cardiff : House of Mercy and Refuge. (13) St. Margaret's, Miles Platting : parish work. (14) St. Margaret's Home, Kingsland : Convalescent Home for Ladies. (15) St. Margaret's, Polwatta, Colombo, Ceylon : Orphanage, Ladies' School, Middle-class School, and Mission work. (16) St. Alban's Home, Worcester : Certified Industrial Home. (17) St. Tydfil's Mission, Merthyr Tydfil : Mission work. (18) Home of the Good Shepherd, Hoar Cross, Burton-on-

Trent : Boys' Orphanage and Parochial work. (19) All Saints', Ennismore Gardens ; Parochial work. (20) St. Columba's, Southwick, Sunderland : Parochial work.

Sisters of the Holy Cross.—Mother House : Holy Cross Home, Hayward's Heath, Sussex (Diocese of Chichester) : Orphanage ; Training School ; Convalescent Home for Women, and visiting. Branch Houses : (1) Holy Cross Mission Home, Old Gravel Lane, London Docks. (2) Dover Holy Cross Mission Home : Mission work. (3) 37 Monkgates Park. (4) Holy Cross Mission, Winchester. The Convalescent Wing in the Mother Home was added last year; there are two divisions—one for ladies, and the other for middle-class patients.

Sisterhood of the Holy Ghost the Comforter, Worthing.—A community formed to provide "Sisters" to visit the sick in the hospital and infirmaries, and to attend private cases.

St. Raphael's Home and Hospital for Consumption.—Accommodates thirty patients—men, women, and children—on a small weekly payment. Patients ineligible for other hospitals or homes in consequence of advanced stages of phthisis are admitted. About 400 cases have received treatment, and several restored sufficiently to return to their homes and employment.

St. Michael's Repository.—For rendering assistance to the distressed families of the clergy by affording them an opportunity of partial support in selling their needlework, paintings, and carvings.

Embroidery taught by the Sisters, and orders executed. Also plain needlework undertaken.

Home of Rest for Church Workers, &c.—For nurses and others needing rest and sea air ; also ladies in distressed circumstances. Accommodation for twenty on payment of 7s. 6d. a week. Ladies must have reached the age of fifty at least, and be able to obtain references from two beneficed clergy and one lady well acquainted with their position and circumstances.

St. Mary's Home, 2, Queen Square, Brighton, founded 1855. The following works of mercy are carried on by the Sisters. (1) The Reformation of fallen girls and women ; over sixty are maintained without payment. (2) A Nursery is provided for orphan or destitute children. (3) School for older girls. (4) The Industrial School at Buxted, St. Margaret's Cottage. (5) A School for boys who form the choir at St. Paul's Church. When apprenticed, a separate home is provided for them, under the supervision of one of the clergy and the Sisters. (6) An Infirmary, which is chiefly occupied by the inmates; when there are vacancies other cases are taken. (7) The Dispensary annually relieves about 1000 of the poor. (8) A large amount of church embroidery is executed. (9) The Middle School is intended for the daughters of gentlemen of small means; a thorough education is given. Number of pupils, forty. Day-scholars are received. Full particulars can be had on application. The work is carried on by Sisters, assisted by associates and other ladies living in the town.

Gloucester and Bristol.—The Sisters of Charity, St. Raphael's, Bristol. (1) House of Charity, St. Raphael's, Bristol. (2) Infant Day Nursery, Philip Street, Bedminster. (3) Convalescent Home, Walton, Clevedon. (4) St. Agnes Industrial Home, Upper Knowle, Bristol. Accommodation for sixty children, £12 a year. (5) House of Charity, St. Saviour's, Leeds. (6) Mission House, St. Jude's, Bristol. (7) Mission House, St. Simon's, Bristol. (8) House of Rest, Convalescent Home, Plympton St. Mary, South Devon. (9) Magila, Central Africa, in connection with the Universities' Mission. (10) Mission House, Knowle.

Sisterhood of St. Michael and All Angels.—The Sisters have charge of the Bussage House of Mercy, which receives twenty-four penitents, and also work in the Parish of Bussage.

London.—Sisterhood of All Saints, 78 to 83 Margaret Street, W. Founded in 1851 for the care of aged and infirm persons, of the poor, and to train up orphans to useful employments. The following Works of Mercy are carried on by the Sisters: (1) 74 Margaret Street, W.: Orphanage for thirty-six girls, age six—fourteen. (2) 77 Margaret Street, W.: Training school for girls, age fourteen upwards. (3) 37, 59, and 61 Mortimer Street, W.: St. Elizabeth's Home for incurable women and children. (4) 4 Margaret Street, W.: ten small boys, age two—eleven, Hospital for incurable boys. (5) St. John's House, Norfolk Street, Strand: Trained nurses are sent out into private families. New Metropolitan Hospital, Kingsland Road. (6) All Saints' Convalescent Home, Beckenham : For married women with their infants. (7) Maternity Home for married women, 10 Queen Anne Terrace, Battersea : The poor are taken in for their confinement, and there is also accommodation for poor ladies. (8) 3 Fitzroy Square, W. ; Nurses' Home for trained nurses. (9) Edinburgh : All Saints' Mission. (10) Eastbourne : All Saints' Convalescent Hospital. (11) St. Leonards-on-Sea : All Saints' Convalescent Home. (12) 3 Margaret Street, W. : St. Agnes Hospital for fallen women in need of medical aid. (13) Cowley St. John, Oxford : St. John the Evangelist Hospital for incurable women of the middle and upper classes. (14) Lewisham : All Saints' Orphanage (boys). (15) Liverpool : St. Margaret's Home : an Industrial School Orphanage. (16) Leeds : St. Saviour's Orphanage for thirty girls, age three—fifteen. (17) The nursing of University College Hospital is managed by the Sisters. There are besides Mission Houses at Wolverhampton, Lewisham, Helmsley, Bradford, Nottingham, Chatham, Westminster, Hammersmith, Finsbury Park, and Liverpool ; Coloured Sisterhood, Schools and Mission work —Baltimore and Philadelphia, U.S., Cape Town, and Bombay.

The Sisters of Bethany, House of Retreat, 13 Lloyd Square, Clerkenwell, W.C. : Primary object, to offer to persons living in the world the opportunity of spiritual retreat. General parochial work. Training girls for service. (1) St. Katherine's High School, Lloyd Square, W.C. : Boarding and Day-school. (2) 9 Lloyd Square, and St. Philip's Mission House, 47 St. Helena Place, Clerkenwell, W.C. Parochial work. (3) 31 Wilmington Square, Clerkenwell, W.C. : Mission House for the Holy Redeemer. Parochial work, 45 Wilmington Square. St. Agnes Crèche for the children of working parents in the districts of the Holy Redeemer and St. Philip's. (4) 6 Lloyd Street, W.C. : School of Embroidery. All kinds of church work undertaken, and lessons given. (5) 4 Newington Terrace, Kennington Park, S.E. St. Katharine's Middle Class Dayschool for boys and girls. The Sisters undertake mission work at St. Agnes', Kennington. (6) 10 Washington Street, Brighton : Mission House of the Church of the Annunciation. Parochial work. (7) 16 London Road, Brighton : Mission House of St. Bartholomew. Parochial work. (8)

Springbourne, Bournemouth: Orphanage and Industrial School; accommodates 110 children, from three to eighteen years of age. (9) Stuffeynwood, Mansfield: Mission work at Shirebrook and Stuffeynwood. (11) Mission to the Nestorian Christians at Umir, Persia, in connection with the Archbishop's Assyrian Mission.

St. Mary and St. Scholastica, Twickenham, Middlesex: A Community of Sisters, who devote themselves to the devotional life. They also undertake church embroidery, plain needlework, and the care of a few aged and infirm persons; a Home of Rest, especially meant for aged or disabled domestic servants, being attached to the Convent, a few orphans also being received. Priests and lay people are admitted as associates of the Convent, and keep a slight rule.

St. Cyprian's, Park Street, Dorset Square, N.W.: Parochial and school work; an Orphanage for boys; and House of Mercy. Home for aged poor. Guilds for boys and girls.

St. Saviour's Priory, 18 Great Cambridge Street, Hackney Road, E.: Branch of East Grinstead Sisterhood, working in the parishes of St. Mary, St. Augustine, and St. Chad, Haggerston. (1) Day nursery. Dinner kitchen. Workroom. Night Refuge for women. (2) Home of Rest, Herne Bay, for women. (3) St. Saviour's Hostel, Brighton, for men. (4) St. Chad's Cottage, for women and girls. (5) Nazareth Home, Tandridge, Godstone, for fathers and mothers.

Nursing Sisters of St. John the Divine, 68 and 70 Drayton Gardens: To provide nurses for the sick in private houses and in hospitals. (1) 42, 44, and 46 Gunter Road, S.W.: A Lying-in House for respectable poor married women—fourteen beds. (2) Montagu Place, Poplar, E.: East London District Nursing Home. (3) St. John's Hospital, Morden Hill, Lewisham: For men and women—twenty-seven beds, and for paying patients at three guineas a week, in separate rooms.

St. Peter's Home, Kilburn, N.W. The Home accommodates upwards of eighty patients, ladies, women and children: acute cases, those in the last stage of illness, surgical and convalescent cases, and a few chronic and incurable patients. The Sisters undertake all kinds of Parochial and Mission work, church embroidery, and an Industrial School for girls from twelve to sixteen years of age. *Branch Houses.*—(1) Woking : This Home accommodates about fifty patients—women and girls—acutely ill, convalescents, and long cases of illness. (2) St. Saviour's Mission House, 21 Penn Street, Hoxton. (3) St. Columba's Mission, Haggerston. (4) St. Mary's Mission House, Golden Lane, E.C. (5) St. Augustine's Mission, Kilburn, N.W. (6) Ormesby House, Littlehampton : Convalescent Home, and Cottage Home for girls between three and twelve. Free Home at Littlehampton for girls, from the East End of London, ages between six and twelve, who want a few weeks' change and sea-air, yet who are not actually ill. (7) The Beauchamp Almshouses, Newland, Malvern. (8) St. Michael's Home, Cheddar, for consumptive men and women.

Sisters of the Church, Randolph Gardens, Kilburn, N.W. : Work-room in which sixty poor women are employed. School for church embroidery. Halfpenny dinners for 3000 poor children. Winter soup dinners and Sunday tea for upwards of 600 unemployed men. Classes for religious instruction. Annual Retreats for ladies. (1) Orphanages of Mercy : Free Orphanages at Kilburn, Broadstairs, and Swansea, receive 500 destitute girls. (2) 27 Kilburn Park Road, N.W. : Office of the Church Extension Association and of the Education Union. (3) St. Augustine's Day and Sunday Schools : For girls and infants (including an Upper Grade School), and capable of accommodating 1300 children ; Gordon Memorial School, 1000 children ; Princess Frederica, Kensal Green, 700 ; Wilberforce School, Kilburn, 800 ; Keble School, Harlesden, 500 ; People's College, Willesden, 150; Waterloo College, Kilburn, 120; St. Gabriel's School, South Bromley ; Saltram Crescent, Paddington. (4) St. Augustine's House of Rest, Randolph Gardens, Kilburn : A temporary home for missionaries on their return to England, also for clergy from the country who may be in London for short periods of time. Annual Retreat for clergy. (5) Lady Adelaide Home, Brondesbury : A free Orphanage for destitute boys. (6) Colonial and Foreign Missions, Randolph Gardens, Kilburn : Free grants of altar furniture, church embroidery, books, &c., made to clergy in all parts of the world. (7) Broadstairs : St. Mary's Convalescent Home, for 300 children of the very poor. (8) London

Docks: St. Katharine's Restaurant for sailors and working men. Food trucks despatched to the Docks and also to the unemployed to supply food at a nominal cost. A Night Shelter is opened for about 160 men; and a Workroom for poor women. General Mission work in St. John's, Whitechapel. (9) Rotherhithe: The Lady Gomm Memorial Mission House and Accident Hospital; also a Dispensary, and general Mission work. (10) Shoreditch: Breakfasts and dinners for destitute children, Sunday-schools and general Mission work. (11) St. Michael's, Bromley: Sunday-schools and general Mission work. (12) St. Augustine's, South Hackney: Sunday-schools and general Mission work. (13) Schools at York, Nottingham, Salisbury, and Croydon, and Toronto and Hamilton, Canada. (14) Eastcombe, Gloucestershire: Small Sanatorium for the use of the orphans. (15) 5 and 6 Paternoster Row: Church Extension Publishing House and Education Agency. (16) Ormerod House, St. Anne's-on-Sea, Lancashire: Convalescent Home. Liddon Memorial Orphanage, Park Town, Oxford, for upper-class boys. Depôts for the sale of clothing to the poor at 229 Edgeware Road, London, W., and elsewhere.

St. Katharine's, Fulham, Normand House, North End, Fulham. (1) Prison Rescue work for young women of good moral character convicted of a first theft. (2) Preventive work. (3) Parish work in St. Matthias', Earl's Court, under the parochial clergy. (4) Church needlework. (5) St. Katharine's Mission House, Earl's Court. (6) St. Cyriac, Bexhill-on-Sea, House of Rest and Home School for Indian and other children.

Norwich. — Sisterhood of All Hallows, Ditchingham, Bungay. House of Mercy. Thirty penitents received. Parochial work. Church embroidery. (1) Carnarvon Road, Heigham, Norwich: Rescue Hospital. Grey Friars Lodge, King Street: Rescue work. (2) Rescue work. Lodge of the Good Shepherd. Ipswich: Training School for respectable girls for service. Ditchingham: All Hallows' Orphan School, for girls of better class who have lost one or both parents, where they will receive a good education on very moderate terms. All Hallows' Country Hospital, accommodates twenty patients. (3) British Columbia: Mission work. (4) Norwich: Mission House for the parishes of St. James, with Pockthorpe, St. John's, Timberhill, and St. Clement's with St. Edmund's. (5) In Ditchingham : Mission House for parochial purposes. Guilds of Holy Family and of St. Agnes. Classes for factory girls.

Oxford.—St. Thomas the Martyr, Oxford. Parish work. (1) St. Anne's School, Rewley House, Oxford : School for the daughters of clergymen and others. (2) St. Scholastica's School : Girls' Middle-class School. (3) Girls' Home : Orphanage and Industrial Home for Girls. (4) St. Thomas's, Basingstoke : Diocesan Penitentiary. (5) St. Katharine's, Southsea : Orphanage for daughters of clergymen and others. (6) Parochial work, St. Peter's, Canterbury.

Sisterhood of St. John the Baptist, Clewer. Founded in 1849 under a Rule approved by the Bishop of the Diocese for works of mercy of various kinds. More than 200 Sisters are employed. (1) House of Mercy, Clewer : Penitentiary. (2) St. John's Home, Clewer : Orphanage and Industrial School, established in 1855, for 66 : payments per head are supplemented by subscriptions and donations ; some cases are received free. At fourteen the children pass on to the Industrial School. (3) St. Andrew's Convalescent Hospital, Clewer : Convalescent Hospital for men, women, and children ; established 1861. Accommodation for 85. Annual subscription of £1 5s. admits an adult for three weeks or a child for a month. In 1887 a small ward for incurable cases (chiefly consumptive) was added to the men's ward. Admission by payment of 12s. 6d. per week ; the ordinary subscribers' letters not being available for this ward. (4) St. Andrew's Cottage, Clewer : House of Rest for ladies of limited means ; accommodation for eight. (5) St. Stephen's Schools, Clewer : Schools ; College for the upper classes ; also High School and Boarding House for girls ; National School for boys, girls, and infants. Mission House for parish work. (6) St. John the Baptist's School, 33 Hamilton Terrace, Kilburn, N.W. : Ladies' School, eighty guineas per annum. (7) St. Barnabas', Pimlico : Orphanage and Mission House for parish work. (8) Pimlico : The Refuge for the reception of fallen women. (9) 9 Rose Street, Soho, W. : Orphanage and Industrial School for 65 girls. (10) All Saints' Home, Hawley, Blackwater, Hants : Branch of the work at Rose Street, Soho, and Sanatorium for the children. (11) 72 Gower Street, Bedford Square, W.C.:

Ecclesiastical embroidery establishment. (12) House of Charity, 1 Greek Street, Soho, W.: House of Charity for the temporary relief of the homeless. (13) St. Alban's, Holborn, E.C.: Parochial work of all kinds. (14) Manor House, Holywell, Oxford: Penitentiary. (15) House of Mercy, Bovey Tracey: Penitentiary; 90 inmates. Also a Mission House for parish work. (16) St. Raphael's Home, Torquay: Convalescent Hospital. St. Luke's Lodge adjoining for men. (17) St. Anne's School, Baltonsborough, Glastonbury, Somerset: Ladies' school. (18) St. Lucy's Home, Gloucester: For orphans and mission work in the town. (19) St. Lucy's Hospital, Gloucester: Free hospital for children from all parts. (20) St. Andrew's Home, Folkestone: Convalescent Hospital. (21) St. Eanswythe's Mission House, Folkestone: For general parish work. (22) St. Saviour's Mission: also for parish work. (23) All Hallows' Mission, 127 Union Street, Borough, S.E.: General mission work. Working Girls' Home, 49 Nelson Square, Blackfriars: accommodation for fifty. (24) St. John Baptist Mission, Newport (Mon.): For parish work, and Preventive Home for Children, accommodation for fifty. (25) St. John the Baptist, New York and Newark, U.S.A.: Mission and Orphanage. Ladies' School, &c. &c. (26) At Poplar, near East India Docks: Mission House (Oxford Christ Church Mission). (27) Lady Canning's Home, Calcutta: Home and Hospital. Charge of the nursing at different hospitals. Eurasian School. European Orphan Asylum. Native Mission work. (28) Hackney Wick: Mission work in connection with the Eton Mission. (29) St. John's, Westminster: Mission House for parish work of all kinds. (30) Mission work in the parish of Cowley St. John, Oxford.

Sisterhood of St. Mary, Wantage. The work undertaken by these Sisters includes: (1) Wantage: A Home for Penitents. St. Michael's Training School for schoolmistresses, pupil teachers, and industrial school for girls. St. Mary's School for young ladies (boarders) and day scholars from Wantage. (2) Lostwithiel, Cornwall: St. Faith's House of Mercy. (3) Plymouth: St. Peter's. Parochial work. (4) 34 Delamere Terrace, Paddington: St. Anne's House, parochial work in St. Mary Magdalene's parish. (5) Paddington: St. Mary Magdalene's Penitentiary. (6) Kennington: St. Mary and St. John the Divine, parochial work. (7)

Fulham : St. James's Diocesan Home, Penitentiary. (8) 5 and 6 St. James's Terrace, Paddington : College for the daughters of gentlemen. (9) Poonah, India : St. Mary's Mission, Orphanage, High School, and Anglo-vernacular School. The Sassoon Hospital. (10) St. Andrew's, Worthing : Parochial work. (11) Mission House, Leicester (The Newarke) : St. Mary Magdalene's Refuge and Home for friendless girls. (12) Spelthorne, near Feltham : Sanatorium for inebriate women. (13) Fulham : Holy Cross House, Home for Incurables—women and children. (14) Wigan : All Saints' Mission House, parochial work. (15) Saltash Cottage Hospital. (16) St. Mark's, New Swindon : Parochial work.

Society of the Holy and Undivided Trinity.—The Convent, St. Giles Road, Oxford. The object of this Society is twofold : to pray for the increase and preservation of the True Faith ; and to work under the Bishop and parochial clergy for the instruction and protection of young girls of the city of Oxford, for the visiting of the poor and ignorant, and for the nursing of the sick poor in their own homes. The Schools conducted by the Sisters in Oxford are an Orphanage and Industrial School, established in 1852. A school for the upper classes, established in 1862, the profits of which go to the support of the Orphanage. A Public Elementary Day-school, for the middle classes. The infant department is a Kindergarten taught by a Sister holding a certificate from the Fröbel Society. In Cambridge, with the sanction of the Bishop of Ely, and with the approval of the Visitor, the Bishop of Oxford, a branch of the Sisterhood is now at work in St. Giles Parish and in St. Mary-the-Less.

Southwell.— **The Sisterhood of St. Lawrence**, Belper. Nursing, parochial work, Orphanage for children of professional men, School for ditto, Cottage Hospital. (1) St. Anne's, Derby : Branch House. (2) Scarborough : Convalescent Home for ladies and children. House of Rest for Clergy. (3) Mission House at Ambergate : also Sunday school. (4) Mission House at Lane End : also Sunday-school with Church Day-school and Sunday-school. Mission House at Milford.

Truro.—The Sisterhood of St. James, Kilkhampton. Cottage Home for girls, twelve. Cottage Home for boys, ten. Parochial work. Nursing. School of embroidery, and plain needlework depôt.

The Community of the Epiphany, Home of the Community, Truro. Laundry Home for twenty Penitents. Charge of an Industrial School. Convalescent Home at St. Agnes. Parochial work. Nursing. A Society for working altar linen for the Diocese. Foreign Missions, &c.

Wakefield.—Sisterhood of St. Peter, House of Mercy, Horbury. Objects: Penitentiary for seventy-five cases, parochial work, laundry and needlework, church embroidery, surplices. (1) High School, Horbury. (2) St. Mary's Home, Rusholme, Manchester, twenty-five inmates. (3) Sacred Trinity Mission House, Salford, Manchester, for parochial work. (4) Parochial work in the parishes of St. Peter's, Horbury; St. Mary's, Horbury; St. John's, Horbury Bridge; St. Andrew's, Netherton; and St. Luke's, Middlestown.

Worcester.—Community of the Mission Sisters of the Holy Name of Jesus, Convent of the Holy Name, Malvern Link: Founded in 1865. *Object*—To honour the Holy Name of Jesus in the strength of union, and in the fervour of a devoted life, by winning souls to Him. The works below named are carried on by the Community. (1) At the Convent, ladies and others are received for the purposes of spiritual retreat and retirement, and for training in penitentiary work. The Sisters undertake mission work in the parish of St. Matthias, Malvern Link. School of embroidery. (2) The Home of the Good Shepherd, close to the Convent, accommodates thirty-three fallen women of the middle and lower class. (3) The Refuge, Melrose Cottage, Worcester. (4) The Orphanage of the Holy Family, Malvern Link. To provide a home for little girls of the middle class who have lost one or both parents. Terms £15 per annum, paid quarterly in advance. (5) Home of the Holy Name, Parkstone, Dorset, for those who desire to give themselves to the service of God in the Penitential Order of the Community. They receive into their house patients (ladies and children) who are incurably ill. (6) The principal Mission House, 141 Upper Kennington Lane, S.E. The Sisters undertake mission work in all its branches in the parish of St. Peter, Vauxhall. Ladies and others are trained in mission work. The Sisters also work in the schools. (7) The Mission House of the Holy Name, Victoria Street, Wednesbury, parish of St. James. (8) The Mission House of the Holy Name, 128 Moseley Road, Birmingham, parish of St. Alban.

(9) The Mission House of the Holy Name, St. John, N.B., Canada, Mission Church of St. John Baptist. The Community is composed of Sisters of the 1st, 2nd, and 3rd (or Penitential) Orders, Associates (or outer) Sisters, Associates and Companions. Further particulars may be had of the Warden, the Rev. G. W. Herbert, St. Peter's, Vauxhall, S.E.

York.—The Sisterhood of the Holy Rood, North Ormesby, Middlesbrough: Founded in 1867 to nurse the sick, and perform parochial work of all kinds. (1) North Ormesby: Cottage Hospital specially for working men suffering from accidents. (2) Brotton: Small hospital. (3) Children's Home, North Ormesby: School for orphans or destitute girls, supported by payments, subscriptions, and donations. (4) Liverton Mines Cottage Hospital for men.

A society, called the "Greyladies," has been established by the Bishop of Southwark.

The College was opened on February 2, 1893, and then consisted only of the head (Miss E. F. E. Yeatman), and two members. Before the following winter began, the house was found to be too small. In July 1894 the house next door was added; and the rooms being now all occupied, arrangements are being made to extend still further.

Twenty-two Greyladies are now working in different parts of Battersea, Blackheath Hill, Charlton, Deptford, Greenwich, Peckham, Southwark, and Woolwich. They are under no vow, nor are there any rules to bind them.

There are many ladies with just sufficient means for their personal wants, and who, though not prepared to become Deaconesses or Sisters, yet wish for a sphere of work recognized and organized by the Church. For these the College is a comfortable home, and one where they will find full sympathy and encouragement in the difficulties and sadness of their daily work. Each member has her own bedroom, in some cases furnished by herself. The dining and drawing-rooms are common property. The chapel adjoins the dining-room, and shortened Matins and Evensong, also mid-day prayers, are held there every day except Saturday, when an Intercessory Service, for the different parishes in which the ladies work, takes the place of Evensong.

Any one desiring to become a member of the College is usually invited to stay there for a week or two before making her decision.

When admitted as a member she wears the uniform of the College, which is grey dress and cloak, and black bonnet; but this need not be worn when off duty.

Each member pays £1 1s. per week, or £50 per annum, to the College, and this covers board, lodging, and service; but not wine, dress, or personal washing.

There are also numerous Societies of Deaconesses.

London.—The London Diocesan Deaconesses' Institution was founded in 1861 to revive the primitive Church order of Deaconesses. The Deaconesses are trained in teaching, nursing, and in managing the various branches of parochial work. Ladies are received on probation, part of which consists of three months' training in the Berkshire Hospital at Reading. When fully qualified the Deaconesses are set apart for their office by the Bishop by the "laying on of hands." All who become Deaconesses, are required to have an earnest purpose of *life-devotion*, and should regard themselves as entirely dedicated to their office for life. In connection with the work proper—parochial work—there is an Industrial Home for Girls, and a Convalescent Home at Westgate-on-Sea for men and women.

The East London Diocesan Deaconesses' Home was opened in 1880, to extend the Order of Deaconesses in the Church, and to provide Deaconesses and Church workers for East London. There are eighteen Deaconesses, thirty-three Associates, and ten Church-workers connected with this Home. Work is being done in nineteen parishes. There are twelve Branch Homes, where the Deaconesses and workers live, so as to be near the parishes in which they work. The Central Home is at Sutton Place, Hackney. The work is carried on by payments of Deaconesses and Associates, subsidized by subscriptions and grants from the "East London Church Fund," and by payments from the Clergy.

Winchester.—The Sisters are employed in nursing the sick, and in all such parish work as is within the province of women. Training is also given in penitentiary and outdoor rescue work. The Sisters are working in the parishes of St Thomas, Portsmouth; St. Mary's, Portsea; All Saints', Landport; St. George's, Portsea; and Eastney: amongst the soldiers' wives in the Portsmouth and Aldershot garrisons: also in the parishes of Alverstoke, Forton, Gosport, and Eastleigh (Bishopstoke). The refuges at Aldershot and Forton, and the Diocesan House of Mercy at Chester, are placed under the care of the Winchester Deaconesses; two are also engaged in mission work in Kaffraria. There are thirty-seven Deaconess Sisters, Probationers, and resident Church workers connected with this Home at the present time.

The Chapel and two portions of a new Home, which, when completed, will be capable of receiving fifty ladies, have been built at Portsmouth, and are now occupied by the Sisters. The total cost of the proposed building is estimated to be £8000.

St. Andrew's Home, for the rescue of neglected children, receiving fifty little girls too young for admission to other Houses of Mercy, is worked in connection with the Deaconesses' Home.

Chester.—This Institution has been reorganized by the present Bishop for the training of Deaconesses for service in all parts of the Diocese, either directly under the clergy, or as heads of Religious Institutions. The training extends over two years, and is (1) Religious and Devotional, and (2) Technical;

nursing, district visiting, class teaching, temperance, rescue, and other kinds of work are included.

There is a District Nursing Home in connection with the Institution, with a staff of six trained and certificated nurses, for the nursing of the sick poor in their own homes.

Chichester.—St. Mary's Lodge, Halton in Hastings; a Communion of Deaconesses under rule. The work (besides district and Sunday-schools) undertaken by them is: To provide in this house a home for, and to teach and train, girls who have fallen from the path of virtue, and having shown some signs of penitence, desire to remain under protection; to nurse, in St. Mary's Ward, sick, chronic, and incurable girls, five to ten years of age; to take women and children at their Cottage Convalescent Home. At Chapel House, Atherstone, Warwickshire, they have eighteen girls, from three to fifteen years of age, who, when they are old enough, are sent daily to parochial schools, till they are fit to be trained for service. At St. Mary's Home, Reading, they have twenty penitents.

Durham.—Diocesan Mission Ladies.—These ladies are licensed by the Bishop of Durham to work in the Diocese under the direction of the Canon Missioner, after training in doctrine, theory, and practice of teaching; nursing, cooking, and general parochial work. Their special works are nursing the sick poor in epidemics, and ordinary parish work. There are about forty-four workers now employed on the mission staff, and there are twenty-five parishes waiting for workers.

Ely.—The Ely Diocesan Deaconesses' Institution was established in the year 1869, to afford opportunities to faithful women of dedicating themselves to the special service of God in the work of the Church. Those employed act immediately under episcopal sanction, and the control of the clergy of the respective parishes within which their work is undertaken. There are also Associates, who in various ways render help to the Institution. A Children's Association has been formed. There is also an Orphanage in which children after leaving school are trained for service. Several Retreats have been held since the chapel was built in 1890.

Exeter.—Diocesan Deaconesses' Home.—This Home provides the systematic training of Deaconesses. No vows are required, but the Deaconesses are expected to have an earnest purpose of consecrating their lives to the ministry of the Church.

Lichfield.—The objects of the Deaconesses' Institution at Walsall are—1. To train and send forth devout women, duly set apart by the Bishop with the laying-on of hands, for active ministrations under the parochial clergy in the Diocese of Lichfield. 2. To provide a Home of Rest, to which those thus sent forth may periodically return.

Rochester.—The Rochester Deaconesses' Institution was opened by the Bishop on April 16, 1887, and a larger Home on December 1, 1891. The object of the Institution is to train Christian gentlewomen for the work and office of Deaconess. They are set apart by laying-on of the Bishop's hands, and are sent forth to live and work in parishes to which they are licensed by the Bishop. Seventeen Deaconesses are already at work.

Salisbury.—The Deaconesses' Institution exists to give practical training, with religious instruction, to women who desire to devote themselves to nursing the sick, teaching, and visiting the poor. Every candidate must reside in the Home on trial for three months; and if approved as a Probationer receives practical training, and is afterwards admitted to the office of Deaconess by laying-on of hands of the Bishop. The Deaconesses are bound by no vows. There is an Institution for training girls for service, a Home for friendless girls, a club and recreation rooms for business girls, and four Deaconesses are engaged in parochial work.

In the Colonies similar institutions are being founded.

"In December 1892, with the sanction of the Bishop, a Sisterhood was founded in Brisbane, under the name of the Society of the Sacred Advent. Some twenty girls have been trained each year for domestic service. Children have been placed by parents under the Sisters' charge, some being sent long distances for the purpose. Other work has also been undertaken. The first school belonging to the Church of England was opened by the Sisters, and already numbers 100 scholars. The nucleus of a high school has been formed, so that parents may no longer have to choose only between the secular Government schools and the Roman convents. Mission work has been steadily carried out, one Sister giving all her time to visiting the police-court, the hospital, the haunts of vice, and from house to house in many poor streets, and a rescue-home has been opened." [1]

Another community, called "The Sisters of the Church," is doing good work in Adelaide, Melbourne, Sydney, Hobart, and Dunedin.

There are also numerous Communities for women in the United States. The following are some of the larger and more important societies, enumerated in *The Living Church*, December 1893—

"All Saints Sisters of the Poor, Baltimore, U. S. A. Founded in London, 1853; established in America, 1874. Home House, Baltimore; mission houses in Baltimore for white and coloured poor; training house for coloured women for a Sisterhood; embroidery and work-rooms for young ladies; industrial home for girls; home for coloured boys; the mission and day-schools of Mount Calvary Church, and St. Mary's Chapel, and St. Andrew's Church; children's summer house; mission house and house for nurses, St. Clement's, Philadelphia; home for nurses and a school for girls, Germantown; instruction in embroidery; altar linen for mission station and poor churches; mission parochial schools, and parish visiting, at Hoboken, N. J."

[1] *Guardian*, June 13, 1895.

"The Sisters of St. Mary and All Saints, Baltimore, U. S. A. A Sisterhood of coloured women, trained to work among their own people, and at St. Mary's home."

"The Sisterhood of St. John the Evangelist, Long Island, U. S. A. The Sisterhood have the charge of the Church charity foundation, St. John's hospital, house for the aged, orphanage, St. Catherine's hall for girls; summer house for poor women. They also devote themselves to missionary and parochial work in several parishes. A body of Associates is attached, who are engaged in a great variety of Church work."

"The Sisterhood of the Holy Child Jesus, Albany, N. Y. The Sisters work in the Cathedral parish, St. Agnes' School, St. Paul's, Troy; and they have the charge of the children's hospital and St. Margaret's home for infants, St. Christopher's house, East Line; and St. Christina house, Saratoga."

"The Diaconal Community of St. Martha, Louisville, Ky. The Community has charge of the Boys' Orphanage of the Good Shepherd, and of the Home of the Innocents."

"The Sisterhood of the Holy Communion, New York. The Sisters have charge of the shelter for girls, and work in the parish of the Annunciation."

"The Sisterhood of the Good Shepherd, St. Louis, Mo. The Sisters have the charge of the schools of the Good Shepherd."

"The Sisterhood of St. Philip and St. James, Diocese of Louisiana. The Sisters have the charge of the children's home, New Orleans."

"The Order of the Deaconesses, Diocese of Alabama, has the charge of the church home, Mobile."

"The Sisterhood of the Holy Cross, Kansas City. The Sisters are in charge of All Saints' Hospital, and devote themselves to teaching."

"The Sisterhood of the Holy Nativity. The Sisters are engaged in all kinds of parochial and mission work. They also prepare vestments and altar linen and church embroidery. Their houses are open to Associates and others for spiritual rest and retirement. They keep up a daily intercession for the conversion of sinners, and the progress of the Church. The work of the Sisterhood is chiefly of a spiritual character, and is especially adapted to ladies drawn to dedicate themselves to an interior life and an extension of the faith. They have a house at Fond du Lac for missionary work in that Diocese."

"The community of the Holy Rood, under the direction of Canon Body. There is a branch of the Order in Philadelphia for coloured cripples and mission work among coloured people."

"The Order of the Visitation of the Blessed Virgin, New York. This Order is incorporated for the care of the sick, needy, and fallen; for the education of the young, and other works of charity and mercy."

"The Order of St. Monica, Fond du Lac, Wis. A religious Order of widows having charge of the Mission of our Merciful Saviour, a home for penitents, and St. Luke's Mission, Utica, N. Y."

"The Sisterhood of St. Mary, New York City, U. S. A. Founded, 1865. There are four schools: St.

Mary's, a boarding and day-school for young ladies, New York; another at Memphis, Tenn.; a third at Kenosha, Wis.; and a fourth at Peekskill, N. Y. There are also: the House of Mercy, St. Agnes' House, and St. Saviour's Sanatorium, Inwood, N. Y., a penitentiary for women. St. Mary's free hospital for children, New York; and a convalescent house for children, at Rockaway Beach, Long Island, and the Noyes' Home, Peekskill, N. Y. Trinity Hospital, New York, for adults; and a seaside home at Islip, Long Island. Trinity Mission, New York; the Laura Franklin Hospital, New York; the Church Home, Memphis, Tenn.; and St. Mary's Mission, Chicago."

"The Sisterhood of St. John Baptist, Clewer. Founded, 1851. Affiliated branch in New York, U. S. A., 1881. Mother house and noviciate, New York; St. John's school, New York; a boarding and day-school; St. Hilda's school, Morristown, N. J., for young ladies; St. Andrew's Hospital for convalescent women, New York; mission work among the German population, New York; girls' day-school in connection with the Mission of the Holy Cross; St. Ann's Cottage, home for women and children; midnight mission and refuge; St. Michael's home, Mamaroneck, N. Y., partly preventional; ecclesiastical embroidery, Christ Church home for children, South Amboy, N. J."

"St. Margaret's, East Grinstead. Founded, 1855; established in Boston, 1873. The Mother house is Boston. The Sisters have two infirmaries for private patients; a school of embroidery; an orphanage for girls. They work in connection with the mission church of St. John, and with St. Augustine's church for coloured people, and have a hospital for them. They have also the charge of the children's hospital, Boston; St. Barnabas' hospital, Newark, N. J.; St. Katherine's home, Jersey City; St. Mark's home, Philadelphia; the House of Prayer, Newark, N. J.; St. Mark's, Jersey City; St. John Evangelist, Montreal, with a home for incurables; several summer homes."

"The Sisterhood of the Good Shepherd, New York. The works of the Sisterhood are, a home and training school for children; a boarding-school for girls; summer homes for women and children, and for working girls, and clothing bureau for the worthy poor; also parochial work."

"The Sisters of the Annunciation. Incorporated, 1893. The Sisters have the charge of the House of Annunciation, New York, where incurable and crippled girls are received."

"New York training school for deaconesses."

"The Society of St. Johnland. Incorporated, 1870. This is a Church Community at Long Island, near New York, and maintains homes for aged men and children."

"The Order of the Daughters of the King. Founded, 1885, for the spread of Christ's kingdom among young women, and the strengthening of parish life."

Many guilds and other societies.

There has been also an approach to revived Monasticism in the Lutheran Church. The work of Pastor Fliedner at Kaiserworth, begun in 1836, is most interesting and successful, and is carried on much upon the old lines, the Deaconesses taking their rule and dress from those of the Hospitallers.[1]

The conclusion then seems certain and inevitable that it is desirable that Monasticism, in some form or forms, should be adopted by the Church of England. We may sum up the reasons for this something in this way—

1. Monasticism has been adopted by the Catholic Church from the early ages, in the East and in the West, among all nations, under almost every variety of circumstances, and for different purposes, in spite of failure and abuses, with every degree of asceticism, from the oriental hermit and the severe Cistercian, to "the Brothers of the Common Life," the Beguines, the Sisters of Mercy, and the Christian Brothers. The Church of England never abolished Monasticism. The Religious Houses were swept away by Henry VIII. for political reasons, for State purposes, and because their wealth was coveted by himself and his courtiers. Bishops, and statesmen, and the common people protested against the destruction. Cranmer endeavoured unsuccessfully to persuade Henry VIII. to spare some of the greater Abbeys; Latimer desired that one monastery at least might be preserved in each county; and a continuous series of regrets, protests, and aspirations may be found in the writings of sober and earnest English Churchmen, lamenting the destruction of the monasteries, and

[1] Note N, p. 391.

desiring their restoration with some reformed constitution. Thomas Fuller, in his *Church History*, says of convents—"They were good she-schools wherein the girls and maids of the neighbourhood were taught to read and work. . . . Yea, give me leave to say, if such feminine foundations had still continued . . . haply the weaker sex, besides the avoiding modern inconveniences, might be heightened to a higher perfection than hitherto hath been attained." Archbishop Leighton "thought that the great and fatal error of the Reformation was, that more of those houses, and of that course of life, free from the entanglement of vows, and other mixture, was not preserved; so that the Protestant Churches had neither places of education, nor retreat for men of mortified temper."

The same desire manifested itself in the life of prayer and regulated duties carried out by Nicholas Ferrar at Little Gidding. In 1625, Mrs. Ferrar, a lady of means, purchased a large house at Little Gidding, in Huntingdonshire, which had a small chapel adjoining it. Her son Nicholas had lately been ordained deacon, and was licensed by the Bishop to officiate in the chapel; having some time before devoted himself to a celibate life, after having held important public appointments, and with a certain prospect of advancement if he had continued a layman. The household consisted of some forty persons, Mrs. Ferrar, her two sons, her grandsons, her son-in-law Mr. Collet, with his wife and daughters, three school-masters, and the servants. Besides the chapel, a large room within the house was set apart as an oratory, and two others, one for men, the other for women, for night oratories. Some outbuildings were converted into a school-house, where instruction was given to the children of the house, and to any others of the neighbourhood, free of charge, in English, Latin, writing, arithmetic, music and singing, besides regular and definite religious teaching. Every Sunday about one hundred children came to the chapel to be catechized, and to repeat the Psalms, which they gradually learned by heart. A substantial meal was provided for them after the sermon, a hymn being sung before, accompanied by an organ; the Bible, or some devotional book, being read aloud during the repast. The household rose every day at four, and at five went to the oratory for prayers; at six the Psalms of the hour were said, with some portions of the Gospels and a hymn; at half-past six they went to the chapel for matins; at seven, said the Psalms of the hour, and sang a hymn, and then went to breakfast. After this the younger members went to their school. At ten Litany was said in the chapel. Dinner was at eleven, during which there was devotional reading. Recreation followed till one, when school recommenced till three. Evensong was said in the chapel at four; there was supper at five; recreation till eight; then prayers in the oratory, after which all retired for the night. The Holy Communion was celebrated on the first Sunday in each month by the Vicar of the parish. Mr. Collet's daughters were instructed in pharmacy and the dressing of wounds, and a sort of dispensary was provided for all the poor of the neighbourhood who applied for medicines and advice, as Nicholas Ferrar had been Physic-Fellow at Clare Hall, Cambridge, and had studied medicine at Padua. Each member of the household held some office, and was responsible for certain duties. There was also a system of services for the night. Two or more persons continued from nine at night till one in the morning repeating the Psalter antiphonally, men in one oratory, and women in the other, and saying certain prayers. At one o'clock they called Mr. Nicholas Ferrar, who then took up the watching and prayer till four. Neighbours and others often joined in these devotions, and introduced them elsewhere.[1]

It is recorded of Dr. Johnson that he said, "I never read of a hermit but in imagination I kiss his feet; never of a monastery, but I fall on my knees and kiss the pavement."

The desire for some recognized form of religious life has grown with the revived life of the Church of England, and is still growing, and becoming more intense and more general, and has already taken a practical shape in the establishment of numerous Sisterhoods, which have grown and prospered with remarkable vigour and healthy development.

"The Church of England has felt various movements of asceticism. Wesleyanism gained its moral vigour in the ascetic principles which are still com-

[1] See *Memoirs of Nicholas Ferrar*, by D. P. Peckard. A.D. 1790.

memorated in the very name of Methodism. The Evangelical movement was distinguished by the abstraction from the world and the rigorous simplicity of life which its leaders exhibited. The Tractarian party put forward asceticism yet more definitely and prominently. Teetotalism is, under one aspect, a form of asceticism, as also is Vegetarianism."[1]

2. Monasticism offers to devout souls that which many at present desire and seek for in vain—more complete separation from the world, and the opportunity of cultivating the higher spiritual life without distractions.

There is in the present day a remarkable awakening to the value of self-sacrifice, and to the power which a strong nature can exercise over the many weak natures that distinguish the majority of mankind. We meet with indirect testimony on all sides, and often in most unlikely places, which proves that the time has come for the production once more of those forces which Monasticism displayed, and by which such vast results were obtained. History repeats itself. There is an ebb and flow in the manifestation of certain human qualities. Monasticism was discredited by the Renaissance, and the revival of pagan ideas of life and morals; these principles have in their turn lost favour with many who are inspired with lofty aims, and who are sometimes Christian without knowing it. Thus Mr. B. Kidd says—

"Natural selection seems, in short, to be steadily

[1] Blunt.

evolving in the race that type of character upon which these forces act most readily and efficiently; that is to say, it is evolving religious character in the first instance, and intellectual character only as a secondary product in association with it. The race would, in fact, appear to be growing more and more religious, the winning sections being those in which, *cæteris paribus*, this type of character is most fully developed. . . . A preponderating element in the type of character which the evolutionary forces at work in human society are slowly developing, would appear to be the sense of reverence. The qualities with which it is tending to be closely allied are, great mental energy, resolution, enterprise, powers of prolonged and concentrated application, and a sense of simple-minded and single-minded devotion to conceptions of duty."[1]

And again—"If asceticism were to come into vogue again, it would exercise an influence over men of the present day quite as great as it did in former ages, not because it is right or wrong, but because, from a positive point of view, it has a condensed dynamic force which will bowl down all the feeble and foolish who fritter away their energies, and make no effort to concentrate their will on the cultivation of the nobler faculties. . . . The sacrifice of all excess of life is the science of life; the sacrifice of the present caprice and pleasure ensures future prosperity; the sacrifice of the straggling tendrils of sentiment strengthens

[1] *Social Evolution.*

the vital stem. Far from destroying the distinct forces of life, sacrifice gathers them up, unites, and maintains them." [1]

Count de Maistre said—" Whoever is able to subdue human will, without degrading human nature, has rendered service to society beyond price. There has never been a happier idea than that of uniting pacific citizens, who laboured, prayed, studied, wrote, cultivated the ground, and asked nothing from those in authority."

"Work in these days fills so large a space in our thoughts, that the inner life of devotion is apt to suffer. Our thoughts, words, and actions tell upon the whole body of the Church, either lowering the whole system or strengthening it." [2]

"Intellectual men allow that the body is rightly subordinated to the intellect, and the Church adds that the body and the intellect are rightly subordinated to the perfection of the will, the moral and spiritual nature." [3]

Napoleon said that "there were circumstances where convent life might have its advantages, that the cloisters must often be very well suited to tender minds, resigned and weary of the world; that these retreats might be opened with advantage, for example, to the widows of colonels and general officers . . . that in his opinion perpetual vows should be

---

[1] *The Origin and Development of Religious Belief.* S. Baring-Gould.
[2] *The Training of Workers by Anglican Sisterhoods.*
[3] *Essays on Religion and Literature.*

forbidden, and that in any case nobody should be admitted under the age of forty."[1]

J. S. Mill said—"The social problem of the future is to unite the greatest individual liberty of action with a common ownership of the raw material of the globe."

"Monasticism kept alive the great thought which philosophy in all ages has proclaimed—that the world exists not in time but in thought; that happiness, if it is to be found, must be sought elsewhere than in sensual enjoyment and the fleeting affections of life; that it lies in each man's breast to cherish it or to cast it away, as he will, and not in the fortuitous circumstances that surround him; that the voluntary extinction of the old Adam of egoism, the self-imposed tearing-out by the roots and fibres, of that which is above all things most difficult to extirpate—the self-assertion of the individual—are the only conditions whereby the mind catches glimpses of other horizons—horizons of moral beauty and perfection, which must for ever remain veiled to those who have not undergone the same fiery discipline. It is the victory of spirit over flesh, of mind over matter; the just appreciation of the meanness and grossness of the details of a sordid and self-absorbed existence; a recognition of the moral force which, breathing in us for a moment between the cradle and the grave, links us to the great Spirit which informs the Universe. . . . Whether it be Christian or philosopher, a Pythagoras, a Buddha, or a Fr. Juan de la

[1] *Memoirs of Napoleon,* by Méneval.

Cruz, who speaks, they are but links in the great chain of philosophic thought, who under their specific teaching have lighted the torch of Idealism to be a beacon for the faint-hearted who sink by the wayside of life; to light each man who comes into the world, and lead him, if he will but listen, to a felicity which none can take away. The lives of those obscure monks, those unknown nuns, have not been lost. They still live: drops lost in the vast ocean of human endeavour, mingled inseparably with the great current which at given moments has purified the earth of its lowest elements, and shown to what heights man can rise."[1]

"The fretfulness, impatience, and extreme tension of modern literary life; the many anxieties that paralyze, and the feverish craving for applause that perverts so many noble intellects, were unknown to the monk. Severed from all the cares of active life, in the deep calm of the monastery, where the turmoil of the outer world could never come, the monkish scholar pursued his studies in a spirit which has now almost faded from the world."[2]

"The right of self-development and social responsibility, which the woman of to-day so persistently asks for, is in many ways analogous to the right which the convent secured to womankind a thousand years ago. The woman of to-day, who realizes that the home circle, as at present constituted, affords insufficient scope for her energies, had a precursor

[1] *Life of St. Teresa.* G. Cunningham Graham.
[2] Lecky, *Morals*, vol. ii.

in the nun who sought a field of activity in the convent."[1]

"There are truths lying below the surface of things, half-hidden beneath the folds of heart and conscience that scarcely admit of being recognized in the midst of a gregarious existence, or by such as can ill brook a day's real seclusion, unbroken by external excitement. Shallow mediocrity prefers fussiness to quiet thoughtfulness. Now-a-days bustling go-ahead activity, commercial, social, political, is set up as the standard of excellence by a generation that has no more marked characteristic than its dead level of commonplace."

3. The Church of England suffers from the want of such members who aim at, and in any degree attain to, perfection. "A little leaven leaveneth the whole lump." All the members partake of the grace which some members receive and use. There are so many great sinners because there are so few great saints. To those who have, more will be given. The sight of Christ-like lives is the most powerful instrument for converting the sinful, and for rousing the inferior and commonplace to make efforts after a higher standard of spiritual life.

"During eighteen hundred years in which Christians have professed to believe in the Cross, nothing really elevated, beautiful, or good has been done upon earth, except at the cost of suffering and self-abnegation."[2]

---

[1] *Woman under Monasticism.* L. Eckenstein.
[2] Dora Greenwell.

"It takes a soul
To move a body ; it takes a high-souled man
To move the masses, even to a cleaner stye ;
It takes the ideal to blow a hair's-breadth off
The dust of the actual."

"A monk is a Christian who puts himself apart from the world, in order more surely to work out his eternal salvation. He is a man who withdraws from other men, not in hatred or contempt of them, but for the love of God and his neighbour, and to serve them so much better, as he shall have more and more purified and regulated his soul. . . . It was not the sick souls, but, on the contrary, the most vigorous and healthful which the human race has ever produced, who presented themselves in crowds to fill [the monasteries]. What was this life, if not a permanent protest against human weakness, a reaction renewed every day against all that degrades and enervates man, a perpetual aspiration towards all that soars above this terrestrial life and fallen nature."[1]

"The Church of England has never been without many individuals cultivating in unobtrusive ways the principles of asceticism, but she has lacked communities devoted to this high aim. He who would triumph in anything must begin by triumphing over self, and no community which is not pledged to this fundamental endeavour can achieve collective glory or progressive victories in any department."[2]

It has ever been found that heroism in any form is attractive even to the lowest and most degraded.

---

[1] *Monks of the West*, vol. i. Montalembert.
[2] J. H. Blunt.

In theatres it is the gallery that hisses the villain, and cheers the self-sacrificing man. In gaols and penitentiaries tales of bravery and noble endurance command attention, and often elicit tears.

An experienced celibate mission-priest writes—" I believe we are not nearly awake to the fact that the Religious Character and ascetic discipline win the faith of the Hindus, and of other races, with a direct force which no other form of life can. Nothing struck me so much in India and Africa as the power the Dedicated Religious had as missionaries in dealing with heathens, civilized or wild. The Sisters can and do, I believe, in India, what no one else can do, as pioneers of Christianity."

The lady known as A. L. O. E., who had much personal experience in missionary work in India, said—" I think what is wanted here is missionaries' graves. Not the graves of young missionaries who have died here, but the graves of old missionaries, who have given their whole lives for their people."

The following is a letter from an All Saints Sister in Bombay—

" I was taking a Hindoo doctor over the Children's Hospital the other day, and the little ones, as is their habit, gathered round me, playing with me, and inviting me to notice them, quite like little English children. The doctor seemed quite astonished that they were so friendly, and remarked, ' This is an object-lesson to me. I wish we could get our countrywomen to nurse as you do. We want them to learn charity.' To this I answered, that charity meant the Son of God, and that that was the difference between their religious acts and ours—that ours was done from the love of God, and theirs from the fear and dread of their gods. The doctor himself has read the Bible intellectually, and he says he is held back from Christianity by the half-hearted lives of the Christians he sees. He told me that if we wanted to convert India, the people must see *lives* given up to God, and that what he wanted to see was missionaries going about as their Master did, not having where to lay their heads—not people living in large bungalows, and driving about in carriages."

Speaking of the work of Sisterhoods in the present day, Montalembert says—" In this age of luxury and universal languidness, these gentle victors have kept the secret of strength, and in the weakness of their sex they exhibit the masculine and persevering energy which is wanting in us, to attack in front and to subdue the egoism, cowardice, and sensuality of our time and of all times. . . . All that is noble and pure in human nature is led to the fight against all our baseness, and to the help of all our miseries. . . . They rush forth to the rescue of the most repulsive and tedious infirmities of poor human nature, lavishing upon them unwearied cares ; they swarm wherever they are wanted to cultivate the deserts of ignorance and of childish stupidity, often so intractable and restive. Braving all disgusts, all repugnances, all denunciations and ingratitudes, they come by thousands with dauntless courage and patience, to win, caress, and soothe any form of suffering and of poverty. . . . Where this is done, they assure us that they have found peace and joy, and in the sacrifice of themselves the perfection of love. They have kept their hearts for Him who never changes and never deceives; and in His service they find consolations which are worth all the price they have paid for them—joys which are not indeed unclouded, for then they would be without merit, but whose savour and fragrance will last to the grave. . . . It is only a false spirituality which makes the soul hard, arrogant, and pitiless. When religion dries up or hardens the heart it is but a lying tyranny. . . . The blessedness of belonging to God will never close a noble heart to the griefs of others, or deprive it of any generous emotion. . . . Young and innocent hearts give themselves to Him, in return for the gift He has given us of Himself; and this sacrifice by which we are crucified is but the answer of human love to the love of that God who was crucified for us."[1]

" I know not what faint aroma of that peace which the world cannot give creeps through these homely joys and sorrows of convent life, and fills me with a poignant regret that such an existence should ever have been condemned by the so-called utilitarian principles of which to-day we see the failure in the ever-increasing misery, vulgarity, and restlessness of

[1] *Monks of the West*, vol. v.

the world. Of all the types of existence that have ever been consecrated by time and human longing after peace, that of the monastery seems to me the noblest, however relaxed its discipline may have become in the times I treat of. No wonder that perturbed spirits, and consciences troubled with many scruples, looked forward to its rest as a distant foretaste of the celestial repose ; that young minds found in it the serene and innocent impulses, that sympathy with others, shed and glow over the darker features of the society around them."[1]

4. The Church's work can be best done by souls who are above those whom they teach, in experience, in spiritual attainments, and in the conquest of the lower nature. As there are specialists in other pursuits, so there ought to be men of exceptional gifts and powers in Evangelical labour. As there are athletes in physical contests, so in the struggle against the Church's rivals, there must be champions, leaders, and heroes, able both to command and to show the way to victory.

" The notion that Sisterhoods are a useful shelter for discontented women, a kind of *pis-aller* for those who cannot find husbands, is probably nearly exploded. A cursory glance at the list of works undertaken by the Sisters will show that they could not be carried on but by a band of thoroughly capable women, strong in health, and vigorous in mind. Indeed more than half of those who offer themselves to Sisterhoods are rejected as unfit for

[1] *Life of St. Teresa*, vol. ii. G. C. Graham.

the life and work, while long and careful training is given to those who are admitted as probationers. There does come a call, a real 'vocation' to some souls, which they cannot but obey, and of which the reality is proved by a life of self-sacrificing devotion to work, which is often difficult, often monotonous, and not seldom painful and perilous. To this life many amongst the very flower of England's daughters have given themselves."[1]

"None need enter upon the life of a Sister of Mercy from a disgust of the world. The work calls for no love-lorn damsels with hearts full of spleen, but women with fresh hearts who wish to love better the Lord who bought them, and for His sake, all for whom He died. Any other motive will be found miserably inadequate to sustain the soul of the Sister of Mercy, and to prevent her, after putting her hand to the plough, from looking back."[2]

Montalembert, with all his passion for Monasticism, says—"To transform the world into a cloister, peopled by unwilling monks, would be to create beforehand a counterfeit hell."

The Church's work can be more quickly, efficiently, and happily executed by men banded together, than by the isolated and unsupported efforts of lonely men. Union is strength. It is promised that "where two or three agree together" that the desired gift is bestowed.[3]

---

[1] *The Training of Workers by Anglican Sisterhoods.*
[2] *Experiences of an English Sister of Mercy.*
[3] Note O, p. 392.

The Church's work is best done by those who are free from worldly and human ties. The Church militant should be provided with soldiers who are not entangled with the ambitions, the motives, the distractions of the things and persons of this life.

So Prof. Allies says (*Formation of Christendom*) —" Exactly as marriage provides for the animal increase of the race, so the virginal life provides for the Christian society."

5. The hurrying spirit of the age demands a counteracting spirit of rest and detachment. Its selfishness requires absolute self-sacrifice. Its scepticism must be met by implicit faith. Its demand for luxury and material comfort must be confronted with asceticism, thorough, but bright and joyous. Every characteristic fault and failing must be rectified by the exhibition of the extreme opposite virtue and grace. The Church and the world are irreconcilable enemies. Every principle and practice of the world ought to have its direct contrary patent and active in the Church.

"The one object of modern progress," says Mr. Mallock, " is to produce those pleasures which Socialism seeks to distribute; in short, the aim of the whole civilized world is to elude the destiny which, according to the doctrines of Christianity, all men ought to welcome, and which those who would be perfect ought to court."[1]

We are threatened with Disestablishment; let us reply by establishing Monasticism. Christianity is

[1] *Studies of Contemporary Superstition.* 1895.

declared to be a "worn-out Syrian superstition"; let us show that it lives in the lives of Christ-like men. Science, they tell us, must be the death of the Faith; let us display the life of faith by works that shall compel the admiration of all noble minds. Socialism is imminent; let us forestall it; let us permeate it; let us elevate it to the level of the first socialism of the Apostolic age, and of the Monasticism of Benedict, Bernard, and Francis. Chivalry, they say, is dead; let us have men ready to live and die for selfless aims, soldiers of the Cross, "not counting their lives dear to them."[1]

There is a specific for every spiritual disease in the treasury of the Good Physician. The fact that the spirit of the age scouts the very idea of Monasticism is proof positive that Monasticism is wanted. Our Lord by His words and His life put Himself into antagonism to the spirit of His day; "as He was, so are we in the world"; the Church will not convert the world by conformity or compromise, but by fighting, by overcoming evil with good. Many worldly people have now been almost, if not quite converted to the toleration at least of Monasticism in its active capacity, but they still misunderstand and decry the contemplative and enclosed life. The work of Sisters in hospitals, orphanages, penitentiaries, and among the poor, is praised, but that men and women should shut themselves up that they may pray, and meditate, and commune with God, and raise their souls to the higher

[1] Note P, p. 393.

ranges of spirituality, this is ridiculed, or declared to be cruel, or wasteful, or mere fanaticism. But such lives form the very salt of the earth and of the Church, saving them from corruption; gaining victories as Moses procured the defeat of the Amorites by his ever uplifted hands, armed with no sword. If men may, without blame, retire from the world to pursue their studies, or to indulge a taste or a hobby, why may not the man who has a passion for God, retire that he may obtain his heart's desire, without hindrance or rebuke? If societies are formed the better to carry out secular schemes of all kinds, why may not men band together for spiritual objects? If money is subscribed and buildings are erected to be the homes of learning, of art, or of pleasure, why may not houses of retreat be set up, and be safe from confiscation, where the soul's aspirations may be realized, and where spiritual science may be studied and enjoyed? Liberty is praised; liberty is claimed by all sorts of persons, and for every kind of pursuit; let the monk and the nun have liberty also to go their own way, which does the world no harm, and which is as dear to them as the life-choice of others whom the world honours and applauds.

St. Augustine said, "The less a monk labours in anything but prayer, the more serviceable is he to man. Did not God Himself judge that cause when He took the part of Mary against Martha?"

That the retired life has strong attractions for many who never obtain the enjoyment of it, is certain. For example, Miss F. P. Cobbe writes of her own early predilections—" In one of our summer excursions, my father and one of my brothers and I lionized Winchester, and came upon an exquisite chapel, which was at that time a sort of sanctuary of books, in the midst of a lovely silent cloister. To describe the longing I felt then, and long after, to spend all my life studying there, in peace and undisturbed, 'hiving learning with each studious year'—would be impossible."[1]

"Probably some are kept back from offering themselves to join a Religious Society by a false idea that such an offer presupposes exceptional natural endowments. That idea must be entirely put away. The humblest souls are better Religious than the cleverest. . . . If we think by our natural gifts to add any glory to a Religious Community we shall be certain to meet with signal failure. . . . Too many efforts have failed probably because men have wished to promote some special aim, instead of purely desiring themselves to be filled with the Holy Ghost. . . . However little any of us may be able to do, we can each one of us grow in holiness, and this must be the *sole* aim of the Religious. . . . In these days men look for quick returns. It is difficult to make men yield themselves up to a Divine vocation in the expectation of a result to be acquired in some distant future. Men want their reward in this world as well as in the next."[2]

6. Monasticism has shown itself capable of development, and of modifications which adapt it to every

---

[1] *Life of F. P. Cobbe*, vol. i.
[2] R. M. Benson, *Literary Churchman*, April 1889.

age and to all kinds of most varying circumstances; it is certain therefore that it is suitable for our own Church, and for these times, and that we suffer loss from the want of it, and that we should gain much by its adoption.[1]

7. Monasteries would afford a retreat and a place of safety for the weakly in mind and body, for the drunkard, the criminal, the poor, the friendless, and the aged.

A few suggestions may be made as to the characteristics of Monasticism which seem to be desirable in our own Church.

1. There must be no slavish copying of mediæval Orders in Rule, in discipline, in dress, in buildings. The first Gaulish monks rebelled against the meagre diet of the Orientals. The climate of Europe demands clothing and shelter which the southern climate renders unnecessary. The Sister's dress is a safeguard to her when she penetrates the slums, but a monk may wear the vestments of common life when he goes abroad, and yet pursue his vocation without hindrance. The Roman Catholic monks of to-day wear their traditional dress within their house, but go about like other people when they are in the streets.

"Benedict did not invent a new habit, but that which he wore himself and his disciples was the habit of a plain honest layman; neither did Francis invent a new dress, but it was the dress of poor country fellows."[2] A badge on the arm, like the Geneva cross of the

[1] Note Q, p. 394.
[2] *Colloquies of Erasmus, The Rich Beggars.*

ambulance, or some simple device upon the cap, would be quite enough to distinguish the Brother of Mercy, without the adoption of any conspicuous costume which would be inconvenient, and often an object of ridicule. The cowl does not make the monk. If we first get the essential vocation and life of the Religious, the dress will come by some law of natural selection.

So too it is neither necessary nor desirable that a thirteenth-century abbey should be built before we can have a body of monks. If we get the men, they may, at first at any rate, be housed in any way that is most convenient. In past times monks and nuns lived in Gothic buildings, when Gothic architecture was in vogue. When the Renaissance came, their houses followed the prevailing style. In later times abbeys and convents were just like domestic buildings, mere dwelling-houses of a larger size. It seems wiser, more real and practical, that religious houses to-day should be merely ordinary houses in all things external. The religious life must take root and grow side by side with the ordinary life of the day, and must not be an exotic transplanted from a distant period, and surrounded by artificial romance and unfamiliar trappings.

2. There must be various Orders, contemplative and enclosed, and active in the world, for men, and for women, for education, for penitentiary and rescue work, for study and writing of books, for missions at home and abroad, for parochial duties, and for all the numerous other objects that demand such systematic

and organized aid. Vincent of Lerins, the author of the famous phrase, *Quod semper, quod ubique, quod ab omnibus*, nevertheless says, " Shall there be no progress in the Church of Christ? There shall be progress, but not change. With the progress of the ages, there must be a growth of wisdom. But religion must progress as the human body grows, yet never ceases to be the same."

So Benedict is reported to have rebuked the extravagant mortification of an Oriental ascetic, who caused himself to be chained to the ground, by saying, " The servant of God is bound not with a chain of iron, but with a bond of love." And Basil used to say to his monks, " If fasting incapacitates you in your labours, it is better to eat, and be a good workman of Jesus Christ."

It is recorded of St. Francis of Sales, that when he was consulted as to the advisability of enjoining that the monks of some reformed monastery should go about barefooted, he said, with much warmth, " For goodness' sake, let the men have their shoes. It is their heads you must try to reform, not their feet!" On the same principle he would not allow his Sisterhood to practise any extraordinary austerities, always insisting that mortifications were not an end in themselves, but only a means to an end, desirable in certain cases, but not to be forced upon every one. And he said with his usual regard for common sense and reasonable and calm judgment, " Nothing is more unworthy than the mind which cannot extol celibacy without condemning marriage; admire voluntary poverty without despising even well-applied wealth; or obedience without depreciating those whose lot it is to rule; or community-life without sneering at those who do their duty in the world." In like manner Gregory the Great, in his instructions to Augustine respecting his mission to England, gave him great liberty, and bade him select from the usages of Rome and those of Gaul and Britain, those which seemed most suitable to the circumstances of the times, and the habits and customs of the Saxons; for he said, "It is not possible to change all at once the habits of men's minds; a mountain is not climbed by one leap, but by gradual steps." St. Vincent of Paul instituted his Order of Sisters of Charity in 1634, to meet the wants of the times, and took care to modify the old regulations of Sisterhoods with a very free hand. He said to those who wished to join the new Order, "Your convent must be the houses of the sick; your cell, the chamber of suffering; your chapel, the parish church; your cloister, the streets of the city, or the wards of the hospital; your Rule, the general vow of obedience; your grille, the fear of God; your veil, to shut out the world, holy modesty." He followed the same course with respect to his Order of Mission Priests called Lazarists, and made them also successful and useful by this means.

"Probably the physical change of our nature through the habits of later ages makes it impossible for men now-a-days to attain even to any approximation to the austerity of earlier days. In the East, where there has been less of this social development, there remains also a greater capacity of austere devotion."[1]

The old Orders were adapted to the wants of their age, but even they were from time to time modified. As Fuller says—"As mercers, when their old stuffs begin to tire in sale, refresh them with new names to make them more vendable, so when the Benedictines waxed stale in the world, the same Order was set forth in a new edition, corrected and amended, under the names first of Cluniacs and secondly of Cistercians."

"The Little Sisters of the Poor" originated with the charity of one good woman, who took a poor destitute person into her house.

3. Vows should be made for a certain number of years, or for life, but dispensation should be possible under proper authority. There would of course be a period of probation or noviciate, and no one would be admitted without his or her own unbiased wish and consent.

4. The Bishop of the Diocese would be *ex-officio* the Visitor of the Religious House, and there would be an appeal to him in all cases of dispute or difficulty.

5. It would be absolutely necessary to guard against the acquisition of wealth. Most of the decay of Religious Orders, and the abuses that have grown up round Monasticism, and which have crippled its powers, and finally caused its suppression, have arisen, directly or indirectly, from the accumulation of in-

[1] R. M. Benson, *Literary Churchman*, April 5, 1879

ordinate wealth, in the irresponsible hands of the head of the convent, or the General of the Order. Apostolic poverty was an indispensable element in primitive Monasticism. The missioners to the poor should be poor themselves. Money is necessary for all work in this world, and plenty of money is sometimes essential at particular crises; but it would be best that the treasurers and the paymasters should be outside the Religious Community, and that the members should, like the Apostles, be free to give themselves wholly to prayer and the ministry of the word.

"The continual touting for money is a terrible scandal to religion, such as no amount of success in works can justify; but works must be maintained, and until the Church learns to be more liberal in endowments, this is a feature of weakness which our Religious Communities can scarcely escape. What would the founders of the early communities have said to the various expedients by which our present Communities seek to sustain their work? . . . The Pope has lately reminded the Carthusians of the incompatibility of their commercial enterprise in liqueur with their vow of poverty." [1]

The greatest want, in the present day, displayed by the Church of England, is heroic self-sacrifice; the spirit of the apostles and martyrs of the first age; the spirit that has always distinguished leaders of men, reformers, enthusiasts; the spirit that has never failed to create the like spirit in others; that

[1] R. M. Benson, *Literary Churchman*, April 5, 1889.

has commanded obedience and devotion; that has wrought conversion from hostility to union, from indifference to zeal, from selfishness to self-abnegation—in a word, the spirit of Jesus Christ, who, for love of others, gave Himself living and dying. Christendom seems to be settling down into commonplace, uninteresting mediocrity and apathy. *Surtout point de zèle*, the motto of an apostate bishop, has more acceptance than the words of Jesus Christ. There has, thank God, been wonderful revival in the life and work of the Church in England. Bishops are no longer altogether unfitted for their high calling, the nominees of party premiers, the worn-out college dons, the feeble juniors of titled familes. We have spent millions in church building and in church restoration. Our services are more frequent, more reverent, more varied. We have missions in the slums; we have Retreats, Diocesan Conferences, Congresses, and a timidly tentative Convocation. But with all this there is a conspicuous want of absolutely devoted and spiritual men, living evidently by a higher rule than that of respectable virtue; men who have given up all desire for self-advancement, self-aggrandizement, self-pleasing; men dead to the world; men who have crucified the flesh; men who count not their lives dear to them, to whom to live is Christ, to die is gain. Just as a man of genius will do that which ten thousand ordinary men never can do; so one man full of the Holy Ghost will by his acts, and even by his silent example, advance the Kingdom of Christ in the world, and make Christ reign supreme and without rival or rebellion in the hearts of Christians. "O God, give us saints!" was the perpetual prayer of a great and wise servant of God. Like all men great in their specialty, saints are created by God. But small gifts may be cultivated and developed, and wherever the Spirit of God is, there is power. The pursuit of holiness by the old path of asceticism is always blessed, and always more or less crowned with success. But men do not follow the old ways. From highest to lowest there is a shrinking from mortification of the flesh that the spirit may be emancipated and become paramount. A recent biography of an excellent bishop proves him to have been a sincere Christian in heart and life, a conscientious and earnest priest, a man of influence and power; but all his life through he is seen anxious for preferment, ready to give up any employment for another more honourable and lucrative, rising from post to post, till he was translated from one important bishopric to another; and yet at the age of seventy-two, he is disappointed and troubled because he is now passed over as too old for a yet higher and more responsible position. There is no *nolo episcopari*, no shrinking from the responsibilities of high place, no fear of wealth and worldly greatness; much less is there any craving for the lowest place, for the loss of all things, that Christ may be glorified in his weakness and obscurity. The good clergyman's work is hindered, his attention is distracted, his motives are swayed, because he has sons to bring up, and a sick daughter to provide with expensive carefulness. The Christian warrior has been "entangled with the things of this life."[1]

Our cathedrals again and their staff do but little for the Church. The present Archbishop when he was Chancellor of Lincoln wrote an admirable and most suggestive book on *The Cathedral*. St. Paul's is doing a really telling work in London. We have Mission Canons here and there. The fabrics have been saved from ruin, and have been adorned with costly and beautiful work. There are popular and attractive services in several cathedrals. But after all the living man is wanted, the Carlo Borromeo, the Savonarola, the Wesley. Our residentiary Canons seem to be the descendants and living presentments of the later mediæval Benedictine monks. Gentlemanly and most respectable men, moral, generous, high-minded, scholars, men of taste and culture; priests whose ministerial duties have been reduced to a minimum; who for the most part pass away, generation after generation, and leave no trace of their existence, no work for which men will call them blessed. Dean Kitchin, in his recent *Life of Bishop Harold Browne*, truly and sadly says—

"The old notion of 'learned leisure' ranks with those of the 'endowment of research.' It is beautiful in theory, it breaks down in practice. What has the leisure of all the cathedral precincts produced in all these years? Where are our monumental books, our contributions to the advance of knowledge, our learn-

[1] Note R, p. 396.

ing leavening the fabric of the Church? There are no such things."[1]

"A strict community life has much to say for itself, on economical, sympathetic, disciplinary, and enthusiastic grounds."[2]

If we turn to the ordinary rank and file of the clergy the same characteristics are evident. There is no body of clergy in the world, either now or in former times, in our own Church or the Church in other countries, more respectable, moral, and decently learned. Now, more than ever, it may be said, "*Clerus Anglicanus stupor mundi.*" It is the exception where the parish priest is not conscientiously trying to do his duty. Churches are built or restored, services are multiplied, music and art are called in to help to make them attractive, all kinds of parochial schemes are devised and carried on, and it is even alleged by some that the clergy are too busy and active, both for their own health's sake, and for the comfort of those who would rather be let alone a little more. But in the meantime the social rank and status of the English clergy is on the whole lower than it was fifty or a hundred years ago, and this in itself makes them less acceptable to and influential over the higher classes. Education has made such advances that many men and women look down upon the pulpit and the mental qualifications of the clergy, feeling themselves better equipped already in knowledge and argument than those who occupy the place

---

[1] *Life of Bishop E. Harold Browne*, by Dean Kitchin (Murray). [2] Bishop of Chester.

of teachers. A preacher of ability or of eloquence will still attract an attentive audience, but it is a lamentable fact that the English clergy have no special training for the pulpit, and that really good preachers are not numerous. The clergy are no longer respected and reverenced because they are clergy, but each individual is weighed and valued according to his personal gifts and qualifications; and the man of very moderate ability, with *res augustæ domi*, and a wife who thinks herself "the first lady in the parish," is not likely to have much influence, or to become a power in the Church. The lower classes too distrust the clergy, and compare their lives of comfort with their own needs, and with the principles which the Church professes to inculcate. They want to see practice correspond with preaching. As Cardinal Newman once said, "The quasi-heathen of large towns will not be converted by the sight of domestic virtues and domestic comforts in the missionary; but the evident sight of disinterested and self-denying love and elevated firmness will influence and rule them." This has been proved by the lives and work of such men as Mackonochie, Lowder, and Herbert, and by the reverence and affection which Sisters earn by their quiet and enduring ministrations among the lowest and foulest regions of crime and misery. As has been well said, "Somehow the idea of marrying, building, or improving their parsonages, and showing forth the charities, the humanities, and the qualities of a family man, did not suggest itself to the minds of the first missionaries of Christianity."

So Robertson of Brighton said, "I wish we had a little more soldier's spirit in our Church. But, alas! the Church of England will endure no chivalry, no dash, no enthusiasm. She cannot turn it to account as Rome does with her Loyolas and Xaviers. We have nothing but prosaic routine, and the moment any one with heart and nerve fit to be a leader of a forlorn hope appears, we call him a dangerous man, and exasperate him with cold and unsympathizing reproofs till he becomes a dissenter and a demagogue." And Coleridge wrote, "There is upon the Church of England a curse; we call it prudence; it is in fact fear."

Bishop Harold Browne wrote—"There is a danger that the English Church should die of respectability. I confess to have a lingering love for respectability. I should choose for myself a gentleman-clergy, sober and solemn, yet warm and hearty services, and sermons full of thought and wisdom, though earnest and home-thrusting and spirit-stirring. But we want mission-work of all kinds in our towns and alleys, on our heaths and hills. Mission chapels, open-air services suited to untrained tastes, sermons that tell on the feelings without offending the intellect; above all, the enlisting of a much larger army of workers from every class, rich and poor, high, middle, and low, to work as sub-deacons, lay readers, district visitors, deaconesses, mission women. There is nothing in the National Church unfavourable to all this, though there may be in the prejudices of her members."[1]

[1] *Life of Bishop Harold Browne*, by Dean Kitchin.

A clergyman who signed himself "One Worker with Eight Thousand People," recently wrote to the *Guardian* complaining that in answer to his advertisement for a curate, he "only succeeded in getting applications chiefly from elderly men, or from men who refused at once to come when they found there was 'no society' or attractions, but only the honour to be had of managing a difficult outpost for the Church in the face of desperate odds. The men cannot be found, and the cry from all sides is the same, 'Where can I get help?' If only incumbents of large parishes cry out, something, surely, in the name of Christ, and for the sake of His Church, may shortly be done."

"The typical Evangelical managed to make life exceedingly comfortable; nobly, indeed, doing his duty towards his fellow-men, but leaving a wide margin for enjoying himself after his own fashion. Instead of living in a cave or on a pillar, he might live in a luxurious villa at Clapham or elsewhere. He might keep a most abundant table, and at that table might be found some of the best table-talk of the day."[1]

"In fifty years," said Thomas Carlyle, "atheism will be the new religion of the whole tribe of hard-headed and hard-hearted men who bear rule in the world's affairs. All Christian religion is nodding to its fall in Europe."

One of the greatest impediments in the way of the success and progress of foreign missions is the godless

[1] *The English Church in the Nineteenth Century*, by Canon Overton.

living of Englishmen abroad. The Mahometan, the Hindoo, and the Buddhist, live stricter lives as regards prayer and self-discipline than our countrymen, and they say that conversion to Christianity would for them be the adoption of a much more lax and indulgent way of life. In the same way members of the Roman and Oriental Churches are astonished and scandalized at the easy and mundane habits of many English missionaries; and the members of the Archbishop of Canterbury's mission to the Assyrian Church say that they would not be respected or listened to if they were not celibates, and more or less ascetic in their lives and habits.

Suarez says—" We call this state Religious by reason of the last and principal end to which it tends, and this end is God Himself. The worship of God and His service is its first object. Those who embrace it consecrate themselves especially and totally to God, and therefore it is that the name of Religious is given to them by pre-eminence."[1]

And Mgr. Gay, speaking to Sisters, says—" As to your country; you do not abjure it; it is also your mother. You do not forget it; far from it. You serve it in your own way, and better than many others; but you go beyond it, and live in a higher region, in the country which is interior, in the mystical Jerusalem, in the universal city, where there is neither Jew nor Gentile, neither Greek nor Barbarian, but where all are in Christ. Wherever you may be, as to the body, it is a matter of little

---

[1] *De vist. et Statu Relig. Tract.* vi. lib. ii. cap. 1.

consequence; according to the spirit, there is your abode." [1]

"The most philosophical mode of viewing it, relative to Christianity, is to recognize that Monachism has made a part of every creed which has attained a certain stage of ethical and theosophical development; that there is a class of minds for which it always has a powerful attraction, and which can otherwise find no satisfaction; and consequently that Christianity, if it is to make good its claim to be a universal religion, must provide expression for a principle which is as deeply seated in human nature as domesticity itself, albeit limited to a smaller section of mankind." [2]

Do we not want then some recognized system by which those eager spirits may find scope for their energies, and instead of being frowned down, may be encouraged, directed, and sustained? There is stirring in the heart of many a man and woman the passionate desire for a higher spiritual life, and for absolute self-surrender, and for devotion to any work to which God calls them. But the impulse is not understood either by the soul that experiences it, or by others. There are no instructors and guides; there is no place of retreat or education; there is no one to say to obedient and able spirits, "Go, and do that."

It is not pretended that such a vocation is for every one. It is not denied that there is work enough and to spare for the ordinary middle-class

---

[1] *The Christian Life*, vol. i.
[2] *Encyclopædia Britt.* 'Monachism.'

of devout and earnest souls. It is not demanded that we have a celibate clergy, or even a celibate episcopacy, but let us not have one hard procrustean rule; let it be honestly and plainly confessed that there is a more perfect way for those whom God has fitted for it; let them not drift into the common run, unconsciously carried away by the tide of public opinion and universal practice, because "no man hath hired them" for honourable and difficult work. The whole Church suffers because the standard of spiritual life is not the highest standard, the standard of perfection, which Christ Himself promulgated.

"We cannot raise the temperature of a thawing mass of ice till the whole is thawed. Till then all heat is absorbed, and becomes latent. So the few earnest Christians are enough to keep the rest from freezing, but their life is spent in keeping up their life." [1]

"Every great and commanding movement in the annals of the world," said Emerson, "is the triumph of enthusiasm." There are heroic souls who cry—

> "O Lord! that I could waste my life for others,
>   With no ends of my own,
> That I could pour myself into my brothers,
> And live for them alone!"

There are soldiers of the Cross ready to fight and to die for their Great Captain and His cause—

> "Each stepping where his comrade stood,
> The instant that he falls."

---

[1] *Two Friends*, by Dora Greenwell (James Clarke & Co.).

But a smile, or a sneer, or a counsel of imperfection, brings down the ardent spirit to the prevailing dead level of commonplace, and the Church loses an opportunity, and thus another vocation for great things is wasted.

"There is no recognized place in our ecclesiastical system for men who wish to give their lives to the service of the Church, and yet shrink from parochial work. A man is practically debarred from ordination unless he is prepared to go for some time as a curate. He may feel himself entirely unfitted for this; he changes his mind, and goes to the Bar, or enters some other profession."[1]

Bishop Fraser said we must not be deterred from the revival of Brotherhoods by "the silly and irrational dread of Monasticism" (1853).

Bishop Lightfoot, in a sermon on "Disciplined Life," 1860, advocated the revival of some form of Monasticism. Dean Farrar says—"There is nothing which will make Romanists smile more disdainfully than to see this proposal fall dead. . . . You say you dislike vows. Be it so. Then create Brotherhoods like the Brethren of the Common Life, or the Order of St. Philip Neri, or the Rosminians, who are not bound by vows. He must, indeed, be ignorant of Church history, who is not aware that my principle advocated in the formation of Brotherhoods existed long before Romish corruptions, and has continued to this day in communities like the Moravians and the Methodists, who are most fundamentally opposed to

[1] G. S. S. Vidal, Esq., Church Congress at Southampton, 1887.

the Church of Rome.... Our parochial system, transcendently valuable for pastoral work, breaks down hopelessly and on every side for aggressive and missionary purposes.... Already in America the suggestion has been carried out by the 'Brothers of Nazareth.'... I would give tons and cart-loads of caution for one sand-grain of real enthusiasm. Even the enthusiasm which flares like fire in straw, is better than the valley which is full of dry bones.... It was enthusiasm which first kindled the flame of Christianity; that enthusiasm with which St. Paul called on all Christians to be Ζέοντες εν πνεύματι, 'boiling in spirit.' All England has just been ringing with eulogies of that great son of the English Church, whom she lost to the Church of Rome. Why did she lose him? She lost him because, as the hard-headed historian has told her, she has never learnt the wisdom of that Church which neither submits to enthusiasm, nor proscribes it, but uses it; 'because,' as another of her sons has said, 'the Church of England is even in danger of dying of respectability.' .. And again, 'Oh, my mother, what is this to me, thou that bearest children, yet darest not own them? How is it that whatever is generous in purpose, and tender and deep in devotion, falls from thy bosom, and finds no home within thy arms?'... One of the weightiest voices in our own Church has told us that the Church of England failed to retain the splendid intellect and glowing spirituality of John Henry Newman, because he desired a mode of life which seemed nearer the ideal of the New Testament than what he called the 'smug and comfortable' life of the English Church, and its 'vulgar success in making the best of both worlds.' . . . The great regenerative movements, at the most decisive crises of Church history, were the work of Brotherhoods. In the third century Brotherhoods of Hermits saved the Church from lethargy; in the sixth century Brotherhoods of Benedictines prevented her from being overwhelmed by the deluge of barbarians; in the thirteenth century, in a wealthy and easy Church, whose symptoms were fatally like our own, the Brothers Minor of Francis of Assisi supported her collapsing pillars by taking Christ literally at His word. When, after the taking of Rome, Garibaldi published his famous proclamation, 'Soldiers, I have nothing but rags, wounds, hardships, and beggary to offer you; let him who loves his country follow me,' the youths of Italy sprang to their feet in answer to that appeal. Were there thousands in Italy to sacrifice all for their country, and shall there be none in the Church of England to sacrifice all for Christ?"[1]

"I think," said Mr. F. W. Faber, "that monasteries would form a safety-valve for much to escape that now condenses into dissent . . . men would be monks who are now field-preachers. Picture to yourself the huge moral wildernesses of countless souls, who throng the earth around the English factories. In each district two or three churches, with perhaps four priests, men of soft habits, elegant manners, and refined education . . . but set down amongst them

[1] Church Congress, Hull, 1890. See Note S, p. 397.

one or two monasteries; combine in them much of the rough, rude energy, which now evaporates in chartism and dissent, and you will soon see a very different state of things.... Send the poor monks out among the poor from whence they have been taken, interfere for the weak against the oppressor, let charity and sympathetic watchfulness, which is even more prized than almsgiving, run over exuberantly, and be flowing night and day from the gates of the monastery."[1]

If ever the question of reunion with other branches of the Church assumes any appearance of possibility, the fact that the Church of England, like all the ancient Churches, has Monastic Orders, and encourages the practice of the precepts laid down by our Lord in the Sermon on the Mount, would constitute an argument that would not fail to be appreciated by those from whom we are at present separated, and would take away the power which they might otherwise exercise of saying that by our entire want of the "Religious Life" we proved our doctrinal disagreement with the Catholic Church in her best days.

"The Salvation Army has given an impulse to our efforts at home evangelization. It has forced us to see clearly that the pastoral, parochial, and edificatory theory of Christian work, though good, is one-sided. Before the Reformation, this theory was corrected by the wide spread of such bodies as the Preaching Friars; but since that time the parochial theory has had

[1] *Lights and Thoughts.*

exclusive possession of the Church, and we see now the disastrous extent of the failure. The parochial theory lacks the spirit of aggression, and wherever Christianity ceases to be aggressive, there Christianity recedes. The result of three hundred years of reformed Christianity (which ought to be the most potent) is that we find ourselves in the midst of what is called 'heathen England.' . . . It is not the craze of a few extreme partisans; holy Archbishop Leighton passionately lamented that the old monasteries had been destroyed, and not reformed."[1]

"In all probability the very increase of unbelief and immorality in the world will result in forcing many devout persons to seek for greater separation from it. We may look for the growing evils of the days of Antichrist to be accompanied by a growing manifestation of supernatural sanctity in the Church of God. As the world withdraws from the restraints of the Church, the Church gains a higher sanctity by the mere fact of such withdrawal. This may not improbably lead to a fuller acceptance of the spirit of Carmel, so that the Church may be prepared, along with the Elias of the last days, to bear the loud witness necessary before the coming of Christ."[2]

"Monasticism has fared very much like Christianity itself. Whenever its profession involved the certainty, or in any high degree the probability of self-sacrifice, none sought it but men of earnest and devout minds; and then its career was resplendent with glory.

[1] Canon A. J. Mason, Church Congress, Derby, 1882.
[2] R. M. Benson, *Literary Churchman*, April 5, 1889.

When it conferred honours and respectability, it was embraced by a certain proportion of brethren who had neither vocation nor sincere piety; and then it grew feeble and secular. But it was never deserted by the grace of God, and its archives teem with more or less successful reforms."[1]

The rise and the extraordinary growth of Monasticism can only be understood when the conditions of human life in the early Christian ages and in mediæval times are investigated, and all the surroundings of modern civilized society are put aside from the mind. The accounts that have come down to us of the prevailing depravity during the reign of the Roman emperors, whether described by heathen writers, or sketched by St. Paul, enable us to appreciate the action of those who became convinced that it was impossible to lead a godly life in the midst of such an atmosphere of all-prevailing vileness; and that the message of Christ to His people dwelling in the spiritual Babylon, was, "Come out of her." In the succeeding centuries the successive invasions of the barbarians reduced the cosmos of the Roman world to chaos; and again despair drove the lovers of peace into the wilds, beyond the reach of fire and sword, to watch for the coming of Christ; to destroy the enemies of God and man, and establish a kingdom of righteousness. In still later times Christianity was professed but not much practised. The lower passions of unregenerate human nature still

---

[1] *Ecclesiastical Chronicle of Scotland*, Rev. J. F. S. Gordon, D.D., vol. iii.

held almost unchecked sway. Wars, pillage, cruelties, lust, hate, ruled the rulers of the world, and the cloister seemed to be the only sphere where the practice of Christian virtues was practicable. As Dean Church says (*Life of St. Anselm*), " That which of itself presented itself to the thoughts of a man in earnest, wishing not only to do right, but to do the best he could to fulfil God's purpose and his own calling by self-improvement, was the monastic profession." As civilization advanced, and Christian principles became influential, not only in the hearts of kings, but among all classes of society, the practice of religion became easier in the midst of the occupations of daily life, and Monasticism began to decline, because its necessity was no longer so evident, because, unhappily, it no longer presented a higher and purer example to the world outside the Cloister. In the present day the old, dreadful heathenism seems to have revived; and the need of an adapted Monasticism becomes once more apparent—not in the form of flight from the world so much as a campaign of soldiers of Christ, not entangled with the things of this life, giving themselves without one selfish reservation to fight the enemies of God and man, and to overcome evil with good.

A very devout priest of the Church of England, entirely devoted to the higher spiritual life, thus writes—" I think that what the Religious Vocation may be intended to do for the Church is (1) To teach the idea of Vocation as giving its significance to every life. The monk takes his life from God, in response to a Divine call. Everything in his discipline reminds him of this Divine basis of every-day life; so the idea becomes understood generally throughout the Catholic Church, and keeps its place in family and public life. (2) To be an object-lesson from which the unlearned and heathen can take in at a glance certain great principles. (3) To be a hospital and shelter for weaker souls, and penitents, who need more spiritual help and protection than others. (4) To be a training for the noblest. (5) To be a practical school of prayer. The great teachers in prayer have been *Religious*—Thomas à Kempis, St. Theresa, St. John of the Cross. (6) To be a shelter from the all-penetrating vanity and distractions of the world, for some who would otherwise find no privacy, or opportunity for retirement.

"If any sort of impression were given that truest Christianity requires celibacy, solitude, and renunciation of possessions, and that this is now only to be found in religious communities, and that the rest of humanity is thrown back upon a state of life which can be of little moral value, it would certainly be very irritating to Protestant sensibilities; but, besides, I do not think it would be true. My impression is that an exaggerated estimate of the Religious Vocation was very natural in ages when the brutalities of ordinary semi-pagan Christian life was contrasted with the order and lofty aim of the monasteries. Men came to imagine that God could raise any one He liked by a call, or a state; and probably the exaggerated estimate was one cause of decay in Monastic

Orders; it flooded the monasteries with men who wanted to find salvation given away as a privilege, and did not want to have to fight for it. And then the over-estimate created the reaction."

It has been objected that the Contemplative Life is unsuited to the spirit of the nineteenth century. And yet Contemplative Orders exist and flourish before our eyes. The Carthusians, who boast that their Order has never been reformed or reconstituted, because it has never degenerated, live and pray at the Grand Chartreuse in France, and at Cowfold in Sussex, and in other places where they are allowed to exist, exhibiting exactly the same practices, and acting upon precisely the same principles as those which St. Bruno established. The Cistercians of La Trappe in France, and of Mount St. Bernard in Leicestershire, and elsewhere in Europe and America, carry out to the letter the Rule of St. Bernard, and display the very same results that have ever followed their ascetic routine of prayer, silence, and labour. Their meagre diet, their night services, their poverty and hard work, do not prevent their enjoying sound health, and living to a good old age; they are bright and happy; they make friends of their animals; they are successful farmers; they give alms without stint. Nor is this all; there are seen in their midst the gifts of the Holy Spirit of God, the fulfilment of Christ's promises to those who take Him at His word, and follow Him literally, fully, and without reserve. This is especially the case with the Lay Brothers, men taken from the lower ranks of life, peasants, labourers, and artisans, men without education, poor, but rich in faith, displaying visibly the likeness of Christ.

"The hidden life of the Church is to be found in the Cloister, among those whose vocation is primarily —in many cases only—a life of prayer. Behind all the active life of the Church stand these great religious orders devoted to prayer and penitence, witnessing to the world that Christianity is not merely a philanthropic society, but that it is devotion to a Person. These men and women devote themselves not to active work for their brethren—in many cases they shut themselves out from the possibility of any such work—but believing that the closer they are to God the more real help they can bring to the world, they give up everything else that they may draw ever closer to Him. . . . Who can tell the power that from age to age has gone forth from these unknown lives?—men and women literally buried out of the world's sight and knowledge, who, while the world has gone on its way and enjoyed itself, and often sneered at the selfish lives of those who fled from it to save their own souls, little knew that they were the world's saviours, whose lives are a living sacrifice for their brethren."[1]

Is it then altogether a preposterous anachronism to express a hope and belief that religious associations of men for the work of the Church are not a thing of the past only? The tide of opposition has run strongly against the idea; but tides turn after a time,

[1] *Some Principles and Practices of the Spiritual Life*, by Rev. B. W. Maturin, p. 142.

and set the opposite way. Is it indeed impossible that a system which grew up from the literal acceptance of our Lord's own words; which was the chief instrument for founding and extending the Church in Europe, not to say the whole world; which recovered a lost civilization; which has shown such marvellous power of adapting itself to various places and times and circumstances, that such a system should rise from its ruins and be again a blessing to the world, a saviour to the Church, a restorer of a dying Christ: unity? No sensible person desires to revive antiquated Orders, much less quaint costumes, or fanatical asceticism. There must be no silly imitation, no sentimental nonsense. But we do want once more the Apostolic life, the simple, absolute, unconditional self-sacrifice for God and for man, the life of Christ; life for life; the life of the good to save the bad, the life of the innocent and pure to reclaim the lost and the vile; the best for the worst. We want the imitation of Jesus Christ, Who gave Himself in life and in death to redeem and restore fallen and lost mankind. "Every great movement against evil," said F. W. Robertson, "has begun by a minority of one, or rather of two, of whom one was God."

Take this picture, and say whether it is mere sickly mediævalism. "Let us suppose an institution of the kind proposed settled in a building away from the bustle and excitement of a town, yet within reach by rail of populous places, such, for instance, as Fountains, or Rievaulx, retired nooks where the brethren might take sweet counsel together, and walk in the House of God as friends, but ready at a moment's call to be at Leeds, Bradford, Halifax, Sheffield, Manchester, or Liverpool. . . . In this house there would reside the Superior and the Clerical Brethren, conducting the training of the Probationers in dogmatic theology and in popular elocution, at the same time that their spiritual training in self-denial, humility, prayer, and meditation was being conducted. From Advent to Easter the major part of the Society should be dispersed over the country conducting missions; the Lay Brothers working in hamlets under the parochial clergy; the Clerical Brothers preaching Advent and Lent courses in any parish whither they are summoned, each Brother in Priest's Orders taking with him a Probationer to assist, and to learn the manner of carrying on the spiritual revivals. In summer, from Easter to Advent, the whole body would be reunited in the Central College, unless some of the Lay Brothers were sent about the country on fixed rounds, preaching in the open air, and book-hawking; occupying the position of the primitive evangelist."[1]

Speaking of the restoration of one of our great abbey churches, a writer in the *Guardian* said some time ago—"Why should not some function be found for Collegiate Churches? Why should not a body of clergy be gathered in them, perhaps a diocesan body of 'Evangelists,' as might well find abundant scope for service under Episcopal sanction, especially in the

[1] *The Church and the World*, 1866.

great towns? When we see magnificent structures standing ready for immediate occupation, we cannot but hope that, sooner or later, the right occupiers will be found. 'Pull down the nests,' said a shrewd old revolutionist, 'and the rooks will fly.' Now that we have built or restored the nests, may not a new spiritual progeny wing their way thither?"[1]

When shall we cease to be afraid to learn something from those who "follow not with us"? When shall we dare to say, "Teach me something good and true and useful, and I will listen and thank you, whoever you are, be you Ignatius Loyola or John Wesley; be you Marcus Aurelius or Gautama Buddha; be you the 'man of '93' or John Stuart Mill"? When shall we learn that the Christian Church did not begin in the sixteenth century, and that England is not the whole world? When will it strike us that men who lived as near to Apostolic times as we live to the Reformation did know something about Apostolic doctrine and practice, and that they had a living tradition of that which our Lord Himself taught concerning the Kingdom of God? When shall we arrive at the conclusion that the means which converted wild savages into sober citizens and God-fearing Christians, may, after all, have been Christ's own appointed method of establishing His Kingdom upon earth? When shall we learn from history and from the sight of our own eyes, that it is Christ-like men who can best carry on the mission of Christ; and that those who have been crucified with Him will,

[1] Note T, p. 397.

like Him, draw men after them? It is not money that is wanted to spread Christianity; it is not fine churches and manifold parochial organizations; it is not societies and Acts of Parliament; it is not eloquent preachers and books of argument: we have these, and they are good and helpful in their proper place; but it is Christ who is needed; Christ living still in this every-day world, speaking by men's lips, looking out from men's eyes, making men's hearts burn as they walk side by side with these "wayfaring men"; it is Christ still "with us to the end of the world," dwelling, reigning without rival, without limit, without hindrance to His mighty working in those who have cleansed the temple of their souls of all things unworthy, so that He can teach there and manifest His whole Self, doing "greater works" than those which He did when He trod this earth in human flesh—it is this that the world needs; it is this that the Church needs; it is this that Christ is ready to give us, if we make ourselves worthy of it; if we compel Him to come in and to abide with us in this the eventide of the world.

> "Ah, could you crush that ever-craving lust
> For bliss, which kills all bliss; and lose your life,
> Your barren unit life, to find again
> A thousand times in those for whom you die—
> So were you men and women, and should hold
> Your rightful rank in God's great universe,
> Wherein, in heaven or earth, by will or nature,
> Naught lives for self. All, all from crown to base,—
> The Lamb, before the world's foundation slain—
> The angels, ministers of God's elect—
> The sun, who only shines to light the worlds—

The clouds, whose glory is to die in showers—
The fleeting streams, who in their ocean graves
Flee the decay of stagnant self-content—
The oak, ennobled by the shipwright's axe—
The soil, which yields its marrow to the flower—
The flower, which feeds a thousand velvet worms
Born only to be prey to every bird—
All spend themselves on others. And shall man,
Whose two-fold being is the mystic knot
Which couples earth with heaven, doubly bound,
As being both worm and angel, to that service
By which both worms and angels hold their life,
Shall he, whose every breath is debt on debt,
Refuse, forsooth, to be what God has made him?
No; let him show himself the creature's lord
By free-will gift of that self-sacrifice
Which they, perforce, by nature's laws endure."

C. KINGSLEY, Health and Education.

NOTES

Note A.

JOHN CASSIAN was one of the great promoters of Monasticism in the West, which began to be established there during his lifetime. He had been a monk at Bethlehem, and, with another monk named Germanus, he visited the hermits and monasteries in Egypt. Going to Gaul, he instructed those who were founding monasteries in the principles and practices of the monks of the East. In order to do this more generally and more effectively, he wrote down his Egyptian experiences. These were contained in twelve books, called the *Institutes of the Cœnobia*, and in twenty-four *Conferences*. The subjects treated of in the *Institutes* are very numerous and varied, *e.g.* the dress of monks; the prayers and psalms used by them; the services for the Canonical Hours; the training of novices, and their after life as monks; the eight principal sins against which monks have to contend. The *Conferences* give an account of the conversations of Cassian and his companion Germanus with some of the abbots of the famous Egyptian monasteries, and with solitary hermits, respecting many religious and spiritual subjects. Questions are asked and difficulties are stated, and the venerable recluses give replies and discourses, illustrated by anecdotes, and by the experiences of saints and eremites. These Books seem to have been written early in the fifth century, and were extensively copied, and were placed in the libraries of most of the monasteries in the West, where they long continued to be regarded as text-books of the religious life. Cassiodorus and St. Benedict both esteemed the works of Cassian highly, and recommended their use in their monasteries.

Note B.

"The extant buildings, wonderful as they are, can only be a small fraction of the whole number of edifices which once covered the land. It seemed as if the world had shaken itself, and throwing off the slough of age, had clothed itself with a white robe of churches."[1]

Note C.

An example of the remarkable increase in the value of monastic lands through centuries of cultivation, and improvements and other causes, may be seen in the case of Westminster Abbey. Thorney Island, which was given as its site, was a barren marsh, unproductive and unhealthy, and the remainder of the original landed property was open fields. Sir Walter Besant, in his *Westminster*, thus describes the grant of land bestowed upon the Abbey by King Edgar—"Take a map of London; run a line from Marble Arch along Oxford Street and Holborn, till you reach St. Andrew's, Holborn; then follow the Fleet river to its mouth—you have the north and east boundaries. The Thames is the third boundary. For the fourth, draw a line from the spot where the Tyburn falls into the Thames, to Victoria Station, thence to Buckingham Palace, thence to Marble Arch. The whole of the land included belonged to the Abbey. A little later the Abbey acquired the greater part of Chelsea, the manor of Paddington, the manor of Kilburn, including Hampstead and Battersea—in fact, what is now the wealthier half of modern London formerly belonged to the Benedictines of Westminster . . . more than half of it was marsh land. In Doomsday Book there are but twenty-five houses on the whole estate. Waste lands, lying in shallow ponds, sometimes flooded by high tides, only the rising ground between what is now St. James' Park and Oxford Street, could then be farmed. The ground was reclaimed and settled very slowly; still more slowly was it built upon."

If Westminster Abbey had not been suppressed by Henry VIII., this estate, which originally was so valueless, would now be the most valuable in Europe.

[1] Lightfoot, *Hist. Essays*, p. 153.

Note D.

The nuns, as well as the monks, occupied themselves in literary pursuits. Some of the most elaborate and beautiful MSS. were the work of these gifted women.

Note E.

In Denmark, King Canute, in the eleventh century, invited monks from England, where his ancestors had virtually destroyed all the monasteries, and he and his successors founded and endowed many flourishing abbeys. In Norway, soon after, King Olaus followed his example; and Sweden, about the same time, established the monastic system throughout the country.

Note F.

Before the reformation undertaken by Pope Gregory VII. (Hildebrand), the Church was in a miserable state. Simony was common, preferments were bought and sold, the clergy were frequently openly immoral, kings and nobles made their relations or dependents bishops and abbots, or boldly took possession of Church revenues, and kept the preferments vacant. St. Peter Damian wrote a book, called *Liber Gomorrhianus*, which revealed such a terrible picture of depravity among the clergy of Italy that the Pope locked it up, and would not permit its publication.

Note G.

The abbey of Luxeuil was within the walls of a Roman encampment, and was built on the site of a Temple of Diana, with the *débris*, the pillar columns and mutilated statues of a former religion scattered all around.

The monasteries were the means of breaking down narrow and jealous feelings of nationality. Monks from different countries were found in all large monasteries. A monk could travel all over Christendom without passport, and without police interference, and be received everywhere as a brother; while the common use of Latin in the Church services would enable him to worship in foreign countries just as intelligently as if he were in his own abbey.

"In the monasteries," says the historian Bernold, "one saw counts cooking in the kitchen, and margraves leading the pigs out to feed."

In or near many monasteries there was often the cave of an anchorite. These recluses lived a still more strict and mortified life than the monks. They were clothed, and inclosed in their cell by a bishop or an abbot with a special service, like the Burial of the Dead. An interesting account of an anchorite in Westminster Abbey is given in Sir Walter Besant's *Westminster.*

One hundred and five monasteries were founded by the disciples of Columbanus in France, Germany Switzerland, or Italy.

An account of the present condition of some of the monasteries founded by St. Columbanus and his Irish companions will be found in *Six Months in the Apennines* (1892), and *Three Months in the Forests of France* (1895), by Margaret Stokes. The authoress not only describes the churches and ruined abbeys, but searches out hermitages, legends, relics, and remains of Irish art and literature, and compares them with similar survivals in Ireland itself.

Note H.

As soon as a monastery was founded the peasants came and lived near it, to escape from the cruel exactions of lay landlords; and traders sought the protection of the abbot from the plundering raids of the lawless chieftains. The wrath and curse of a saintly abbot was more feared than the sword of a neighbouring rival count, or even the threats of the King or the Emperor himself.

In the tenth century there were five hundred monks at St. Gall; and all alike, priests and lay brethren, poets like the Notkers, learned men like the Ekkehards, those who had been men of rank and title, and those who had been but peasants, all went in turn to the fields and laboured side by side; all ate at a common table, and worshipped in the same church.

Note I.

The idea originated at Cluny was that of a wide system of monasteries entirely subject to one great central house and abbot. The Abbot of Cluny was in reality a general, whose army was quartered under lieutenant-generals in different places, and even in different countries. All authority originated and remained with the Abbot of Cluny; all subordinate officers were appointed by him; thus traversing the fundamental Benedictine principle and rule that the abbot of each convent should be elected by the universal suffrage of the monks. There was a vast power in this system, so long as a vigorous and capable authority ruled at Cluny, but as soon as weakness and incapacity prevailed there, the whole fabric was rendered insecure and the seeds of dissolution were sown.

The Cistercian system resembled that of Cluny in establishing a central authority, and in the formation of an " Order," rather than in the creation of a number of independent communities, each managing its own affairs in a Chapter presided over by its own abbot, and subject to the Bishop of the diocese. The idea thus inaugurated was but the first step towards the formation of the orders of Mendicant Friars and that of the Jesuits, each of which was governed by a General in Rome.

NOTE J.

"The Puritan preachers of the thirteenth century," says Bishop Lightfoot, "were the Franciscan friars. . . The shaven crown and bare feet of the one, the straight hair and sober-coloured suit of the other were only accidents. The spirit is the same. The Franciscans were the earnest fanatical preachers of their day, the dreaded opponents of the parochial clergy, and the great innovators upon the traditional usages of the Church."—*Historical Essays*, p. 111.

"I protest against Hallam's language, who curtly and scornfully discusses 'the swarms of vermin, the mendicant friars, who filled Europe with stupid superstition.' What! Nothing but stupid superstition? With far deeper knowledge and truer insight, Professor Stubbs describes them as 'always in extremes; sometimes before, sometimes after their age.' They were first in the van of political progress, and then in the van of intellectual progress."—Bishop Lightfoot, *Historical Essays*.

NOTE K.

Sir Walter Besant, in his book on *Westminster*, thus speaks of the state of English monasteries in the latter part of the fifteenth century—" It was now extremely difficult to enter one of the richer abbeys; a lad of humble origin had no chance of admission. Sometimes founders' or benefactors' kin possessed the right of nomination ; sometimes admission was bought by money, or the gift of land ; sometimes it was obtained by the private interest of some great man. . . . The wars had greatly damaged the value of the monastic property, so that an abbey no longer supported so many monks as formerly. Thus the number of monks decreased steadily ; at Westminster there had been eighty ; before the dissolution the number sank below thirty ; at Canterbury a hundred and fifty became fifty-four ; at Gloucester a hundred went down to thirty-six. Probably those who remained had no desire to return to the former and longer roll, which would involve a diminution in the splendour of their establishment. We must remember that the external splendour of the Abbey, which does not necessarily involve luxury and gluttony, was a thing always greatly regarded by the brethren ; it magnified the Order ; it glorified the religious life. Even the most ascetic desired a splendid service, rich robes, vessels of gold and silver, gorgeous tapers, a fine organ, a well-trained choir of glorious voices, troops of servants, and stately buildings. So that this remarkable diminution of numbers may have been due, in some measure, to the increase of this kind of luxury. . . . Some of us can remember how under the old system at Cambridge the Senior Fellows remained in College all their lives, their interests centred in the Society, dining in hall every day, sitting over the College port in Combination Room every day. Few among the Seniors, as one remembers them, were any longer capable of intellectual work ; they had never had any ambitions ; they played bowls in the garden ; they walked every day the customary round ; they were in Orders ; they were regular at chapel, and they led decorous lives. . . . Such as were these aged dons, so were, I believe, the monks of Westminster—dull and respectable, decorous, obedient to so much of the Rule as they could not escape, and stupid and ignorant, since they had been locked up within these walls from childhood."

Note L.

The Lichfield Diocesan Mission, besides employing clerical agency, has a Lay Brotherhood, which works in the diocese and elsewhere. The following statement describes the aims and work of the Brothers—" The Evangelist Brotherhood is an order of laymen. Its object is to help the mission work of the

Church, at home, in the Colonies, and amongst the heathen. It now numbers forty-four members, six of whom are helping in the foreign mission field, and the rest in the Home. The Brotherhood welcomes men from any rank of life, but no difference is made, all are equal: it is a democratic society. No member of the Brotherhood is sent into a parish to work until he has had *at least twelve months' training* at head-quarters."

Mr. Thomas Hughes, in his *Vacation Rambles* (1885) mentions the work of an American Brotherhood on shipboard. He says—

"Attracted by a crowd on the fore part of the deck, I became one of a motley group assisting at a sort of moral 'free-and-easy' got up for the three hundred steerage folk by two ecclesiastics, whom I took at first for Romish priests from their costume. I found I was mistaken, and that they were the Principal and a Brother of 'the Fraternity of the Iron Cross,' an Order of the American Episcopal Church, which, it seems, has taken root in several of the large cities. The Brethren are vowed to 'poverty, purity, and temperance' (or obedience, I am not sure which); and these two were crossing in the steerage to comfort and help the poor folk there—no pleasant task, even in so airy a ship and such fine weather. One can imagine what power this kind of fellowship must give the Iron Cross Brethren with their rather sad fellow-passengers, to whom they could say—one of them indeed did say it—'We are just as poor as the poorest of you, for we own no property of any kind, and never can own any.' This brother (a strapping young fellow of twenty-five, who I found had been an athlete at Oxford) waxed eloquent to them on his experiences in Philadelphia, especially on the working-men brethren there. One of these, a big, rough chap, with a badly-broken nose: he had rather looked askance at first, till he heard that the broken nose had been earned in a rough-and-tumble fight with a fellow who was ill-using a woman. 'Now they were the closest friends, and he looked on the broken nose as more honourable than the Victoria Cross, and hoped that none of them there would fail to go in for the decoration if they ever got the same chance.'"

Note M.

The Rev. N. Goreh (who has recently died) was a member of an ancient and noble family in India, and a Brahman of the highest caste. Endowed with great intellectual gifts, he received the best education that could be obtained. By a gradual process, and through his wide course of study, he became acquainted with the true principles of Christianity, and ultimately, in spite of the strongest family opposition and the traditional prejudice which is so difficult to overcome in the higher ranks of Hindoos, he became a Christian, and after a time was ordained to the priesthood, and ultimately he joined the Brotherhood of St. John at Cowley. The following is a short account from the *Guardian* of a speech made by him at the Missionary Conference in May 1877—

"The Rev. N. Goreh thought that the 'religious life,' with its vows of celibacy, poverty, and obedience, was best fitted for mission work in India. He was far from disparaging other modes of life, but as a native of India, he felt that the work was not progressing as it should among his own people, who, though essentially religious men, were not attracted to the Gospel. The professors of other religions passed outward lives which bore witness to their professions, while the English missionary led a life, which, however simple, was one of luxury compared with native habits. Mr. Goreh then drew a vivid picture of the simple, self-denying life which he had shared with Fr. O'Neill, but said that this did not disarm the suspicion of the educated natives, one of whom told him in reference to Fr. O'Neill that 'elephants had two sets of teeth—one to show, and one to chew with.' . . . Still even now the natives are struck by the ascetic life, and the attention to the Seven Hours, constituting a course of life more like the Indian notion of what is meant by a religious life. He would urge that many Englishmen should follow the example, which is much needed among native Christians, to counteract the example set by European luxury so much imitated by native converts. The religious life with its freedom from the encumbrances of family life would qualify the natives to become the best and cheapest missionaries."

NOTE N.

Theodore Fliedner was born in 1800, the son and grandson of Lutheran clergymen. At the age of twenty-two he was appointed Protestant pastor of Kaisersworth, near Düsseldorf, a small manufacturing town, the inhabitants of which were for the most part Roman Catholics. One day, a poor woman who had been lately in prison, and who was homeless and friendless, came to him, and he could not find it in his heart to send her out into the hard world, but lodged her in a small building that belonged to his parsonage. Other outcasts followed, and he took them in. In 1836 he rented an old house, and transferred his poor women to it. Then he conceived the idea of providing nurses for his pensioners, and training them as deaconesses. To obtain funds for his work, he made a begging expedition to Holland and England, and was successful in raising sympathy and eliciting considerable sums of money. "The Kaisersworth Deaconesses' Institution" made steady progress, till at the present time there are two hundred beds for the sick and aged; there is a training home for deaconesses, a Magdalen Home, a large Kindergarten, a training college for school-teachers, an orphan asylum, an old woman's home, and a home for worn-out deaconesses, besides workshops and other undertakings. There is a farm of several hundred acres and a publishing establishment. Money is received from benefactors, but the institution is nearly self-supporting. Fliedner's deaconesses may be found all over Germany, in America, at Jerusalem, at Constantinople, and several other Oriental cities; 10,400 deaconesses have been trained and sent out to 3640 different places. Three years are occupied in training, and then the deaconess is sent out as a nurse in a hospital, or in some poor parish, or for private nursing, and a moderate payment is made to the mother-house for her services. There are no vows, and each deaconess can leave the institution when she wishes.

NOTE O.

"There is a power in united numbers altogether greater than that represented by the sum of the individual units. . . . The monk is secluded from the world. . . . What a power does not this give him over the man of the world, who is perhaps the slave of the little pleasures, the frivolous vanities, the busy interests, the all-engrossing ambitions which the monk leaves and ignores! The power to withdraw is a mark of strength, and we worship strength in spite of ourselves. The man who can show himself perfectly independent of us at once places himself in a position of superiority, and the feeling of inferiority is the first step towards submission. Again, there is a simplicity about the true monastic character. One thoroughly imbued with that spirit has no end to serve save only the one.

"... If he lacks calculating shrewdness, an art which the world affects but despises, by this his way is opened to the only sure road to the human heart.... The monk, too, dwells in a world that has lasted long. By his traditions he has learnt the Divine art of patience, and can wait in peace and faith for God's own time. In the monastic order the action of the individual is sunk in that of the corporate body.... Individual members pass away, but the self-same life goes on, and the self-same influence continues to manifest itself on those brought within its sphere.... The Romans effected the subjugation of countries to their empire, not so much by the force of arms as by the gradual influence of the 'colonies' they planted among the conquered races. These bodies of men were the real but unobserved conquerors of the world.... So by the mere fact of settling among them, and exhibiting to them the excellence and beauty of the Christian life, the monks won them insensibly to adopt the Christian creed....

"The burning fire of enthusiasm and heroic self-devotion can alone reanimate the fallen and depraved soul.... It is the life of the preacher, or rather the fact of his aiming at a higher ideal than that to which he invites his hearers, that touches the heart, subdues the will, and finally leads the intellect to accept the faith of Christ. It was not the learning of the Apostles, but the fact that they had left all to follow their Master, that drew after them the largest hearts and intellects of the empire of Rome.... But a single man, though a saint, is but one. The Christian life is not merely the life of an individual, it is the life of a society. To establish a Christian nation, it is necessary to present for the imitation of the people an actual pattern of a Christian Society. This is found preeminently in the monastic life, and it is the monastic order which has proved itself the apostle of the nations."[1]

NOTE P.

"The religious orders, whatever be their special purpose, grew always out of a keen sense of passing evils, and a consciousness, sometimes instructive, sometimes confessed, that the Church was at the time powerless to cure those evils by corporate, general, and normal action. To establish an Order pledged to poverty was a testimony against the covetousness and

[1] Rev. F. A. Gasquet.

worldliness which had overspread the Church—a partial remedy for it—a witness that the Church ought to have purged herself from the vice, and could not. To set up an Order of preachers is a declaration that an urgent Church duty is neglected, and a mark that that watchful and rigorous discipline is declined which would have provided against neglect by universally effective methods. So in our day to establish and propagate the Church of England Temperance Society is to tell forth in no ambiguous terms that intemperance is a special bane of our nation and our times; and also that, inasmuch as normal and ordinary modes of checking the vice either fail us or cannot be applied, there is need for a new and special organization to acquit ourselves of what is an elementary duty of our Christian covenant."—Chancellor Espin, at the Annual Meeting of the *Society for the Propagation of the Gospel in Foreign Parts*, April 30, 1877.

Note Q.

A very remarkable book has lately appeared, entitled *En Route*, by J. K. Huysmans, which describes the conversion of a Frenchman who had been an atheist, and one who had formed habits of degrading vice. This man is a scoffer, who despises Christianity because of the inconsistent lives of professing Christians, and especially the clergy. He is induced to visit and spend some time in a Trappist abbey, and there the ascetic lives of the monks, together with their bright happiness, convinces him that there are true Christians in the world of to-day, and that the religion of Christ is a reality and a mighty power. The following extracts will give some idea of the line of thought that pervades the work, and how it illustrates and confirms the theory that Monasticism is not dead, but that it is a possible and powerful instrument for the promotion of Christianity both to-day and in the future—

"pour sauver l'Église il reste le moine que le prêtre abomine, car la vie du cloître est pour son existence à lui un constant reproche."

"Le clergé séculier ne peut être qu'un déchet, car les ordres contemplatifs et l'armée des missionaires enlèvent chaque année la fleur du panier des âmes. Ainsi écrèmé le reste du clergé n'est évidemment plus que le lait allongé, que la lavasse des séminaires."

"Quand vous verrez des hommes qui, après avoir tout abandonné pour servir Dieu, mènent une vie de privations et de pénitence telle qu'aucun gouvernement n'oserait l'infliger à ses forçats, vous serez bien obligé de vous avouer que vous n'êtes pas grand'chose a côté d'eux."

"nous entrons ici pour faire pénitence, pour nous mortifier, et nous avons à peine souffert que déjà Dieu nous console."

"Puis, songeant à tous ces Trappistes, à la sérénité de leur visages, à l'allégresse de leurs yeux, Durtal se disait que ces Cisterciens n'étaient nullement, ainsi que le monde croit, des gens douloureux et funèbres, mais qu'ils étaient, bien au contraire, les plus gais des hommes."

"Les moines atteignent ici-bas le paradis en y cherchent l'enfer."

"Si vous pouviez causer avec ces paysans et ces illettrés [the lay Brothers] vous seriez surpris des réponses souvent profondes que ces gens vous feraient ; puis ils sont les seuls qui soient réellement courageux à la Trappe ; nous autres, les pères, lorsque nous nous croyons trop affaiblis, nous acceptons volontiers le supplément autorisé d'un œuf ; eux pas ; ils prient davantage, et il faut admettre que Notre Seigneur les écoute, puisqu'ils se rétablissent et ne sont, en somme, jamais malades."

"une tâche qui consiste non plus à purger les fautes d'autrui, mais à les prévenir, à les empêcher d'être commises, en supplantant les personnes trop faibles pour en supporter le choc."

"Le monde se demande à quoi servent les ordres contemplatifs. Ils sont les paratonnerres de la société. Ils attirent sur eux le fluide démoniaque, ils resorbent les séductions des vices, ils préservent par leur prières, ceux qui vivent dans le péché. Les sœurs qui se vouent à la garde des malades et des infirmes sont admirables, mais combien leur tâche est aisée en comparaison de celle qu'assument les ordres cloîtrés, les ordres où les pénitences ne s'interrompent jamais, où même les nuits alitées sanglotent."

"Le monde ne conçoit même pas que les austérites des abbayes puissent lui profiter. La doctrine de la suppléance mystique lui échappe complètement. Et Dieu sait pourtant de quels cataclysmes ce monde inconscient serait menacé, si par suite d'une disparition soudaine de tous les cloîtres, cet equilibre qui le sauve était romper."

"Qui sait si les folies démoniaques d'un Carrier où d'un Marat ne concordent point avec la mort d'une abbaye dont la sainteté préservait, depuis des années, la France."

" La Revolution n'a détruit que des ruines. Le régime de la Commende avait fini par sataniser les monastères. Ce sont eux, hélas ! qui, par le relâchement de leurs mœurs, ont fait pencher la balance et attiré sur ce pays la foudre."

" Après le siège de 1870, prudemment, l'on enveloppa Paris dans un immense réseau d'infranchissables forts ; mais ne serait-il pas indispensable aussi de l'entourer d'une ceinture de prières, de bastionner ses alentours de maisons conventuelles, d'édifier, partout, dans sa banlieue, des monastères de Clarisses, de Carmélites, de Benedictines du Saint-Sacrement, des monastères que seraient, en quelque sorte, de puissantes citadelles destinées à arrêter la marche en avant des armées du mal."

This opinion, that the Regular Orders are superior to the secular clergy, is not universally held. The late Cardinal Manning, in his book on *The Eternal Priesthood*, maintains that the secular clergy enjoy liberty from vows, which is the highest state of perfection. Christ and His Apostles were not under vows. Christ founded the Priesthood and the Episcopate Himself, but the Religious Orders are merely an ecclesiastical institution *ad auxilium*.

The Rev. B. W. Maturin says—" The idea of Vocation must not be limited to one or two of the more clearly marked calls of God, such as the call to the priesthood or the religious life ; we read in the Gospels of one who thought he had a call to such a special following of our Lord as the Apostles had, and our Lord forbade him. . . . He would have mistaken his Vocation if he had given up everything for Christ ; his Vocation, therefore, was as distinctly to the home life as was St. Peter's to the Apostolic life."—*Some Principles and Practices of the Spiritual Life*, p. 64.

NOTE R.

A recent painting in the Salon, by Jehan-Georges Vibert, illustrates the contrast between the ordinary spirit of the clergy and that of the enthusiast who sacrifices himself for Christ. In a spacious apartment, upon the walls of which hangs on one side the portrait of Cardinal Richelieu, and on the other a painting of the martyrdom of St. Bartholomew, several cardinals are reclining on luxurious seats, sipping their after-dinner coffee.

In the midst is a poor friar missionary, who is recounting his experience, and showing the wounds which nearly caused his death, while he eagerly tells how he has vowed to return to his post as soon as his health is restored. The prelates languidly listen, one plays with a dog, and all evidently consider that the martyr is at liberty to go his way so long as he allows them to go theirs.

Note S.

See an account of the self-sacrificing devotion of Brothers who ministered to the wounded during the Franco-German War, in *L'Heroisme en Soutane*, and in the Memoirs of Fr. Damien, who gave his life to the lepers.

Note T.

The following is an abridgement of a picturesque and suggestive imaginary picture of a modern Religious House of Retreat for aged clergy, entitled *The Brotherhood of Peace: an Ideal*, which appeared in *The Church Times* of January 31, 1896—

"I caught sight of a cluster of red roofs, surmounting a low range of grey stone buildings, from one of which a gilded cross flashed the last rays of the setting sun. I looked to Brother Francis for an explanation. 'You have not heard then,' he said, 'of our Brotherhood of Peace? Perhaps that is hardly strange. It was founded a few years ago for poor and solitary priests like myself, who are past active work, and who desire a quiet haven, and a little space of preparation before we die.'

"As we drew near to the little group of buildings it resolved itself into a quadrangle, occupying a low spur of the range of hills which shut in the valley on its northern side. We entered the quadrangle through a large gateway, above which I noticed, deeply cut in the stone, 'Domus Pacis.' In the corner of the quadrangle opposite was evidently the chapel, and as we emerged from the gateway into the cloistered court a bell began to sound from a little bell-cote at its western gable. 'We are just in time for Evensong,' said Brother Francis, and we passed round two sides of the cloister walk and entered the antechapel. Brother Francis pointed me to a *prie-dieu*, and himself passed through the screen into the chancel proper. The chapel, I could see in the dim light, was small, but of excellent proportions. In the canopied stalls on each side brethren were already assembled. They were habited, as was Brother Francis, in cassocks of dark blue serge with a hooded cape. A taper by each brother's desk gave light enough for the recitation of the well-known office, and enabled me to scan the faces of the brethren. Old men they were, grown old in their conflict with the evil in the world, and bearing the marks of conflict in their faces. But each face had something of serenity; they seemed truly brethren of peace. The bell stopped, and a brother, younger than the rest, who occupied a return stall, began the office. The *Nunc Dimittis*, as the brethren recited it, seemed more than ever full of pathos and significance.

"Evensong ended, Brother Francis showed me the guest-room which I was to occupy, and returned to fetch me to supper. The refectory in the north cloister was a large, low room, with an open hearth, on which a cheerful wood fire burned. Brother Francis, in the absence of the sub-warden, said a familiar Latin grace, and sat at the head of the table. The meal was of the simplest, and was served by two lay brethren in brown habits. Brother Francis explained to me that the community numbered more than the ten or twelve who were present, as two of the brothers were in the infirmary, and others were so feeble as to be waited upon in their own rooms. We spent a short time after supper in the fratry, or common room, where I renewed my acquaintance with one or two of the brethren whom I had known when they were in active work. But I was eager to hear from Brother Francis some account of the foundation of the community, and so he took me to his rooms in the south cloister. The sets of rooms consisted each of a sitting-room, approached through a small lobby, and a bed-room above, with a tiny oratory in a recess. They were lighted by electricity, of which the mountain stream was the motive force, and heated by hot air. The Brother's rooms were comfortably but plainly furnished, and there he talked to me of the Brotherhood and its origin until the bell summoned us to Compline. The community was founded and to a certain extent endowed, he told me, by the present warden, whose lodgings were in the north cloister. There was a sub-warden, who was responsible for the services in the chapel, and for the general well-being of the community. Under him the more able-bodied of the community held various offices, serving by course in each office for a month at a time. There were, for example, a sacristan, an infirmarian, a porter, and a librarian. The work of the house and the garden was undertaken by lay-serving brethren, though the Brethren of Peace often shared in it if they were able. The warden ruled the community, and from his decision, when confirmed by the chapter, no appeal was possible. 'But we dwell together in unity,' said Brother Francis, 'and there has never been any difficult question of discipline to decide.' The brethren were under no obligation to attend other services than Matins and Evensong, though as a matter of fact the lesser hours were almost invariably frequented. The conditions of admission were inability to undertake or continue parochial work, poverty, and want of relatives with whom the priest might live; and election to the Brotherhood was by the whole community. 'And for the rest,' he concluded, as the bell summoned us to Compline, 'we pass our few days in peace, though not inactivity. Some of us find leisure for literary work, and to each of us comes the opportunity of slight occupation, and of small deeds of charity. And so we await our end, thanking God continually that He has put it into the heart of our Founder to make provision for the old age of some of His priests.'

"Next morning we visited first the two brethren in the infirmary. They were being nursed by two Sisters of Charity, from a Community which had undertaken the work, and had a small branch house hard by. From the infirmary the patients could look down through two large bay windows into the chapel, and join in spirit with their brethren in the offices and the Holy Sacrifice. Above the altar of the chapel the Blessed Sacrament was continually reserved, lest any sick brother should depart without the Viaticum. We went up into the library, a roomy chamber lined with books old and new, with pleasant alcoves for writing and reading. Above the great fire-place was the one word which I had everywhere seen graven or painted, 'Pax.' Here one brother was writing, the librarian was posting up the catalogue, another was looking up obscure references for a correspondent, a fourth was reading the month's reviews. 'We are little fettered by rule,' said Brother Francis, 'and we employ ourselves, as you see, as liberty and conscience allow.' Round the inner court ran the cloister walk, by which any part of the building could be reached without going into the open air, and in which the more feeble brethren could take exercise in boisterous weather. Smooth, well-kept sward made a cool cloister-garth, and the murmur and plash of a fountain in the middle lent it life.

"Outside the quadrangle, south and east, the slope of the hill was terraced into gardens of a formal type, in complete accord with the buildings. Here and there in sheltered nooks brethren were sitting and reading. 'Here is our best garden,' said Brother Francis, as he led me through a wicket in a pleached hedge, into an open space eastward of the chapel, where two or three grass mounds told of brethren departed. At the head of each grave was a simple cross of oak, with the name of the brother and the date of his departure incised. In the middle of the cross rose a great marble Calvary, with the inscription, *Animæ fidelium, per misericordiam Dei, requiescant in pace*, cut on the lowest step. Everywhere peace reigned."

Note U.

"A certain monk, being asked why he had fled humankind, answered, on account of his great love for it, and the impossibility of loving God and it at the same time."

"The early monks, however useful and venerable as tillers of the soil and students of all sciences, were, nevertheless, only agglomerated hermits, retired from the world for the safety each of his own soul; whereas the preaching, wandering friars are men who mix with the world for the sake of the souls of others."

"The universal brotherhood, preached by Francis of Assisi, is a brotherhood, not of suffering, but of happiness, nay, of life and of happiness."[1]

[1] *Renaissance Fancies and Studies*, Vernon Lee, p. 26.

INDEX

ABELARD, 98
Abuses, early, 152; seventh century, 170; Hume on monastic, 173; in everything, 218; showing them up, 230; no argument against use, 275
Abyssinians, 90
Acedia, 223
Adamnan, 150
Ælfric, 155
Africa, Church in, 142
Aidan, St., mission, 26; at Lindisfarne, 147
Alacoque, Marie, 5
Albertus Magnus, 121
Albigenses, 118
Alcantara, Order of, 110
Alien Priories, founded, 156; seized, 159; suppressed, 176
Allies, Prof., on Human Society, 25; on Marriage and Virginity, 349
All Saints' Sisterhood, 308; in India, 337
A. L. O. E., 344
Alpine Club, 13
Ambrose, St., 61, 84, 85
America, Brotherhoods in, 298, 390; Sisterhoods in, 328
American Indians, 13
Ammonius, 51
Anchorites, 387
Angelico, Fra, 121
Annales Minorum, 176
Anselm, St., the object of monasticism, 7; joyfulness of monks, 33; torn from his cell, 35; intellectual power of, 98
Anthony, St., his conversion, 7; author of monasticism, 42; said to be a myth, 43; St. Jerome on, 44

Anthony, St., of Padua, 116
Antonio de Guevara, 7
Aquinas, St. Thomas, on perfection, 3; a Dominican Friar, 121
Argyle, Bishop of, on the Religious Life, 309
Arians, 91
Armagh, 65
Armenians, 90
Arnaud, Angelique, 124
Arnold of Brescia, 98
Asceticism, universal, 12, 336, 338; in unlikely places, 19, 369; carried to extremes, 259
Asia, 15
Athanasius, St., on St. Anthony, 45; introduces monasticism in the West, 57
Athos, Mount, 89, 289
Augustine, St., of Canterbury, a missionary, 26; his mission, 95; revives British monasticism, 140
Augustine, St., of Hippo, his conversion, 7; on St. Anthony, 45; favours monasticism, 61; his Rule, 100; condemns bad monks, 225; discourages labour among monks, 351
Augustine's, St., Canterbury, 143
Augustinian Canons, incorporated, 104; in England, 159; in Scotland, 214

Bacon, Friar, 98
Bangor, in Ireland, 65, 134; in Cheshire, 132, 145
Barbarians, invasions of the, 26, 374; in Africa, 81
Bards, the, 139
Barras, Memoirs of, 242
Bartolomeo, Fra, 121
Barton, Elizabeth, 179

3 F

Basil, St., influence of, 26; one of the fathers of monasticism, 41; life of, 53; Rule of, 67; on the eremitical life, 175; on fasting, 355
Beaton, Cardinal, 216
Bede, St., at Jarrow, 148; his history, 150; on monasticism, 170
Bega, St., 86
Beggars, Supplication of, 178
Beghards, the, 123
Beguines, the, 123
Benedict, St., Rule of, 6; promoter of monasticism, 41; like St. Paul, 70; Order of, 100; on asceticism, 355
Benedict, St., of Aniane, 96
Benedict, St., Biscop, builds monasteries, 148; life, 155
Benson, Fr., on male and female communities, 310; on the aim of Religious, 352; on austerities, 357; on touting for money, 358; on the Church and the world, 373
Bernard, St., a saying of, 9; Abbot of Clairvaux, 103; his letters, 226
Bernardin, St., of Sienna, 116
"Bernardus valles," etc., 123
Bernold, 387
Bertha, Queen, 142
Besant, Sir W., 385, 387, 388
Black Book, the, 187
Black Death, the, injured monasticism, 176, 254
Blunt, J. H., on asceticism, 10, 330, 337, 343; on monasticism, 16; on slander of monks, 173; on English monks, 195; on the destruction of monastic libraries, 201; on the suppression of English monasteries, 204; on the Friars, 250; on the revival of monasticism, 274
Bonaventura, St., a Franciscan, 116; on the Friars, 249
Bonhommes, the, 160
Boniface, St., a missionary, 26; the founder of Fulda, 95
Borromeo, Carlo, 354
Bossuet, on the Rule of St. Benedict, 6; on solitaries, 44
Brandon, pilgrimage of, 136

Brewer, J. S., 178
Bridget, St., founds nunneries, 135, 208
Britain, monasticism in, 131
British Church, 144
Brotherhoods, needed, 36, 397; Anglican, 294; American, 298, 390; literature on, 302; Convocation and Diocesan Conferences on, 303; Dean Farrar on, 369
Brothers, Christian, 281
Brothers of Nazareth, 370
Browne, Bishop Harold, 357
Browne, Matthew, 230
Browsers, 52
Bruno, St., his conversion, 7; founds the Carthusian Order, 104
Bryce, Prof., 292
Bucer, 261
Buddha, flees the world, 12; a leader of men, 40
Bulteau, 9
Burke, A. R., 239
Burnellus, the Ass, 239
Byron, Lord, 271

Cadoc, 137
Cædmon, 148
Calatrava, Order of, 110
Calvin, 12, 263
Camaldoli, 104, 279
Camden Society's transactions, 185, 189
Canons of the East Syrians, 127
Canons, Regular, 107
Canterbury, St. Augustine at, 142; cathedral rebuilt, 157; a dinner at Christ Church, 178
Canute, 155, 386
Capistran, St. John, 116
Capuchins, 116
Carlyle, Thos., on monks, 31; on Christianity, 365
Carmelites, claim Elijah, 43; come to Europe, 111; come to England, 161; come to Ireland, 211; come to Scotland, 214
Carthusians, the, founded, 104; Ruskin on, 105; came to England, 161; accused of treason, 185; put to death, 198; driven

from Perth, 217; of to-day, 279, 377
Cassianus, 64, 384
Cassino, Monte, founded, 71; titles of the Abbot of, 81; burned, 91; suppressed, 94
Cassiodorus, 62, 384
Cathedrals, Benedictine, 158
Catherine, St., of Sienna, 121
Celtic Church, the, St. Patrick's influence on, 65, 100
Celtic usages, in the Saxon Church, 144; St. Wilfrid opposes them, 149; in the Irish Church, 209
Certosas, 105
Chalcedon, Council of, 57
Chantal, Jane Frances de, 86
Chapuys, 200
Charity, Sisters of, 123
Charlemagne, 235
Charles, St., Oblates of, 123
Chateaubriand, 17
Chaucer, 172
Chester, Bishop of, 362
Christian Brothers, 281
Chrysostom, St., on virginity, 4; a monk, 26; on monastic joy, 33; on the Thebaid, 50; on monasticism, 56, 86, 90, 225
Church Army, 297
Church of England, her present wants, 351, 370
Church, Dean, on reforms, 234; on Camaldoli, 279; on monasticism, 375
Cistercians, the, founded, 103, 388; come to England, 159; come to Ireland, 210; their schism, 226; of to-day, 280, 377
Citeaux, 103
Clairvaux, 103
Clares, the Poor, 114
Clergy, the English, 355
Clewer, the, Sisterhood, 313, 325
Clotilda, 85
Cloveshoe, Council of, 153
Cluny, founded, 103; Cluniacs come to England, 159; controversy with Citeaux, 226; Visitation of Order, 228; new idea, 387
Cobbe, Miss F. P., on self-sacrifice, 19; on monasteries, 32; on Mar Saba, 290; on retirement, 352
Cockayne, the Land of, 178
Coleridge, 364
Colman, Abbot, 149
Columba, St., his fiery temper, 17; his history, 137; in Scotland, 208
Columbanus, St., his missions, 100, 136, 209, 387
Commende, injurious effects of the, 32, 250, 396
Common Life, the Brothers of the, 124, 306, 369
Communist Societies in America, 20
Comperta, 186
Confucius, 40
Constantine Copronymus, 226
Constantinople, the taking of, 259
Copts, the, 89
Cordeliers, the, 116
Counsels of Perfection, 6, 38
Cowley, the, Brotherhood, 294
Cowley, the poet, 8
Cranmer, 333
Crawford, F. M., 15
Creighton, Bishop, 27, 167, 274
Cromwell, Vicar-General, 182; secret schemes, 184; instructions to Visitors, 193
Croyland, 151
Culdees, 209
Cunegunda, 86
Curzon, visits to Eastern monasteries, 87, 289
Cuthbert, St., his life, 150
Cynics, the, 16

Damasus, Pope, 60
Damian, St. Peter, 386
Danes, the, sack Iona, 140; sack Lindisfarne, 150; destroy British monasticism, 153; in Ireland, 210
David, St., founded monasteries, 132, 137
Deaconesses, Societies of, 324; Kaiserworth, 326, 391
Decian persecution, the, 43
Dissolution of monasteries, Act for the, 187; value of smaller

monasteries, 189; property given to the nobility, 191; misery resulting, 199; injury to the Church, 200; in Ireland, 212; in Scotland, 217
Dixon, Canon, on English monasteries, 196, 203
Dixon, Hepworth, 291
Döllinger, Dr., on the Templars, 256; on the Reformation in Germany, 262
Dominic, St., 118
Dominicans, the, eminent men among, 121; and the Inquisition, 121; in England, 160; in Ireland, 211; in Scotland, 214; quarrels with the Franciscans, 226
"Domini Canes," 120
Donatus, 63
Dubritius, St., 132
Duckett, Sir G. F., 228
Duns Scotus, 116
Dunstan, St., 154

Eanswith, St., 151
Ebba, St., 86, 151
Eckart, 11
Eckenstein, 264, 342
Edmundsbury, St., founded, 155; desecrated, 199
Edward the Confessor, 156
Edwards, O. M., 135
Egypt, 13, 43
Elfreda, 151
Elijah, 43, 111, 123
Elizabeth, St., of Hungary, 86, 116
Ely, founded, 151; restored, 153
Emerson, 368
Emilianus, 63
Encyclopædia Britt., 367
Ephrem, St., 52
Epiphanius, 52
Erasmus, 202, 240, 249, 261, 353
Erigena, 98
Espin, Chancellor, 394
Essenes, the, 15
Etchmiadzin Monastery, 88, 292
Ethelbert, 142
Ethelburga, 146, 151
Etheldreda, St., 86, 151
Eustochium, St., 85

Evolution, social, 83, 338

Faber, F. W., 264, 371
Farrar, Dean, 369
Faure, John, 262
Feckenham, Abbot, 206
Fenelon, Archbishop, 232
Ferrar, Nicholas, 334
Ferrer, St. Vincent, 121
Fliedner, Pastor, 326, 391
Fontevraud, founded, 104
Fox, Samuel, on English monasteries, 35
Francis, St., de Sales, 355
Francis, St., of Assisi, his conversion, 7; his joy, 32; his love for animals, 34; his life, 113
Franciscans, the, founded, 112; in England, 160; their labours, 172, 371, 388; in Ireland, 211; in Scotland, 214; complaints against them, 226, 249
Frankish polygamy, 186
Fraser, Bishop, 369
Friars minor, 116
Friars Preachers, founded, 119; in England, 160
Frideswide, St., 86, 152
Froude, J. A., on enthusiasm, 18; in praise of monasteries, 30, 169; on the Carthusians, 105; on the Irish monks, 133; on St. Alban's, 163; against the revival of monasticism, 273, 277
Fulda, 65, 95
Fuller, 334, 357
Fursy, 148

Gall, St., 102, 136, 387
Garibaldi, 371
Gasquet, Fr., on the Black Death, 177; on the benefit of monasteries, 204, 393
Gay, Mgr., on Sisterhoods, 366
Génevois (newspaper), on Protestantism, 264
Germain, St., of Auxerre, 64, 133
Germany, 259
Gertrude, St., 86
Gibbon, on early monasticism, 31, 69
Gidding, Little, 334

INDEX

Gilbert of Sempringham, 159
Giraldus Cambrensis, 178
Glastonbury, said to have been founded by St. Joseph of Arimathea, 131; rebuilt by Dunstan, 154; description of the Abbey, 167; Abbot Whiting hanged, 198
Gordon, J. F. S., 374
Goreh, Rev. N., 390
Gotschalk, 98
Gould, S. Baring-, on suffering, 14; on services done by the monks, 97; on the Irish missionaries, 134; on prejudiced attacks upon the Church, 233; on the corruption of the Church, 235, 236, 246; on the present state of Lutheranism, 263; on asceticism, 338
Graham, G. C., on joy in convents, 33; on monasticism, 85; relaxation of discipline in Spanish convents, 239; splendour of Las Huelgas, 248; benefits of monasticism, 340; nobility of monasticism, 347
Grandmont, the Order of, founded, 104; in England, 161
Green, J. R., 66
Greenwell, Dora, on the religious life, 342; on Christian earnestness, 368
Greg, Percy, 224
Gregory, St., the Great, describes the Barbarian invasions, 27; his conversion, 91; sends forth St. Augustine, 141; his instructions to St. Augustine, 349
Gregory, St., Nazianzen, 26
Gregory VII., Pope, 99, 386
Grey Ladies, the Society of the, 323
Grinstead, East, Sisterhood, Sisters mobbed, 303; list of works, 306; in America, 325
Grostête, of Lincoln, 171
Gualbert, 104
Guardian, The (newspaper), list of congregations in France, 277; want of zeal in curates, 365; on Collegiate churches, 380
Guthlac, St., 151

Hallam, 245, 388
Halliwell, 198
Harding, Stephen, 76
Hare, A. J. C., 265
Hearne, Thomas, Letters of, 195
Henry VIII., unworthy motives of, 174; cruel measures, 179, 190; attacks the Friars, 185; suppresses the monasteries in England, 197; in Ireland, 212; persuades the King of Scotland to suppress the Scotch monasteries, 215
Hermits, 290, 371
Héroïsme, L', en Soutane, 397
Hilarion, St., a promoter of monasticism, 41, 52
Hilda, St., founds Whitby, 148
Hildegarde, St., 98
Hindu religion, 12, 344, 366
Honoratus, St., 64
Hopkins, Fr., 295
Hore, A. H., on the married clergy, 174; on the cruel results of the suppression of the English abbeys, 190
Hospinian, 238
Hospitallers, Knights, founded, 107; come to England, 160; in Scotland, 214; Pope Clement VI. rebukes their luxury, 227; the Order revived, 297
Hospitals, 161
Hughes, Thomas, 390
Hugo of St. Victor, 7
Hume, 173
Huysmans, J. K., 394
Hypocrisy, 35

Iconoclasts, 22
Inquisition, the, 121
Iona, 65, 138
Ireland, missionary monks from, 100; monasteries in, 133, 209

Jacobite Christians, 90
Jarrow founded, 148, 153
Jeaffreson, J. C., 174
Jerome, St., on the founders of monasticism, 44; on noble monks, 58; his life, 59; on unworthy monks, 224
Jesuits, the, 122

Jews, the, 15
John, King, 158
Johnson, Dr., 334
Joseph II., 268, 271
Julian, Emperor, 53

Kaiserworth, the, Deaconesses, 333, 391
Kempis, Thomas à, 120, 376
Kent, the Holy Maid of, 179
Kentigern, St., 132, 213
Kettlewell, St., 306
Kidd, B., on monasticism, 83; on modern religious character, 337
Kingsley, C., 383
Kitchin, Dean, on learned leisure, 361; Life of Bishop Harold Browne, 364
Knights Hospitallers in England, 160; rebuked by Pope Clement VI., 227
Knights Templars, founded, 108; in England, 160; in Ireland, 207; in Scotland, 211; their suppression, 255
Knox, John, 216
Kuntze, 263

Lacordaire, on Christian love, 25; revives the Dominican Order, 230; dread of monastic wealth, 250
Lamartine, 271
Lanfranc, 157
Latimer, 333
Laura, 104
Lay Brothers, 104; at La Trappe, 377, 395
Lay Impropriation, 200
Layton, 194
Lazarists, the, founded, 123; their instructions, 356
Lecky, on the ideal of monasticism, 6; on the origin of monasticism, 15, 16; on mediæval monasteries, 29; on the ill effects of asceticism, 30; on degraded monks, 47, 226; monastic humility, 55; causes of the growth of early monasticism, 59, 72; on the admission of children to monasteries, 76;
value of monasteries, 83; on monastic acedia, 223; when monasteries became unnecessary, 224; on the suppression of monasteries, 257, 264; on the monastic spirit, 272; uses of monasticism, 341
Lee, Vernon, 400
Leighton, Archbishop, 327, 373
Leo X., 252
Lerins, importance of, 64; St. Augustine at, 141
Liber Gomorrhianus, 386
Libraries, monastic, 201
Lightfoot, Bishop, 369, 385, 388
Lindisfarne, 64
Lingard, Dr., on the admission of Benedictine novices, 75; on Pope Gregory's reforms, 93; on early monastic abuses, 152
Literature, monastic services to, 1, 201
Little Sisters of the Poor, 350
Lollards, the, attack the monks, 176
Lombards, the, 91
Loyola, Ignatius, founds the Jesuit Order, 122; his spirit wanted in the English Church, 364
Luther, not an ascetic, 12; his attack on monasticism, 256, 260; his remorse, 261
Luxeuil, 101, 386

Mabillon, 163
Macaulay, value of monasteries, 99; bad results of the dissolution of English monasteries, 201
Macharius, 51
Maclean, Dean, on East Syrian monasteries, 127
Magdalen, St. Mary, 85
Mahomet, an ascetic, 12; a leader of men, 40
Maistre, de, 339
Malabar Christians, the, 90
Malachy, St., 210
Mallock, on the Renaissance, 258; on modern progress, 349
Malmesbury, William of, 206
Manning, Cardinal, 396
Margaret, St., of Scotland, 214

INDEX

Marist, the, Fathers, 123
Marmoutier, 64
Maronites, the, 90
Martin, St., a promoter of monasticism, 63
Mary, St., of Egypt, 85
Mason, Canon A. J., 373
Maturin, Rev. B. W., 14, 378, 396
Maurus, St., 94
Medeshampsted, 148
Medicis, Giovanni di, 252
Mendicant Orders, 112
Méneval's Memoirs of Napoleon, 340
Merovingians, 246
Methodists, the, 362
Mill, J. S., 340
Milman, Dean, on turbulent monks, 225; on the revivals of monasticism, 229; on the development of monasticism, 237
Milton, John, 271
Minoresses, 114
Monasteries, beautiful situations of, 82, 166; their good work, 167; their wealth, 107, 158, 167, 180, 242; founded by Henry VIII., 190; number founded in England, 158
Monastery, officers in a, 162; daily routine in a, 164
Monasticism, its importance, 1; its motive principle, 2, 37, 275, 374; sanctioned by Christ, 8, 21, 38; not for all, 9, 38, 341, 376, 396; not instituted by the Church, 39; the work of a few gifted men, 39; arose in the East, 43; its rapid growth, 45; Pagan opposition to, 61; in Spain, 63, 94, 110, 239, 247, 262, 268; in the East, 43, 87, 289; in Britain, 131, 279, 280; in Wales, 135; in Ireland, 132, 207; in Scotland, 213, 267; in Scandinavia, 267, 386; in Mexico, 263; in Portugal, 268; in Germany, 266, 279; in France, 276, 281; in Italy, 269, 278; in America, 277, 284, 390; in Russia, 290; in Austria, 277, 279; in Armenia, 292; in Switzerland, 279; converts the barbarians, 98; aids civilization, 152, 379; reforms of, 227, 229, 374; why suppressed, 265, 333; its revival, 270, 274, 333, 337, 349, 375; wrong ideas of, 376
Monastic missions, 14, 72, 88, 95, 100, 113, 134, 209
Monks, description of English, 174, 389; charges against them, 190, 194, 197, 205; happiness of, 32; alleged hypocrisy of, 35; their duties described, 125
Montalembert, asserts the principles of monasticism, 4; describes men's frequent love of retirement, 11; says the monasteries were for strong, not for weak, natures, 336; says that monks were not sad, 32; on the power of self-sacrifice, 83; on Irish monasteries, 134; on the degeneracy of monasteries in France, 253; on monasticism in the present day, 278, 343, 346; monasticism not for all, 348
Moravians, the, 362
Mortmain, the statute of, 175
Morton, Archbishop, 175
Moslems, 142, 366
Mungo, St., 213
Münster, fanaticism in, 263

Napoleon, 339
Neale, Dr. J. M., 88, 237
Neri, St. Philip, founds the Oratory, 123; his principles, 369
Nestorians, the, 89
Newman, J. H., on the original principle of monasticism, 5; on the invasions of the Barbarians, 27; on the admission of children as monks, 76; sketch of daily life in a Cistercian abbey, 164; on the beauty of English abbeys, 167; on the quasi-heathen of towns, 363; why he left the Church of England, 370
Nilus, St., 52

Ninian, St., 136, 213
Nitria, 43
Norbert, St., 104
Nordhoff, C., on communistic societies, 21
Notker, 102
Nuns, 50, 85, 98, 386

Oblates of St. Charles, 123
Observants, 116
Odo, 154
Olcott, H. S., 11
Opus Anglicum, 98
Oratorians, the, 123, 369
Oswald, 147
Overton, Canon, 365
Oxenham, H. N., 262

Paconius, 41, 49
Paganism, 60, 257, 259
Parochial system, 369, 370, 373
Parry, O. H., 289
Passionists, the, 123
Patrick, St., taught at Lerins, 65; missionary to Ireland, 100, 207; history, 132
Paul, St., 22
Paul, the hermit, 44
Paula, St., 85
Paulinus, 146
Peasants' War, 261
Pecca fortiter, 260
Peckard, D. P., 336
Pelagianism, 144
Penda, 146
Peter of Cluny, 7
Peterborough, founded, 148; restored, 154
Philo, 15
Philobiblon, 238
Pilgrimage of Grace, the, 191
Pius IX., on the suppression of the Italian convents, 228
Placidus, 94
Plate, the gold and silver, of the English abbeys, 202
Pliny, 16
Pluralities, 251
Port Royal, 124
Powell, T. Yorke, on Saxon monasteries, 152; on the social benefits of monasteries, 170
Præmunire, the Act of, 181

Prejudice against monasticism, 35
Premontré, the Order of, founded, 104; follows the Rule of St. Augustine, 107; in England, 159
Property of English monasteries, 203
Pudentiana, St., 85
Pythagoreans, 22, 340

Quarterly Review, The, false charges against the English monks, 197, 205
Quignon, Cardinal, 116

Radegund, St., 85
Rancé, de, 124
Rationalism, 259
Recollects, 116
Redemptorists, the, 123
Renaissance, its connection with the Reformation, 233; its principles, 257, 354
Reunion, 372
Revue Benedictine, 9
Reyner, 207
Rites, curious, 163
Robertson, F. W., on enthusiasm, 364, 379
Roland, Madame, 271
Romanism, 35
Romuald, St., 104
Rosary, the, 119
Roscelin, 98
Roses, Wars of the, 176
Rosminians, the, 369
Royal monks and nuns, 151
Rule, the, of St. Basil, 55, 286; of St. Benedict, 76, 103; of St. Francis, 115; of St. Columbanus, 103; of St. Augustine, 63, 106
Ruskin, John, on the Carthusians, 105
Russia, monasteries in, 90
Rutilius on the monks, 68

Sacrifice, self, 337, 358
Sacrilege, the fate of, 206
Salle, de la, 281
Salvation Army, the, 20, 372
Salvian, 66
Santiago, the Order of, 110

INDEX

Savonarola, 121, 361
Scholastica, St., 85
Schools, monastic, 168, 200
Schopenhauer, 34
Seebohm, F., 264
Sellon, Miss, 312
Semeur, Le, 271
Simon Stock, St., 111
Sisters of Charity, the, 123, 348
Sisters of the Poor, the Little, 123, 357
Sisterhoods, 36, 311; in America, 328; in the Colonies, 327
Smiles, Samuel, 200
Social evolution, 83, 338
Southey, 205
Spectator, The (newspaper), 262
Spelman, Sir Henry, 206.
Spirituals, the, 116
Stephen, J. F., 264
Stokes, Margaret, 387
Stone of Fate, the, 139
Suarez, 366
Supremacy, the Royal, 185
Switzerland, Protestantism in, 262
Syrians, the East, 127, 289, 366

Tamerlane, 90
Taylor, A., 272
Telemachus, monk, 26
Teutonic Order, the, 107, 109
Thaïs, 85
Theodora, Empress, 86
Therapeutics, the, 15
Theresa, St., her dread of melancholy in convents, 33; on bad convents, 239; a teacher of prayer, 376
Tintern Abbey, 148
"Tota jacet Babylon," 264
Trail, H. D., 158
Trappe, La, the Order of, founded, 124; in England, 280; at present, 377, 394
Trench, Archbishop, on abbey sites, 82; on the Mendicant Orders, 112; on the degeneracy of the Friars, 249
Trent, the Council of, 232
Troitzka monastery, 391

Ursulines, the, 123

Valens, the Emperor, in conflict with St. Basil, 53; hostile to monasticism, 225
Vallombrosa, 104
Vestal Virgins, the, 84
Vibert, J. G., 396
Vidal, G. S. S., 369
Vincent of Lerins, St., 64; on Church progress, 355
Vincent of Paul, St., 311, 356
Visitation of English Abbeys, 182, 183
Vital, Orderic, 33
Vocation, 348, 375
Voltaire, on good monasteries, 232; on monks, 271
Vows, 357

Wales, 135
Warham, Archbishop, 179
Watson, Bishop, 262
Wealth, 357
Wearmouth founded, 148, 156
Werburg, St., 86
Wesley, John, austerity of, 12; a leader of men, 361
Westminster Abbey, 146, 385
Whitby, founded, 148; conference of, 149, 214
White Friars, 111
Whiting, Abbot, 195, 198
Wilfrid, St., 148
William the Conqueror, 153
William Rufus, 157
Wilson, A., 12
Wilson, Mrs. R. F., 288
Winfred, St., 95
Winifred, St., 86
Wireker, Nigel, 239
Wishart, 216
Wolsey, Cardinal, 176
World, coming out of the, 10, 83

Xavier, St. Francis, 364
Ximenes, Cardinal, 239

Zosimus, 69

RICHARD CLAY & SONS, LIMITED,
LONDON & BUNGAY.

www.ingramcontent.com/pod-product-compliance
Lightning Source LLC
Chambersburg PA
CBHW030601300426
44111CB00009B/1059